THE PHILOSOPHY OF
SAINT THOMAS AQUINAS

The Philosophy of
SAINT THOMAS AQUINAS

A Sketch

Stephen L. Brock

 CASCADE *Books* • Eugene, Oregon

THE PHILOSOPHY OF SAINT THOMAS AQUINAS
A Sketch

Cascade Books
An Imprint of Wipf and Stock Publishers
199 W. 8th Ave., Suite 3
Eugene, OR 97401

www.wipfandstock.com

ISBN 13: 978-1-62564-663-7

Cataloging-in-Publication data:

Brock, Stephen Louis.

The philosophy of Saint Thomas Aquinas : a sketch / Stephen L. Brock.

xx + 196 p.; 23 cm—Includes bibliographical references and index.

ISBN 13: 978-1-62564-663-7

1. Thomas, Aquinas, Saint, 1225?–1274. 2. Thomas, Aquinas, Saint, 1225?–1274—Criticism and interpretation. I. Title.

B765.T54 B76 2015

Manufactured in the USA.

To my teachers

Table of Contents

Preface

"The artist is the man who is more and not less intelligible than other men."
—G. K. Chesterton, "An Apology for Buffoons"

IF CHESTERTON IS RIGHT about the artist, then Thomas Aquinas was one of the greatest artists ever. His whole aim, we might say, was to be intelligible, and few have been more so. As a result, those who have learned something from him, when they set out to convey the thing to others, do indeed risk buffoonery. They are sure that his own way of putting it is better.

Their readers may feel the same way. Chesterton was decrying a tendency that he saw among followers of artists in his own day. It was not their forming factions or cliques; he found these inevitable, and excusable. But now, he protested, the clique "has taken on the character of an interpreter; by hypothesis the interpreter of something unintelligible; and its existence encourages the artist to be unintelligible, when it is his whole function to be intelligible." On this reasoning, if the art is good, to interpret it may even reflect badly on the interpreter's own intelligence.

Chesterton's targets, however, must have been interpreters who were the masters' contemporaries; otherwise his complaint would boomerang. And of his many interpretations of past masters, one of the best—a work of art in its own right—is of Saint Thomas.

Aquinas's very language is dead. As he himself often observed, what is more intelligible in itself may be less so to us. The intellectual signal, however clear at the source, may hit interference in transmission. It might still get through, of course; in fact, Thomas got that thought from Aristotle, who was in various ways even farther from him than he is from us. But the signal may still need a booster, and therein lies the only excuse for a book like this.

For all of its shortcomings, at least it is short. Right now there are several short books on Aquinas in circulation. This one is not meant to replace any; they all fit on the shelf, and they may even support each other. Nor is it meant to favor any school (the academic equivalent of a clique). Saint Josemaría Escrivá, who wished his own followers to form no school, used to commend Thomas simply as "a good friend." I hope this book will be received in that spirit.

Acknowledgments

M Y THANKS TO KEVIN Flannery, Craig Iffland, Christine Jensen, Steven Jensen, and Luca Tuninetti for their very helpful comments on drafts of this book. A special word of gratitude goes to Francisco Fernández Labastida, to whom the book owes its very existence.

Abbreviations, References, and Technical Terminology

EN	Aristotle, *Nicomachean Ethics*
Metaph.	Aristotle, *Metaphysics*

Tʜᴏᴍᴀs Aǫᴜɪɴᴀs:

De ente	*De ente et essentia* (*On Being and Essence*)
De pot.	*Quaestiones disputatae De potentia* (*Disputed Questions on the Power of God*)
De princ. nat.	*De principiis naturae* (*On the Principles of Nature*)
De spir. creat.	*Quaestio disputata de spiritualibus creaturis* (*On Spiritual Creatures*)
De subst. sep.	*De substantiis separatis* (*On Separate Substances*)
De ver.	*Quaestiones disputatae de ueritate* (*Disputed Questions on Truth*)
In De an.	*Sentencia Libri De anima* (*Commentary on Aristotle's* De anima)
In De caelo	*Sententia super librum De caelo et mundo* (*Commentary on Aristotle's* De caelo)
In De gen.	*Sententia super libros De generatione et corruptione* (*Commentary on Aristotle's* De generatione et corruptione)

In De Trin.	*Super Boetium De Trinitate* (*Commentary on* Boethius's De Trinitate)
In Eth.	*Sententia Libri Ethicorum* (*Commentary on Aristotle's* Nicomachean Ethics)
In Meta.	*Sententia super Metaphysicam* (*Commentary on Aristotle's* Metaphysics)
In Peryerm.	*Expositio Libri Peryermenias* (*Commentary on Aristotle's* De interpretatione)
In Phys.	*Sententia super Physicam* (*Commentary on Aristotle's* Physics)
In Polit.	*Sententia Libri Politicorum* (*Commentary on Aristotle's* Politics)
In Post. an.	*Expositio Libri Posteriorum* (*Commentary on Aristotle's* Posterior Analytics)
In Sent.	*Scriptum super libros Sententiarum* (*Commentary on* Peter Lombard's Sentences)
Quodl.	*Quaestiones de quolibet I–XII* (*Quodlibetal Questions I–XII*)
Scg	*Summa contra Gentiles*
STh	*Summa theologiae*

Where possible, references to Thomas's works include the paragraph numbers (signaled by §) of the Marietti editions (see the Bibliography), which many English translations follow. The translations of Thomas in this book, however, are the author's.

Although Thomas strives to adhere to the meanings that words carry in ordinary speech, a number of terms in his lexicon bear technical senses. I have tried to catch and explain those that appear in this book, but if the reader still finds a term unclear, or desires a fuller account, an excellent source is William Wallace's handy reference work, *The Elements of Philosophy*.

Introduction

Manuductio

ACCORDING TO ONE OF his earliest biographies, when Thomas Aquinas was a boy of five or so, he would pester his tutor with the question, *quid est Deus*—what is God?[1] Poor tutor. Sooner or later the youth would come to understand that only one man could possibly answer that question satisfactorily: the God-man. But its hold on him never slackened. That is why he became a theologian. He also never lost his readiness to learn from other, merely human persons about the things they were qualified to teach. That may be one reason why he became such a great teacher himself, eventually dubbed Angelic.

A term that Thomas himself often uses to describe the activity of teaching is *manuductio*, leading by the hand. Teachers bring us from familiar truths, truths that we already know, to others hitherto unfamiliar or unknown. It usually takes time, and patience. Thomas thinks angels take in whole fields of knowledge in an instant, but our earthbound, sense-bound mind is made to proceed gradually, step by step.[2] Thomas finds pedagogical *manuductio* practiced in quite a variety of ways and settings, the chief practitioner being God Himself.[3]

1. Petrus Calo, *Vita S. Thomae Aquinatis*, §3, 19.
2. See George, "Mind Forming and *Manuductio*."
3. See, for example, *De ver.*, q. 14, a. 10.

But there is also a kind of *manuductio* into divine matters that is practiced mainly by human teachers, and in which Thomas especially excelled. It is the kind that he ascribes to philosophy when he considers it from the theologian's viewpoint. Philosophy, he says, regards what can be known by man's natural reason. The things proper to theology, by contrast, are above reason (which does not mean contrary to it). The philosophical things, then, are more familiar or better known to us. Indeed, without reason, neither faith nor any other kind of access to divine truth would even be possible for us, any more than it is for beasts. So the human mind, Thomas judges, "is more easily led by the hand" from philosophical things into the things of theology.[4] Later we will look at his conception of philosophical *manuductio* in more detail. But for a testimony to his own proficiency at it, let us fast-forward to a few weeks after his death.

Thomas died before reaching fifty. At the time of his demise he was traveling in southern Italy, which was the region that had witnessed his birth, his upbringing, and the discovery of his vocation as a Dominican friar. But he had moved extensively over Europe during his short life, and the place where he had spent most time and made most impact, first as a student and then as a theologian, was Paris. So it is not too surprising that authorities at the university of Paris, upon learning of his passing, should have sent the Dominicans a letter of condolence.[5] But the emotion avowed in the letter, even allowing for rhetorical excess, is striking. "For news has come to us which floods us with grief and amazement, bewilders our understanding, transfixes our innermost vitals, and well-nigh breaks our hearts." They went so far as to claim for Paris the right to Thomas's remains.

But two other features of the letter are what interest us most. First, it speaks on behalf of only part of the university's personnel: "the rector and the procurators, and the other Parisian masters presently teaching in the Faculty of Arts." The Faculty of Arts was what we could call the Philosophy Department. Second, other things, besides Thomas's body, were also requested. These included "some writings pertaining to philosophy, begun by him at Paris, left unfinished at his departure, and completed, we believe, in the place to which he had been transferred." Possibly among these was his commentary on Aristotle's *Metaphysics*.[6]

---

4. *STh*, I, q. 1, a. 5, ad 2.

5. See Foster, *The Life of Saint Thomas Aquinas*, 153–57.

6. See Weisheipl, *Thomas D'Aquino*, 332.

The letter made no reference at all either to the Faculty of Theology or to any of Thomas's own theological works. Of course, the theologians might have reacted separately to the news of his death, leaving no record. Still, the omission does bring to mind the doctrinal tensions that had arisen between Thomas and some of the less Aristotelian-minded, more conservative theologians at Paris, including Stephen Tempier, now the city's Bishop.[7] And there is irony here, because it is not that Thomas's relations with the Arts Faculty were always perfectly smooth. Just four years earlier, he had produced a polemical tract against a position that was being promoted by some of the Arts masters themselves (and was formally condemned by Tempier the same year).[8] Thomas attacked the position as at once contrary to the faith, to Aristotle's views, and to the principles of philosophy. Philosophers are an unpredictable lot. Was the Paris letter written despite that tract, or partly because of it?

The intellectual situation today is rather more complex, of course, but with regard to how Thomas is seen, there do seem to be some similarities. Obviously the proportion of Christians among philosophers is lower now than in the thirteenth century, and so is the interest in theological matters. But is there any other theologian, past *or* present, for whom philosophers show anything like the regard they show for Aquinas? A brilliant contemporary reader of Aristotle, for example, talking about commentaries on the *De anima*, says, "For students the only one I found useful is the one by Aquinas. While I disagree with him about some vital issues, I find him somewhat helpful to first readers at every point. He stretches out what Aristotle compresses."[9] (He leads by the hand.) Nor is the esteem confined to the Aristotle experts. Among the heirs of Frege and Wittgenstein there is a current called analytical Thomism.[10] Some of Husserl's students have gone deeply into Thomas. On the practical side, Thomas is present in action theory, virtue ethics, and legal theory. The Straussians respect him. Even some Heideggerians engage him. (I am thinking of Heidegger's hostility toward Aristotle and of his view of faith and philosophy as mutually inimical.) Some may say that the theological intent underlying Thomas's philosophizing detracts from its strictly philosophical value, or from its intrinsic

7. See below, 10–14.

8. The tract is *On the Unity of the Intellect.*

9. Gendlin, *Line by Line Commentary*, vol. 1, Introduction, 8.

10. See Haldane, *Mind, Metaphysics, and Value*, and Paterson and Pugh (eds.), *Analytical Thomism.*

intelligibility (which is almost the same thing). But surely the broad interest that it generates among philosophers at least suggests otherwise.

As for Thomas's relation to contemporary Catholic theology, this is a topic far exceeding the limits both of these pages and of my competence, but I will hazard a few remarks.[11] He does remain a reference-point, though his views certainly do not have the quasi-canonical status they once had. That was, at best, a mixed blessing anyway, especially as concerned the direct study and assessment of his own works in their own setting. Such study now proliferates. But of course it is mostly confined to specialists. The general attitude among the theologians, in a way reminiscent of his own time, seems to be one of wariness. And even those who are favorable to him seem inclined to discount his philosophical thought and, when they must treat it, to downplay the Aristotelian side. All of this is not explained merely by the burgeoning of scriptural and patristic studies (which Thomas would surely have welcomed). In part, it is a reaction to what are perceived as the rationalistic excesses of the Neo-Scholastic approach that dominated Catholic theology in the first half of the twentieth century. But other factors surely figure in as well; for instance, the influence, direct or indirect, of Martin Heidegger. Perhaps, however, the attitude is less pervasive now than it was two or three decades ago.[12]

I have no wish to promote Thomas's philosophical thought to the detriment of his theology. That would be silly. Thomas was a theologian. Period. And he himself denies that theology absolutely needs philosophy.[13] Nevertheless he just happened to find philosophy useful in theology. He also just happened to think that, in order to use it, one first had to master it. And to me it seems undeniable that, in his particular case, the quality of the theology produced was very much a function of the philosophical mastery achieved. Of course, it depended on many other things too, things

11. My acquaintance with Protestant theology is very partial, but my impression is that, within it, Thomas is being read more than ever, and with excellent results. For instance, there is the study by Princeton theologian John Bowlin, *Contingency and Fortune*, and also that of his student David Decosimo, *Ethics as a Work of Charity*.

12. See, for example, Reinhard Hütter's *Dust Bound for Heaven* and Matthew Levering's *Scripture and Metaphysics*. Both theologians have also produced several other fine works. A strong resurgence of high-quality Thomistic theology has been taking place for some time now within the Dominican order, both in North America and in Europe; currently prominent names include Serge-Thomas Bonino, Gilles Emery, Michael Sherwin, and Thomas Joseph White. Very interesting theological studies, mostly in English, are also coming out of the Thomas Instituut te Utrecht in the Netherlands.

13. *STh*, I, q. 1, a. 5, ad 2.

shared by Thomas and other great theologians: a profound acquaintance with Scripture and the Fathers, personal holiness, a keen mind, taste for study, writing skills, and so forth. But I think that a Thomas without his philosophy would have been rather like a young David without his sling.

1

Matrices

Philosophy in the Setting of Thomas's Life,
Thought, and Works

Student

THOMAS AQUINAS WAS BORN in or around 1225.[1] His birthplace, half-way between Rome and Naples, lay on the edge of the kingdom of Sicily, and therefore under the rule of emperor Frederick II, but near the Papal States. The place's name, Roccasecca, is sometimes rendered Dry Rock, but much closer would be Dry Fort or Dry Castle. Or, if we have to have an echo, hardly less accurate than Dry Rock would be Dry Rook, in the sense of the chess piece. In fact, the place's single remaining tower rather resembles one, and the word could serve as a reminder of the Arab influence on medieval culture generally and on Thomas's thought (although he may not have played the game). His father was a knight. His mother, if not a queen, was a noblewoman, a countess.

They had nine children. As the youngest of the four boys, Thomas would have been expected to enter the service of the Church, and the family may have nourished hopes of his succeeding his paternal uncle as abbot

---

1. Most of the biographical information in this chapter is taken from Torrell, *Initiation*.

of the important Benedictine monastery at nearby Monte Cassino. In any case, at the age of five or six he was sent there as an oblate to learn the liberal arts.

Whether on account of his precocity, or because the abbey was drawn more and more into the Guelph–Ghibelline conflict, at about the age of fourteen Thomas was sent to the university that Frederick had founded at Naples in 1224. There the youth continued with the liberal arts and began to study philosophy. It was a lucky circumstance. The university was already a major European intellectual center, and almost nowhere else in Christendom could Thomas have been exposed so fully to the thought of Aristotle.

Only very recently had the bulk of Aristotle's writings been translated into Latin. They were causing a stir throughout the continent, and Church authorities regarded them with some suspicion. This was perhaps in part because they arrived accompanied by translations of the commentaries of the great Arab philosophers Avicenna (†1037) and Averroes (†1198), some of whose readings seemed to favor heretical views. In any case, when Thomas began his philosophical studies, ecclesiastical universities such as the one at Paris did not allow the official teaching of any but a fraction of Aristotle's works, those on logic and ethics. Frederick's civil university had no such restrictions.

A certain Peter of Ireland, himself author of a commentary on one of Aristotle's logical treatises, was Thomas's main guide through the so-called natural books. These covered all the natural sciences then known, and also the master philosophical science of metaphysics. Thomas never acquired more than a basic knowledge of Greek, but eventually he would be counted among Aristotle's greatest interpreters, and his distinctive way of using the teachings of "the Philosopher," both in philosophy and in theology, is a hallmark of his thought.

It was also at Naples that Thomas met the new order of mendicant friars, the Dominicans, founded at Toulouse in 1215. He soon decided to enter their ranks. The decision encountered severe opposition from his family, but his will proved adamant, and eventually they relented. Soon afterwards, in 1245 or thereabouts, his Dominican superiors sent him to their priory in Paris, Saint Jacques, to continue his philosophical studies. He also began the formal study of theology, apparently even before finishing the philosophy curriculum. There is a manuscript containing his own transcriptions of a series of courses on that great Syrian theologian, now known as pseudo-Dionysius, whom the medievals identified with Dionysius the Areopagite (Acts 17:34). The professor was the renowned German Dominican, Albert the Great.

Perhaps Albert's recognition of Thomas's qualities was what led to the young friar's early entry into theology. At any rate, when Albert left Paris in 1248 to assume the direction of a new Dominican house of studies in Cologne, Thomas went along. There, besides studying Sacred Scripture and perhaps writing his first biblical commentaries (on *Isaiah*, *Jeremiah*, and *Lamentations*), he continued transcribing the courses on pseudo-Dionysius, and he also transcribed a course of Albert's on Aristotle's *Nicomachean Ethics*. This is somewhat surprising, since by then he would have finished philosophy. But whatever the explanation, Thomas clearly treasured the course. He kept his notes from it and made use of them even long afterwards, in composing the moral part of the *Summa theologiae*.

It would be hard to exaggerate Albert's influence on Thomas. If the young friar needed any help in learning to value philosophy, no one was more suited to provide it than Albert. Thomas must have been inspired by Albert's gigantic effort to assimilate Aristotle's thought and to integrate it with the Neoplatonism that was more traditional among Christian thinkers. This is not to say that the disciple's mind was in every way like the master's. For instance, Thomas shows considerably less interest in natural history. His real bent and genius were metaphysical. And in his own synthesis of Aristotelianism and Neoplatonism, the former is much more dominant than it is in Albert's. Perhaps on this account, and whether for better or for worse, scholars generally seem to agree that Thomas's synthesis also looks more unified.

Probably while at Cologne, Thomas was ordained to the priesthood. In 1251 or 1252 he returned to the Dominican priory at Paris, now as subregent. At the university he soon began working toward the most advanced degree in theology, that of Master. The program was intense. There were many courses on Sacred Scripture, other Christian writings, and specific theological topics. The candidate also had to deliver a series of lectures of his own, based on the standard theological textbook of the time, the *Sentences*. This was a broad summary of Christian doctrine, weaving together Scriptural texts and opinions ("sentences") of Fathers of the Church, compiled by the twelfth-century Bishop of Paris, Peter Lombard. The commentary on the *Sentences* that resulted from Thomas's lectures was his first major work. His last, the *Summa theologiae*, would be motivated, at least in part, by dissatisfaction with the *Sentences* as a book for beginners in theology.

Before finishing his studies, Thomas also composed two short philosophical treatises, *On the Principles of Nature* and the more famous *On Being and Essence*. The first lays out the main ideas governing the Aristotelian philosophy of nature or of physical reality. We will look at some of those ideas later. The second work offers an extraordinary synthesis, and even development, of the doctrine contained in the daunting middle books of Aristotle's *Metaphysics*. The focus is on the constitution of the essences of things at different levels of reality: substances and accidents, material and immaterial substances, and God. Both works show the influence of the Arab commentators on Aristotle, Avicenna, and Averroes.

Sources

Having finished his formal education, Thomas devoted the rest of his life to teaching and writing. This seems a good place to suspend the narrative and to say something about the principal sources of his thought, which is to say, the writers who chiefly influenced him. Like most of his contemporaries, Thomas considered himself heir to an ancient and venerable intellectual tradition, and to a large extent his own work can be seen as a kind of dialogue with its main representatives, the so-called *auctores*.

The word is not easy to translate. It is certainly weightier than our *author*. But if we say *authority*, we must be careful about the kind of authority we mean. It is not that of a commander or a lawgiver. It is that of a teacher, a person deemed a reliable source and guide in the process of acquiring knowledge. The difference is not small. Following a commander or lawgiver consists mainly in obeying, executing orders. This may sometimes require asking for clarification of the order's meaning, or even of its purpose; but the point is to obey. Of course following a teacher also involves performing assigned tasks. But the point is to learn. And learning is very much a matter of asking questions. A good commander will allow some questions, but a good teacher welcomes, even provokes them. A medieval thinker was always putting questions to the *auctores*. This was not because he doubted whether they knew what they were talking about, but precisely because he was sure that, on the whole, they did.[2]

2. On the medieval attitude toward teaching authority, see the fine discussion in Martin, *Thomas Aquinas*, 1–14.

Thomas's authoritative sources were many and various. First, of course, came the Sacred Scriptures, which because of the divine inspiration attributed to them constituted a class by themselves. Then there were the writings of the Church Fathers and other venerable Christian authors: Ambrose, Jerome, Gregory the Great, Boethius, Origen, pseudo-Dionysius, John Chrysostom, Nemesius, John Damascene, Anselm, Peter Lombard, and especially the one whom Thomas qualifies as *egregius*, outstanding: Augustine.[3] Of non-Christian writers, certainly the most influential on Thomas was Aristotle. Of Plato's works he knew only the *Timaeus*. His conception of Platonic thought was based partly on what Aristotle says about it and partly on authors of more or less Neoplatonic inspiration—chiefly Boethius, Augustine, pseudo-Dionysius, and Proclus. In ethics, Stoicism was important for him, especially as presented in the writings of Seneca and Cicero. Also very influential were a number of Jewish and Islamic thinkers, especially Moses Maimonides, Avicenna (also strongly Neoplatonic), Algazel, and Averroes (called the Commentator, on account of his impressive commentaries on Aristotle). Thomas also cites a large number of lesser authors.

Naturally another major factor in the configuration of his thought was interaction with contemporary thinkers. Tracing this requires some expertise. He almost never names his contemporaries, even in polemical writings. Occasionally he will say that "some persons" hold a given position. And he has passages that seem to be echoing some other writer, but none is cited. At that time there was little or no notion of intellectual property.

Indeed, even though medieval thinkers were as prone to vainglory as anyone else, they seldom went out of their way to seem merely original. If anything, they would downplay their originality and stress their continuity with the tradition. They would almost never directly contradict an *auctor* if they could avoid it; that is, if they could plausibly interpret him in a way that was consistent with their own view. Precisely because the *auctor* was a teacher, the distinction between interpreting what he said on a given matter and inquiring into the matter itself was rather a fine one. A famous remark of Thomas's, that "the study of philosophy is not for the sake of knowing what men thought, but what the truth of things is," actually appears in the midst of a very painstaking commentary on Aristotle.[4] The remark can hardly mean that he cared little for what his sources really thought or was

3. *Contra errores Graecorum*, pars 1, Proem.
4. *In De caelo*, I, lect. 22, §228[8].

ready to foist his own ideas on them whenever it suited him. On the contrary, the concern in his commentaries to get at the author's real meaning is so evident that some scholars have doubted whether these works can be assumed to give us his views about "the truth of things." Nevertheless he does sometimes take the opportunity to carry the discussion of the things well beyond what he thinks the author is saying about them; and on a few occasions, he even disagrees explicitly with the author's position. The most famous case is his rejection of Aristotle's would-be proofs of the perpetuity of motion and time.[5] These points suggest that usually, if he does not say otherwise, Thomas accepts the author's view as true.

If today we tend to take Thomas's commentaries on Aristotle and other philosophers as having only the author's meaning, and not the truth of the matter, for their immediate object, I think it is partly because of how our own philosophy departments typically organize their curricula. In one group are the courses consisting in the direct study of some subject or topic, perhaps with a textbook produced by the professor or by one or more colleagues. Here indeed the aim is to get at the truth of the matter. But what are called the historical course are another group. Their aim is to understand past thinkers and to trace their influences. So we come to assume that is one thing to study metaphysics, and quite another to study Aristotle's *Metaphysics*.

Now, in the medieval university, the courses of instruction were also mainly of two kinds or formats: *lectiones* and *disputationes*.[6] In a *lectio* (whence *lesson*), the professor read directly from some established authoritative text (few students had their own copies!) and commented on it. The *disputatio* format was a sort of cross between a seminar and a debate, in which the students played a very active role. Generally the *disputationes* were for more advanced students, presupposing the knowledge acquired in the *lectiones*. But it is not at all that the *lectiones* were purely historical and the *disputationes* purely thematic. Both were historical, and both thematic. The *Metaphysics* was both a strange old tome for experts to interpret and a current textbook for everyone in the program to assimilate and argue about. Does this mean that medieval scholars were less alive than we are to the historical dimension of the old works? Perhaps so, but they were far from unconscious of it. Thomas himself displays a sharp critical sense

5. *In Phys.*, VIII, lect. 2, §986[16]–90[20].
6. See Torrell, *Initiation*, 87–90.

regarding the attribution of authorship.[7] And his works are rife with accounts of how thinkers have handled a given topic over the course of time. (In this too he is following Aristotle.) In any case, it seems safe to say that medieval scholars were more alive to the historical dimension of their own textbooks than we often are.

But my concern is not with the value of the medieval approach. It is with Thomas's aim in his commentaries.[8] He thought of Aristotle's works not only as historical documents, but also as philosophical sources (albeit human and hence fallible ones). He commented on the *Metaphysics* expecting it to be used as a metaphysics textbook. He was not just doing the part of metaphysics which is the history of metaphysics. He was doing metaphysics *tout court*.

How far Thomas's philosophical thought can be termed Aristotelian is disputed, and I suppose it always will be. While he certainly accepts Aristotle's criticisms of Plato, an influence of Neoplatonism on him is undeniable.[9] The influence is especially strong in what regards the divine nature and its relation to the world. Aristotle says relatively little about that, and of course for Thomas nothing is more important. Still, it seems safe to say that in all areas of philosophy, including that one, he shows a constant and strong determination to keep his teachings in harmony with the principles he finds in Aristotle. Perhaps *determination* is not even the right word, since it suggests deliberate effort. Thinking like Aristotle seems to come almost naturally to Thomas, probably more so than to any other Christian theologian, before or since. At any rate, such is my impression. But what makes this point interesting theoretically, and not just biographically, is that thinking like a Christian also came quite instinctively to him. That, I take it, cannot be dismissed as a mere impression.

Teacher

When we paused to consider Thomas's relation to his sources, our narrative had reached the early 1250s, when he was doing advanced studies in theology and lecturing on Lombard's *Sentences*. At that time the secular clergy who controlled the university were waging a bitter attack on the young mendicant orders—the Franciscans and the Dominicans—and trying to

7. See below, 14, on the *Liber de causis*.

8. On this question see Weisheipl, *Thomas D'Aquino*, 280–85.

9. See Henle, *Saint Thomas and Platonism*.

exclude them from the teaching staff. Moreover, the university's statutes set the minimum age for a master at thirty-five. Nevertheless, thanks to the intervention of Pope Alexander IV, in the spring of 1256 Thomas was granted the title of Master of Theology. He joined the faculty in 1257, the same year as his fellow student and (as it were) Franciscan counterpart, Bonaventure. By another notable coincidence, it was also during the early 1250s that the Arts Faculty obtained ecclesiastical permission to include in its curriculum the entire Aristotelian corpus. This would eventually lead to the controversies between Arts masters and theologians that we glimpsed in the Introduction and will see in more detail shortly.

For about three years Thomas occupied the university's Dominican chair in Theology. During this time he produced the lengthy *Disputed Questions on Truth*, which, despite its title, covers many topics in addition to truth: divine, angelic, and human knowledge; the good; free choice; the passions; grace and justification. He wrote several shorter works as well, including the philosophically important commentary on part of Boethius's *De Trinitate*, and quite possibly the no less important commentary on Boethius's *De ebdomadibus*. There is also a short disputed question *On the Immortality of the Soul* that Thomas may have composed in or around 1259.[10]

In June of 1259, Thomas was called to take part in a general chapter of the Dominicans at Valenciennes, in which important decisions were taken regarding the friars' studies. After the end of the school year he travelled south, spending the next ten years or so at various places in Italy. Between 1261 and 1265 he was mostly in Orvieto at the Dominican convent (not at the Papal court, as is sometimes said). Besides attending to heavy responsibilities as teacher, consultor, and preacher, he composed a long commentary on the book of Job and compiled most of his famous *Catena Aurea*, a "golden chain" of passages from Fathers of the Church connected to form a running commentary on the four Gospels, "as though by a single teacher."[11]

In Orvieto Thomas also completed one of his most original and influential works, the *Summa contra gentiles*. Apparently this title is not his. What the manuscripts indicate is *On the Truth of the Catholic Faith against*

10. This work is usually tagged as of doubtful authenticity, but see Kennedy, "A New Disputed Question," and Torrell, *Initiation*, 619–20. Torrell calls for a comparison with other works of Aquinas. This has been done: Bergamino, "*Quaestio disputata*." The results favor authenticity, especially if the work's dating turns out to be fairly early. On the overall trajectory of Thomas's writings on the topic, see Dewan, *Form and Being*, 175–87.

11. Guilelmus de Tocco, *Ystoria sancti Thome de Aquino*, XVIII, 130.

the Errors of Unbelievers. Occasionally the work (or at least all but its fourth and final Book) has also been misrepresented in a more substantial way, as a kind of *Summa philosophiae*. This fits neither with the stated intention of manifesting the essential truths of the Catholic faith and eliminating contrary errors, nor with the numerous scriptural citations throughout, nor with the fact that it starts with the consideration of God, which for Thomas is where philosophy ends and only theology begins. Clearly its very subject matter is God and what pertains to Him. It is theology.[12] If it is laden with philosophical material, so are Thomas's other theological writings. For various reasons, in the present book I draw much more on the other *Summa*, but I do not in any way mean to belittle this one.

From 1265 to 1268 Thomas was mostly in Rome, setting up and directing a new Dominican house of studies. Here he composed his own commentary on pseudo-Dionysius's *Divine Names*, a commentary on Aristotle's *De anima*, perhaps some of the commentaries on epistles of Saint Paul, and three sizable sets of disputed questions: *On the Soul*, *On Spiritual Creatures*, and *On the Power of God*. All the evidence indicates that he also undertook a new commentary on the *Sentences* during this period.[13] But that project was halted, giving way to a theology textbook of his own devising: the *Summa theologiae*. He produced its First Part while still in Rome.

Though never finished, this work is generally, and justly, deemed Thomas's masterpiece. The only one that he himself called a *Summa*, it is not so much "against the errors of the unbelievers" as for the instruction of believers, although of course such instruction is partly about dealing with errors. Its proem says it is for "beginners" in Catholic truth. Nowadays this makes first-time readers laugh (or moan). For indeed it is no penny catechism. And even a quick skim leaves no doubt of its presupposing a serious philosophical training—if not on the students' part, at least on the part of the teacher basing his classes on it.

The *Summa* is divided into three Parts, with the Second subdivided into two. The work breaks off at Question 90 of the Third Part.[14] The rationale of the *Summa*'s structure has been the object of much discussion.

12. See Torrell, *Initiation*, 598. On the method and purpose of the *Summa contra gentiles*, see ibid., 148–70; also Tuninetti, "L'argomentazione dialettica." On how philosophical and theological treatments of God differ for Thomas, see below, 17–24.

13. Thomas Aquinas, *Lectura romana in primum Sententiarum Petri Lombardi*.

14. There is also the *Supplementum*, a compilation of texts that some disciples of Thomas selected from his (first) commentary on the *Sentences* and arranged according to the apparent plan of the portion never written.

This is surprising, since the work itself provides ample explanations of its structure, both overall and within specific sections.[15] Sometimes readers are surprised by the fact that it leaves the thematic treatment of Jesus Christ for the Third Part. Thomas says that the First Part is about God; the Second, about man's movement toward God; and the Third, about Christ, who as man is our way of tending toward God.[16] He also describes the Third Part's object as the "consummation of all things theological."[17] The treatment of Jesus Christ comes last, then, because it is the most important. Christ is at the summit, and Thomas, we might say, has taken upon himself the task of leading us by the hand toward Him.

In 1268 Thomas was sent back to Paris to occupy the Dominican chair in Theology for a second time. The motive is uncertain, but he immediately found himself embroiled in serious controversies. One of them was a renewal of the struggle between the secular clergy and the mendicants. Others more directly involved philosophical matters. These highlight the extent to which Thomas's thought moved outside the prevalent currents at the university. Let me suspend the narrative again and explain some of the things at issue in these disputes.

Maverick

One of the controversies centered on certain views being put forward by some members of the university's Faculty of Arts. By then the restrictions on teaching Aristotle at Paris had been lifted for quite some time, and in fact the Aristotelian corpus dominated the philosophy curriculum. In expounding Aristotle, these Arts masters—the most prominent being Siger of Brabant—adhered rather closely to the interpretations of Averroes. For this reason, they are often referred to as Latin Averroists. Some scholars, however, prefer to call them radical Aristotelians, or even heterodox Aristotelians. These epithets better indicate the nature of the controversy. For the complaints were not coming from other Arts masters who disagreed with the Averroistic readings of Aristotle. They were coming from the Faculty of Theology.

15. For an account of the rationale based on these explanations, see te Velde, *Aquinas on God*, 11–18.

16. *STh*, I, q. 2, Proem.

17. *STh*, III, Proem.

What troubled the theologians was not that Aristotle was being taken to say one thing or another. It was that everything he was taken to say was being presented as solid philosophy—whether or not it fit with Catholic doctrine. The Arts masters knew very well that some of the theses which they attributed to Aristotle were contrary to the faith. The three most notorious ones were that the world had no temporal beginning; that all human intellectual activity is seated in a single intellect, which somehow interacts with individual human beings but which exists apart from them; and that, inasmuch as the animating principles—the *animae*, souls—of individual human beings are not intellectual, neither are they immortal.

Now, contrary to what is often said about them, the Arts masters did not quite call those theses true. The Bishop of Paris, Stephen Tempier, did eventually accuse them of speaking "as though" there were a "double truth"—one in theology, and a contradictory one in philosophy. And indeed their position seemed to imply such a view. But there is no evidence that they actually asserted it, and really their having done so is scarcely plausible. No self-respecting Aristotelian could uphold such a breach of the principle regarded by Aristotle as the most fundamental truth of all, that mutually contradictory assertions cannot hold together. What the Arts masters held was only that those theses, whether in contradiction with truths of the faith or not, followed validly from necessary rational principles. Naturally, however, this did not satisfy the theologians, or the Bishop. Near the end of 1270, he formally condemned thirteen propositions, most of which are traceable to the Arts masters.

Thomas wasted no time joining the controversy. Shortly before Tempier's condemnation, he produced his most vigorously polemical tract, *On the Unity of the Intellect*. He aimed to show that the existence of only one intellect for all human beings was neither Aristotle's view nor philosophically sound. With this, his theological colleagues could have no quarrel.

There is another tract of his, however, also apparently dating from the second Parisian period, called *On the Eternity of the World*.[18] It too bears on one of those troublesome theses: that the world had no temporal beginning. In this tract, Thomas reiterates a position for which he was already famous, and which set him against not only the Arts masters but also most of the theologians. It was not Aristotelian enough for the former, and it was too Aristotelian for the latter. Aristotle, in his *Physics*, offers proofs of the world's lacking a temporal beginning. Thomas found the proofs

18. On its dating, see Torrell, *Initiation*, 268–73.

inconclusive. In fact, he held that no such proof was even possible. Yet he did think it possible to prove that the world was produced by God, and indeed that it was produced by Him "out of nothing," taking this expression in the sense of "not out of something."[19] This means that God made the whole world and whatever in any way enters into its constitution; nothing in the world is independent of Him. Nevertheless, Thomas insisted, God could have produced a world with no temporal beginning, and only by revelation do we know that He gave it one. Thomas knew quite well that most of the theologians opposed him strongly on this last point, and he aimed *On the Eternity of the World* directly against them.

Moreover, although he agreed with them about the intellectual nature of individual human souls, on other issues regarding the soul he and they differed sharply.[20] His views on the soul involved him in controversy especially during his second stay in Paris.[21] The clash over the soul was complicated, but what particularly troubled the other theologians was how closely Thomas associated the highest dimensions of human life with mere physical matter. For he insisted that each person has just one soul, one fundamental vital principle. It would be at the root of all the person's vital activity, from the contemplation of truth and the exercise of free choice, which are somehow Godlike, down to sensation, which we share with beasts, and even down to the vegetative functions that we have in common with plants. Thomas even insisted that if the human body itself holds together at all—if it is truly one body and not a mere heap—the cause is this one soul. To put it in his terms, the one soul is a human being's sole *substantial form*.[22] In all of this, Thomas was defending the fundamental unity of the human person. But many theologians feared that, despite his claims to the contrary, in making the intellectual soul so involved with the body, he was jeopardizing its immortality.[23]

---

19. See below, 125.

20. For the general picture, see Pegis, *St. Thomas and the Problem of the Soul in the Thirteenth Century*.

21. We see this in some of the public disputations that he held during that period, the so-called Quodlibets (*Quaestiones de quolibet*, literally, "questions on whatever"). In these events, open to the whole university, a master held forth on topics of his colleagues' choosing, and fielded objections to his views. See Torrell, *Initiation*, 273–78.

22. This notion will be discussed in some detail below in subsequent chapters.

23. Some also raised Christological issues. On Thomas's mature approach to the soul's immortality, see below, 114–16.

Thomas's views on matter itself also raised some concerns. For example, he insisted that prime matter was pure potentiality, with no actual existence of its own.[24] It could only have actual existence through some form. Otherwise it would already be a full-fledged substance, and its unity with any form would be merely accidental, not substantial. In itself this idea might not have been problematic. But a corollary that Thomas drew from it was that not even God could cause matter to exist without a form. Some theologians found this to be an unacceptable limitation on divine power.

Thomas also opposed the rather widely held view that all creatures, even the incorporeal or spiritual ones, contain matter. Proponents of this view argued that things are changeable only if they have matter, and that even spiritual creatures can change (with respect to what they understand and will). Thomas agreed that all creatures can undergo change, but he thought that some kinds of change do not require matter.[25] Some theologians also judged that spiritual creatures had to be composed of matter and form so as to differ from God, who alone would be perfectly simple, a pure form. Thomas handled this point with his famous and eventually even more controversial distinction between substantial form and act of being, *esse*.[26] In all creatures, these are really distinct and constitute a real composition. Only in God are they really identical, and so only He is utterly simple.

These and other tensions between Thomas and the more conservative theological majority would come fully to a head only after his death, as would the controversy regarding the Arts masters. In 1277, after what seems to have been a rather hasty investigation, Bishop Tempier condemned a much wider-ranging set of propositions, 219 in all. The Arts masters were again the main target, but several of the propositions sounded very much like things that Thomas was known to have taught. It was probably no coincidence that the condemnation was issued on March 7, his date of death. There is evidence that Tempier also initiated a separate inquiry into Thomas's works, which was cut short by orders from Rome. That same year, a more limited but similar condemnation was issued for Oxford by the Archbishop of Canterbury, the Dominican Robert Kilwardby. Scholars

24. On prime matter, see below, 40–44.
25. See below, 79n73.
26. See below, 126–30.

usually see 1277 as a watershed in the story of Thomas's influence and of medieval thought generally. But this is beyond our scope.[27]

Happy Ending

During the second Parisian period Thomas produced several important works: the Second Part and some of the Third Part of the *Summa theologiae*; commentaries on the Gospels of Saint Matthew and Saint John; the disputed questions *On the Virtues* and *On Evil*;[28] full commentaries on Aristotle's *De sensu et sensato* and *Physics*; large portions of commentaries on the *Posterior Analytics* and the *Metaphysics* (both completed at Naples); and unfinished commentaries on the *De interpretatione*, the *Politics*, and the *Meteorology*. Also at that time he composed most, if not all, of his commentary on the so-called *Liber de causis*. This difficult work had long been attributed to Aristotle. Albert already doubted this attribution, and Thomas correctly identified the work as a compilation, by an Arab author, of excerpts from the *Elementatio theologica* of the pagan Neoplatonic philosopher Proclus.

Thomas could make that identification thanks to a recent translation of the *Elementatio theologica* from the original Greek by William of Moerbeke (†1286). This learned Flemish Dominican translated numerous Greek philosophical works into Latin, including several of Aristotle's. Thomas certainly took ample advantage of his confrere's work. Contrary to what is often said, however, there is no strong evidence of direct collaboration between them.[29]

On the other hand, Thomas's enormous output would have been impossible without a team of assistants helping to prepare his materials and to put his words on parchment.[30] Early biographies speak of his often dictating to three or four secretaries at the same time. This may strain credibility, but the facts are not easily explained otherwise. By a reasonable calculation, taking a page as three hundred words, during Thomas's four years in Paris he averaged about fourteen pages per day.

---

27. See Torrell, *Initiation*, 433–63.

28. The important sixth Question, which consists of a single article on free choice, is generally thought to be a separate composition, of uncertain circumstances.

29. Torrell, *Initiation*, 253–58.

30. Ibid., 350–57.

In the spring of 1272 Thomas left Paris for the last time. His next and final teaching post was in Naples, at the head of yet another new Dominican house of studies. Its location seems to have been chosen by Thomas himself, possibly with the encouragement of king Charles II. Here, in addition to commentaries on Saint Paul's *Epistle to the Romans* and on the *Epistle to the Hebrews*, and perhaps the unfinished commentary on the *Psalms*, he continued with the Third Part of the *Summa theologiae*, brought to completion the commentaries on the *Posterior Analytics* and the *Metaphysics*, initiated a commentary on the *De generatione et corruptione*, and composed a substantial portion of a commentary on the *De caelo*. This last work presents an extraordinary display of both philosophical and astronomical erudition. Perhaps also in Naples, if not previously in Paris, he undertook a treatise, never finished, concerning the angels, the metaphysically penetrating *On Separate Substances*.

On or around December 6, 1273, while celebrating Mass, Thomas underwent an experience of some kind that left him visibly altered. Afterwards he showed no desire to continue writing. According to his closest companion, Reginald of Piperno, he offered only a very brief explanation: "I can do no more. Everything that I have written seems like straw in comparison with what I have seen." What he meant by this has invited many conjectures. A subsequent event, however, indicates that it was in no way a repudiation of his thought, and that the experience had not at all affected his mental faculties. After a few weeks of rest at his sister's home near Naples, toward the end of January or the beginning of February he set out with some other friars for Lyons, where the Pope had convoked a Council for May 1. On the way, Thomas was asked to stop at Monte Cassino and explain to the monks a passage from Gregory the Great on the compatibility of God's infallible knowledge of the future with human freedom. Unwilling to make the detour, Thomas instead dictated a response, the *Epistola ad Bernardum abbatem casinensem*. It is one of his clearest treatments of the topic.

Further on in the trip Thomas struck his head against a low-hanging branch. The incident left him stunned, but he brushed it off. Some days later they stopped at the home of his niece, where he fell ill. It is here that he is said to have expressed a desire for fresh herrings. Normally he did not request special dishes, but he had lost his appetite and was pressed by the physician about what he might be able to ingest. A passing fishmonger was found to have a basketful of them, even though they were unknown in that region and the fishmonger swore that he had been carrying sardines. This episode was recounted during Thomas's process of canonization. There is no indication that it influenced the process's outcome.

After a few days Thomas attempted to travel again, but fatigue forced him to stop at the abbey of Fossanova. There his condition worsened rapidly. On March 7, 1274, two or three days after receiving the Sacrament of Penance and Viaticum, and a day after receiving the Anointing of the Sick, he expired.

Despite the request of the Paris Arts masters, Thomas's remains were kept at Fossanova until 1369, when they were transferred to the Dominican church at Toulouse. Pope John XXII opened his process of canonization on August 7, 1316, and proclaimed him Saint on July 18, 1323. In 1325, the Bishop of Paris revoked the articles of Tempier's 1277 condemnation "insofar as they touch or are said to touch on the doctrine of blessed Thomas." His doctrinal authority grew apace. Until the mid-sixteenth century, the Roman Catholic liturgy celebrated only four Doctors of the Church: Ambrose, Jerome, Augustine and Gregory the Great. On April 15, 1567, Pope Pius V added five names to the list: Athanasius, Basil, Gregory of Nazianzus, John Chrysostom, and Thomas Aquinas. It is striking that the most recent of the other eight Doctors, Gregory the Great, lived seven centuries before him.

According to testimonies given during his process of canonization, in manhood Thomas was of lofty stature, heavy, erect and well-proportioned; his large head was well-shaped and somewhat bald; his complexion, delicate and "like the color of new wheat." He was serenely cheerful and seldom in a bad mood, taciturn and given to abstraction but not aloof, capable of irony but never mordant or sarcastic, patient and kind with his students, modest but firm with his colleagues. Even his staunchest opponents acknowledged the nobility of his character. Although he travelled a good deal, outwardly his life was relatively uneventful, spent largely in prayer, study, preaching, teaching, and writing. He desired no other. In 1265, on being named Archbishop of Naples by the Pope, he begged—successfully—to be excused.

Thomas's staggering production displays a mind as tireless as it was quick. His extant, undoubtedly authentic works total about sixty; a number of others have been attributed to him over the centuries, some of probable authenticity, some dubious, and some spurious.[31] His genres were common

---

31. A very informative catalogue compiled by Gilles Emery, O.P., can be found in Torrell, *Initiation*, 483–525, 611–32. The works have been classified in various ways. Probably the least disputable is by genre, as in Emery's catalogue.

enough in his time, but today readers need to be familiarized with them in order to read the works with ease and profit. Two of the major genres, the textual commentary and the disputed question, reflect those two most usual teaching formats in the university, the *lectio* and the *disputatio*. But not all of Thomas's works in these genres were the result of classroom activity, and the disputed question format is more or less explicitly present in several works of other genres, most notably the commentary on the *Sentences*, the commentary on Boethius' *De Trinitate*, and the *Summa theologiae*. Although his main views were remarkably constant throughout his career, he did change his position on some issues, and even when his conclusions remained the same, his ways of addressing many questions underwent significant development. At the very least, it is important not to lose sight of the chronology of his works.

In scholarly writing Thomas achieved a distinctive blend of rigor, clarity, simplicity, and elegance. The dryness of expression and almost total absence of references to himself are sometimes regarded as the unconscious symptoms of a mere want of feeling. But such a judgment is hard to square with the artful, theologically precise, yet movingly intimate eucharistic prayer, *Adoro te devote*.[32]

Handmaid

The rest of this chapter is about the place of philosophy in Thomas's thought. He studied and wrote about philosophy because he considered it useful for his theological work.[33] His chief philosophical interests were in the areas that overlap with theology—God, the soul, morality, and so on—and theological issues were often what prompted his best philosophical thinking. Nevertheless, as is shown by his commentaries on Aristotle, he cultivated the philosophical sciences quite thoroughly.

In order to understand Thomas's view of the relation between philosophy and theology, a good place to begin is the very first article of the *Summa theologiae*. There he asks whether, in addition to the philosophical disciplines, human beings need any other doctrine. He is taking it quite for granted that philosophy is a valid and even necessary factor in human well-being. He is probably also assuming that his reader has already received

32. See Wielockx, "Poetry and Theology," and Murray, *Aquinas at Prayer*, 239–59.

33. For a helpful synthetic presentation of the role of philosophy in theology for Thomas, see West, "The Functioning of Philosophy in Aquinas."

a philosophical formation. On the other hand, his answer shows that he judges philosophy insufficient, even gravely so. Human beings need another doctrine as well, one that exceeds the power of human reason and is revealed by God; and they need it in view of their very end, the ultimate point and perfection of human life. For the end itself exceeds reason's comprehension. It is something supernatural, the heavenly vision of God "face to face," as He is in Himself.[34] If we are going to play any kind of intelligent role in the process of arriving at this goal, we need information about it, and about the way to reach it, that we cannot obtain on our own.

To be sure, even this thesis, that man's end exceeds reason, is known with certainty only by revelation. Thomas's fundamental account of the need for theology is itself theological. He does not base the need for theology, or what he more commonly calls sacred doctrine, on philosophical or any other non-theological truths. Quite generally, he holds that theology is altogether sufficient unto itself for its validity. Some of its teachings depend on others—it contains both principles and conclusions—but none of them depends on extraneous principles or needs to be verified in the light of non-theological knowledge. Its principles are not things proved by philosophy. They are held on faith, through belief in God's Word, as such.

Thomas also finds it significant that divine revelation has come to our aid even with regard to that limited body of truths about God and about our relation to Him that, at least in principle, reason itself can grasp. These truths, which Thomas calls preambles of the faith, include God's existence, many of His attributes, and the fact that worship is due to Him and to Him alone. Revelation itself teaches that reason can know such truths.[35] And Thomas is sure that some philosophers actually did hit upon them.[36] (He generally restricts the term *philosopher* to pagan thinkers—truth-seekers using reason alone.) But without revelation, these truths "would be known only by a few, after a long time, and mixed with many errors."[37]

This is so even though, at least in Thomas's judgment, almost the whole point of the visible world is to display its Maker to us. The problem is not that the world is intrinsically cryptic. To recall Chesterton's quip, God is the most intelligible artist of all. The problem is that our minds have been dulled by sin. Even before the fall, Thomas grants, man and woman did

34. *STh*, I–II, q. 3, a. 8.

35. Rom 1:19–20.

36. *Scg*, I, cap. 3, §14. See McInerny, *Praeambula Fidei*.

37. *STh*, I, q. 1, a. 1; cf. *De ver.*, q. 14, a. 10.

not actually see God in Himself, since otherwise sin—turning away from Him—would have been impossible. God in Himself is utterly irresistible. But instead of having to go through a process of reasoning, as we do, in order to know anything concerning Him, they understood at once what His created effects show about Him.[38] As for our present situation, Thomas often cites a comparison of Aristotle's: in relation to the things that are most evident or intelligible in themselves, our mind is like the eye of the bat in relation to sunlight.[39]

And yet Thomas judges philosophy—sound philosophy, following its own principles—to be highly useful in theology. Its utility consists, surprisingly enough, in its coming to the aid of our mind's weakness as we grapple with divine truth. Even though theological knowledge does not intrinsically depend on it, it makes this knowledge easier for us to acquire and to manage, because it is rooted in the things that are most intelligible to us: "from the things that are known by natural reason," our mind "is more easily led by the hand—*facilius manuducitur*—into the things above reason that are transmitted in this science."[40] The philosophical sciences thus make for a "greater manifestation" of sacred teaching. They connect supernatural truth, to the extent that such connection is possible, with things that we can see for ourselves.

Thomas says that philosophy is useful to theology in three ways: for providing likenesses or analogies to supernatural things from things that are naturally knowable; for arguing against positions contrary to the faith, either by proving them false or by showing that they are not necessarily true; and for proving those preambles of the faith.[41] We might also add a fourth way in which Thomas seems to find philosophy useful in theology: for weeding out bad arguments in favor of revealed truths, such as the attempts by some to prove that the world had a temporal beginning. Thomas thinks such arguments do more harm than good.[42]

---

38. *STh*, I, q. 94, a. 1, corp. & ad 3.

39. *Metaph.* II.1, 993b9–11; see, e.g., *STh*, I, q. 1, a. 5, ad 1; q. 12, a. 1.

40. *STh*, I, q. 1, a. 5, ad 2. As mentioned in the Introduction, Thomas thinks teaching generally involves a kind of *manuductio*, or rather, various kinds. A full list of passages would include works spanning his entire career, especially the *Sentences* commentary and, above all, the *Summa theologiae*. Some of the *Summa* texts: I, q. 12, a. 12; q. 117, a. 1; I–II, q. 91, a. 5, ad 1; q. 98, a. 6; q. 99, a. 6; II–II, q. 2, a. 3; q. 81, a. 7; q. 180, a. 4.

41. *In De Trin.*, q. 2, a. 3.

42. *STh*, I, q. 46, a. 2.

So, the fact that theology is self-sufficient does not at all mean that it is simply isolated from philosophy, as though they never spoke about the same things or as though their modes of discourse were so foreign to each other as to preclude communication between them. Thomas describes theology's overall relation to the philosophical sciences as that of a superior or architectonic discipline to inferior and subordinate ones. It is like the relation of statecraft to the military arts.[43]

In fact, because the role of the philosophical sciences in theology is to help lead us by the hand, Thomas even goes so far as say that theology uses them all as *ancillae*, handmaids.[44] Does this clash with philosophy's autonomy and dignity? Some theologians might not take the question very seriously, but Thomas would; and his answer would be no. Autonomy is self-regulation. A discipline is autonomous to the extent that its rules and principles are intrinsic to it rather than imposed on it or dictated to it from the outside. Now, Thomas does think that some human sciences get their principles from other sciences. And he thinks that all the principles of the philosophical sciences are "determined"—definitively formulated and de-fended—by one of them, namely metaphysics.[45] But he flatly denies that any of the principles of the philosophical sciences come from or depend upon theology.[46] Sacred doctrine functions only as a kind of touchstone for them, though an infallible one: "anything in the other sciences that is found to be contrary to the truth of sacred doctrine is condemned as altogether false."[47] And Thomas is sure that any such conflict with theological truth in some other science must entail either a violation or at least an overstepping of that science's own principles. As we saw, some of the Arts masters seem to have held it possible that a heretical, and therefore false, proposition be reached as a rationally necessary conclusion. But Thomas insists that what reason necessarily concludes can only be a necessary truth.[48]

As for the dignity of this handmaid, it should almost suffice to recall what was for Thomas the most famous use of that epithet (Luke 1:38). But besides that, the fact that philosophy is being used for the sake of some end

43. *STh*, I, q. 1, a. 5, ad 2; see also I, q. 1, a. 8, ad 2.

44. *STh*, I, q. 1, a. 5, s.c. & ad 2; cf. *In De Trin.*, q. 2, a. 3, ad 7.

45. On the relation of metaphysics to the other philosophical sciences, see below, 101–3, 152–53, 166–71.

46. *STh*, I, q. 1, a. 6, ad 2.

47. Ibid.

48. *On the Unity of the Intellect*, ch. 5.

outside of it does not, for Thomas, exclude its having an intrinsic value of its own or its being desirable for its own sake. Indeed, as he sees it, theology can make philosophy itself even more lovable. "For when a man has a will disposed to believe, he loves the truth believed, and he reflects on it and embraces any reasons for it that he finds."[49] More generally, since the theologian is sure that all truth comes from God, he can judge that "the study of philosophy, in itself, is licit and praiseworthy, on account of the truth that the philosophers have acquired through God revealing it to them, as stated in Romans 1 [v. 19]."[50] In this respect philosophy even constitutes a kind of germ or foretaste of man's last end, which consists in the contemplation of the highest truth.[51]

Ancillary Theology

Thomas of course was by no means the first Christian thinker, nor the only one of his time, to reflect on the relation between revealed truth and philosophy. Thirteenth-century thinkers gave special attention to how philosophy and theology stand with respect to the conception of scientific knowledge that is laid out in Aristotle's *Posterior Analytics*.[52] To compare what Aristotle and the medievals meant by *science* with what we usually mean by it would be a complicated affair. But at least some aspects of the Aristotelian conception are still familiar enough. A science was then, and still is, a body of knowledge about a specific subject matter, verified through rigorous proof. For present purposes this is a sufficient description.

Now, Thomas holds that theology is indeed a science in the Aristotelian sense (albeit with some peculiar features that need not detain us here), and in the *Summa theologiae* he makes a visible effort to observe the canons of the *Posterior Analytics*.[53] But making theology a science raises an issue for him, because, as his conception of the preambles of the faith suggests, he also posits a philosophical science that treats of God. It is the science that Aristotle himself sometimes calls theological.[54] The question is, how

49. *STh*, II–II, q. 2, a. 10.

50. *STh*, II–II, q. 167, a. 1, ad 3.

51. See *STh*, I–II, q. 3, a. 6; I–II, q. 57, a 1, ad 2.

52. For an unpacking of the doctrine of the *Posterior Analytics*, very lucid, and staying very close to Thomas's commentary on it, is Weisheipl, *Aristotelian Methodology*.

53. On the general topic, see Jenkins, *Knowledge and Faith in Thomas Aquinas*.

54. E.g., *Metaph.*, VI.1, 1026a19; XI.7, 1064b2.

can there be two sciences of the same thing? Of course there can be two (or more) sets of opinions, or of hypotheses, or of myths about God or the gods. But a science, by definition, is a set of truths. If they are truths about the same thing, why are they not all in the same set?

Part of the answer will be that one set is revealed supernaturally, while the other is the work of natural reason. But for Thomas that cannot be the whole answer. This is because, on his view, the very subject matter of a science is what chiefly decides how the science works. As he sees it, the subject itself is the principal source of the science of it; the way in which it is known is largely the way in which it makes itself known or presents itself to the mind. The science of numbers and the science of fish proceed in very different ways, and this is mainly because numbers and fish are very different things and present themselves to us very differently.

For Thomas, then, the reason why sacred doctrine is supernaturally revealed and not the work of natural reason is precisely that its proper subject matter is God Himself. God does not naturally present Himself, as He is in Himself, to natural reason at all. He naturally presents Himself in that way only to Himself. He can share His knowledge of Himself with others, but they cannot possibly acquire it on their own. He can also share it more or less perfectly. Sacred doctrine is a rather imperfect share in it, ordered toward the far more perfect share that awaits the blessed in heaven. It is like the way in which a student who has not yet mastered a subject shares in his teacher's knowledge of it, namely, by hearing what the teacher says about it and believing that. Even for the idea of belief or faith as a way of sharing in genuine knowledge, Thomas finds support in Aristotle, who says that "he who would learn must believe."[55]

But what Thomas (rarely) calls philosophical theology is not a share in God's knowledge at all.[56] And despite that designation, neither is God its proper subject matter. Of course it does treat of God. But this is only because, and insofar as, He enters into the account of its own subject matter, which must be something that does present itself to the human mind.

What is the subject of Aristotle's "theological" science? This was itself a matter of dispute in the Middle Ages. Everyone agreed that this science was the one laid out in the *Metaphysics*. They did not know that the writings contained in the *Metaphysics* were put together as a single work only after Aristotle's death, and they simply assumed that all of this book pertained

---

55. Aristotle, *Sophistical Refutations*, 2, 165b3; see *STh*, II–II, q. 2, a. 3.

56. He uses this expression in *In De Trin.*, q. 5, a. 4, *in fine corp.*

to one single science. In some parts of the *Metaphysics*, however, it sounds as though the science's subject is what Aristotle calls the first or primary causes. In other places, the subject seems to be being, inasmuch as it is being, and as common to all things. In still others, it seems to be the divine "separate substances"—that is, the incorporeal beings on which all visible reality depends, and which, being alive and immortal, are duly termed gods.

On this issue the great Arab commentators, Avicenna and Averroes, disagreed. Avicenna held that the subject of metaphysics was common being, *ens commune*. Averroes said it was the divine substances. Thomas sides with Avicenna. The subject of a science, he says, is that nature whose causes and attributes are investigated in the science. The causes are not the subject of the science; rather, knowing them is the science's end or goal.[57] By studying the nature of being, as such, metaphysics is led to the consideration of the divine, as that nature's first and proper cause. This consideration does not lead to an understanding the divine nature as it is in itself. What God is cannot be properly conceived in terms of what being is or of any other created nature. But many true judgments about Him can be formed in light of creatures, and they are the highest achievement of philosophical thinking.

There is still room, then, for another theology, whose very subject is the divine nature. In denying that such a theology can be a human science and insisting that it must be revealed, Thomas is again opposing Averroes. The opposition is strong, since Thomas in fact denies that natural reason can properly grasp the nature of any purely incorporeal reality—not only God's, but also that of the incorporeal creatures, the angels. This is not because we cannot think of such realities at all, but because we can think of them only by comparison and contrast with sensible, corporeal reality, which is where all our thinking begins. "Our natural understanding can extend just as far as it can be led by the hand by way of sensible things."[58] So now let us turn to the part of Thomas's philosophy that regards what is most proper to such things.

Perhaps, however, a preliminary caveat is in order, both for the next chapter and for much of the rest of the book. Thomas certainly thinks that the physical world and its occupants are worth studying, just for their own sake. He thinks that knowing about them is good and pleasant in itself. It is even a kind of wisdom. But it is only a secondary kind, and his strictly physical teachings, despite their considerable thoroughness, are ultimately

57. *In Meta.*, Proem.
58. *STh*, I, q. 12, a. 12. Cf. I, q. 88, a. 2; *Quaestio disputata De anima*, a. 17.

23

intended only as aids to a better vision of reality as whole and, especially, of non-physical things. These are the primary things and the concern of the primary wisdom. And it is only in light of them, Thomas judges, that physical things and physical teachings themselves become fully intelligible. The same holds for the other non-metaphysical parts of his philosophy that we will explore. As one works through them for the first time, one may therefore have the nagging sense of only half getting them. This may very well be as it should. The test, I suppose, is how they look once one reaches the summit and gazes back down.

2

Births

Nature, Natural Philosophy,
and the Hylomorphic Analysis of Change

Back to *natura*

THE WORD *NATURA* AND offshoots of it run throughout Thomas's writings, and they play crucial roles both in his philosophy and in his theology. The word's English cognates are familiar enough.[1] Nevertheless, what Thomas takes to be its most proper meaning is now anything but current. Here is a sign of its strangeness. Using the word in what he considers its most proper sense, he says that a stone's moving upward is "against nature."[2] Would anyone today say that? Would you even feel sure enough of its meaning to disagree with it?

Thomas can hardly mean that such an event is weird or abnormal. Boys make it happen all the time. Nor can he mean that making it happen is wrong or immoral. Picking up a piece of straw would be against nature in this same sense, and yet he judges it, in itself, morally indifferent.[3] Is

---

1. On the history of *nature* and related terms, very helpful is Lewis, *Studies in Words*, chapter 2, 24–74.

2. *STh*, I–II, q. 71, a. 2, obj. 2.

3. See *STh*, I–II, q. 18, a. 10.

it that moving downward rather than upward is what stones usually do? This is closer, but it is still not quite the idea. What he means is that a stone has in itself an inclination to move downwards—that is, toward the earth's center—and that this inclination, which he calls *gravitas* (heaviness), arises from within it, from its *natura*—whatever that is.

Now, we will probably be inclined to say that it does not matter what *natura* is. Such a view of gravity must be wrong in any case. The tendency of stones to move downward, we are taught, is the effect, not of anything within them, but of the force of the earth's gravity acting to pull them down. And we would surely also say that if their yielding to this force is any sense natural, their yielding to the greater force of a throw is so too, in the same sense.

In part, I suppose, this is what is called a merely empirical question. Thomas thought that falling was a rather localized phenomenon, confined to some of the kinds of bodies that exist under the moon. Had he seen the evidence that celestial and terrestrial things differ much less than he thought they did, perhaps he would have accepted the view that *gravitas* affects all kinds of bodies and that it is not strictly relative to the center of the earth.[4] But there is also a broader issue here, not about gravitation, but about the actions of things generally.

We may accept easily enough that a given kind of thing has certain active properties. An electron, we say, has a negative charge. But we probably do not think of the electron itself as giving rise to the charge. Its having the charge is just a brute fact about it. The very word *charge* suggests a load that something just happens to carry. Presumably if it did not have the charge, we would not call the thing an electron. But do we really think of the charge as essential to or inseparable from that thing? Most of us, I suspect, conceive the situation in a rather mechanistic way. We tend to picture energy, forces, and the like as free-floating entities, and bodies as their mere receptacles—quite inert receptacles, ready to be pushed or pulled anywhere, or nowhere, and to be made to do anything, or nothing. Such a body can take a charge or leave it.

A few of us might deny the need to posit such bodies at all. And in fact I think Thomas would be rather sympathetic to that view. Still, he does posit bodies of some sort, and he distinguishes between a body, or the inner makeup of a body, and the active properties that it may have. For its

---

4. This is not to say that he would accept the idea of a force of gravitational attraction. See below, 50.

inner makeup is all its own, while its active properties are relative to other bodies and presuppose its makeup. But he definitely does not think of the makeup as inert. It is not itself an active property or set of properties, but it is a source of them. He does not deny that things can be also subjected to outside forces; he knows that stones can be impelled upward. But the important point, and the main one that I hope to get across in this chapter, is that, in his world, there is an order or a level of power or energy that is distinct from and prior to that of motion and change and process and interaction. We can call it the substantial level.

But let us return to the question of what Thomas means by *natura*. Is it just the makeup of a thing? That would not be so strange to us, would it? But it is not quite right either. For Thomas, the makeup of a thing is not a *natura*, in the proper sense, unless it gives rise to properties that pertain to motion and change. By contrast, we will just as easily call the makeup of a thing its nature, whether or not it has any such properties. We speak of the nature of a triangle, of a concept, of anything. Thomas does grant that *natura* can be used in this very broad sense. But he considers it a merely derivative sense and rather diluted—not to say denatured. *Natura* in the proper sense is for him something exclusively physical.

In a way, of course, this is a mere redundancy, since *phusis* is just Greek for nature. But clearly not everything that we call physical is something that Thomas regards as properly natural. What is more physical than a stone's being thrown upward? And although we do sometimes speak of nature as something exclusively physical, we usually mean either the whole of corporeal reality, or else a single power or force driving and regulating the whole—something like Mother Nature. For Thomas there are many natures, as many as the kinds of physical things. Nor are the bodies themselves nature, in the strict sense. They are *by* nature.

I have only been trying to convey the strangeness of Thomas's concept of nature, not to explain it. Almost inevitably, readers not alerted to its strangeness will either misconstrue much of what he says (or is reported to say) about it, or else find it all hopelessly muddled and defying construal altogether. Now I shall try to explain the concept, along with related notions. I hope that, by the end, even if still strange, it also seems serious. Thomas holds that the order of nature is instituted by divine wisdom, and that reason, virtue, and even grace, imitate it.[5] If his concept of nature is not serious, many of his other concepts are not either.

5. On virtue and grace as imitating the order of nature, see *STh*, II–II, q. 31, a. 3. On

A Branch of Philosophy

In Lewis and Short's Latin-English dictionary, the first meaning listed for *natura* is *birth*. Thomas confirms this. In common usage, he tells us, *natura* refers to *nativitas* (birth) or *nascentia* (things born).[6] English has lost the verbal connection, but as a way of saying that someone is or acts somehow by nature, we might well say that he or she was born that way. Birth or begetting or generation, the bringing forth of another individual of the same kind as the begetter or the generator, is for Thomas, as for Aristotle, the most natural event of all. By it, Aristotle says, corruptible beings share as far as they can in the immortal and the divine, achieving perpetual existence at least for their kind, even though the individuals perish.[7]

For Thomas, natural birth also points to the divine in a way that Aristotle could not have imagined. It reflects the birth in the deity itself, the begetting of the Son of God. However, it is not to this that Thomas refers when he speaks, as he often does, of God's nature. It hardly could be, since the Father too has that nature, and He is not begotten. The Son is begotten, *genitum*, in the proper sense, but His divinity is a *natura* only by extension. This is because it is not physical.

Still, Thomas does find this truth about God putting ordinary physical nature, especially human nature, in a new light. Following the tradition, he holds that our being in the image of God, which sets us off from other bodily creatures, refers chiefly to the spiritual dimension of our makeup. Thomas also holds that, on the whole, angels are in God's image more perfectly than man is. This is because their spiritual makeup, which is their entire makeup, is more perfect. But he also finds two ways in which man alone is in God's image.[8] One is that "man is from man as God from God." Angels do not beget angels. That is a fairly easy idea.

The other way is that man's soul is whole in his whole body and also whole in every part of it, which is how God is in the world. This is rather difficult. It rests on a concept touched upon briefly in the first chapter, that of the human soul as the human body's substantial form. This notion, substantial form, is absolutely fundamental in Thomas's philosophy. It is crucial even for having some positive notion of spiritual things. I mention

---

reason as doing so, see chapter 6.

6. *In Meta.*, V, lect. 5, §808; *In Phys.*, II, lect. 1, §145[5]. I draw on these two *lectiones* throughout this chapter.

7. *De anima*, II.4, 415a28–b7. See *In De an.*, II, lect. 7, §311–17.

8. *STh*, I, q. 93, a. 3.

it now because, in fact, the most proper meaning of *natura* will turn out to be precisely this, a body's substantial form. Seeing how Thomas reaches this conception of nature will occupy most of this chapter.

But returning to the notion of birth, what removes the begetting of God's Son from the domain of *natura* in the proper sense is what I mentioned before: it involves no motion or change. The Son did not come into being. Nor did He grow up. Aristotle associates the word *phusis* with *phuesthai*, to grow.[9] The Son's birth is eternal, and He is eternally equal to the Father. Thomas does call the Son's begetting a procession, but Thomas is no process theologian.[10] In his God, "there is no change nor shadow of alteration" (Jas 1:17). Natural begetting is always a change, a coming into being, as well as the first of many other changes or processes in what is begotten. There is always a last one too, a passing away. For Thomas, subjection to processes or motions is quite generally and formally what defines the field of that large branch of inquiry which he calls natural philosophy. The subject matter of this inquiry is *ens mobile*, mobile being.

Thomas was not as interested in the physical world as Albert was, but he considered natural philosophy absolutely essential to a sound philosophical curriculum, and indispensable as a preparation for the study of metaphysics. Today these convictions may not be easy to appreciate, because the very notion of natural philosophy has become rather unfamiliar. It is not the same as what we call the philosophy of science. That centers on the modes of thinking involved in scientific knowledge. The closest thing to it, in Thomas's philosophy, would be the kind of study offered in Aristotle's *Posterior Analytics*, which Thomas considers part of logic. But what he calls natural philosophy is not *about* natural science. It is about natural reality. Indeed, in his sense of the term *scientia*, natural philosophy *is* natural science.

Obviously if by natural science we mean the type of knowledge that is gained through modern methods of experimentation, there is little or none of it in Thomas, under any name. This, however, does not mean that his natural science is mere armchair speculation, remote from observation or experience. He would not regard armchair speculation about nature as science. But experimentation is only one way of gaining experience of things, and only of some things. As for the modern tools of observation, he would surely have welcomed them.

9. *Metaph.*, V.4, 1014b16–18.

10. See Michael J. Dodds, *The Unchanging God of Love*.

Thomas would also have had no quarrel with our practice of dividing natural science into a multiplicity of disciplines, each concerned with a specific part or aspect of physical reality: physics, chemistry, geology, biology, and so forth. But he would call these disciplines parts of philosophy too; and it seems safe to say that he saw more unity among them, and with philosophy as a whole, than is usually ascribed to them now. The unity among them would be owing to a set of general concepts and principles that all natural sciences use, most of which are treated in Aristotle's *Physics*; for instance, the very concept of motion. Like Aristotle, Thomas thought these ought to be mastered before entering into any specific science. One of his earliest works, *On the Principles of Nature,* offers a brief and lucid synthesis of many of them. Being very general, these principles may seem to us more metaphysical than physical. And they do overlap somewhat with matters that Thomas treats in metaphysics. But even at this general level, he thinks natural philosophy has its own perspective or focus on things—the focal point being, as we said, the mobility of things. The naturalist wants to know why things move and act as they do. This is why those general principles are for him only the beginning. Things move and act in very different ways, and his ultimate aim is an accurate understanding of the specific way of each. The rest of this chapter will lay out some of the general principles. The next will present some of Thomas's views on one specific type of natural, mobile beings: the living ones.

Mobility and a General Definition of Nature

Now, if the field of natural philosophy is physical reality, one might wonder why the primary defining feature of its subject is said to be motion or mobility, and not corporeity. Thomas's answer would be that there is also another kind of science that considers bodily things, but not insofar as they are natural or physical or mobile. A body is a substance with three dimensions. We can consider this in abstraction from any motions or actions, and even any tangible properties, to which it might be subject. That is what Thomas thinks mathematicians do. Their field, he says, is "substance as subject to quantity."[11] Birth and death and the processes in between are not quantities. In abstracting from them, the mathematician abstracts from what makes bodies physical or natural. Of course, natural processes are associated with quantities, and mathematics has many applications in

11. *STh,* I, q. 85, a. 1, ad 2.

natural science. Thomas recognizes such applications, and he thinks they play decisive roles in certain natural sciences, for example, optics and astronomy. But he would not agree with Galileo that the book of nature is written in the language of mathematics. On the whole, Thomas regards mathematics as rather secondary in the study of physical things. Such things have their own proper principles, and these have to be understood on their own terms.

On the other hand, obviously the field of mobile beings does extend beyond those that are born, in the proper sense of the term. Only living things are properly said to be born. In one place Aristotle calls motion a kind of life in the universe, but Thomas says this is a metaphor.[12] Still, he does think there is something like birth among inanimate things, namely generation or coming into being. The generation of non-living things differs from birth, he says, in that what is born, generally speaking, begins as somehow joined or united to what generates it. What is born is, as we say, an "offspring" of its parent(s). For instance, a seed starts off inside, or even as part of, the tree that produces it. Inanimate things usually originate in something detached from what generates them, as a fire is started in one log by the fire in another log. But Thomas also thinks that even inanimate things can be seen to be joined with some kind of source of motion; for example, as we saw, he thinks a stone has in itself a principle of moving downward. (Even we must grant that it has in itself some sort of principle by which it can be pulled downward by the earth's attraction. After all, not everything can. Numbers, and angels, fall only metaphorically.) As emerging from such a conjoined principle, the thing's motion is like a birth. That, for Thomas, is how inanimate things came to be spoken of as natural. It is not that all such things are generated; indeed, he thinks some of them are not, for instance the stars (which we say are born and die). It is that they are joined to principles or sources of motions that they undergo.

This, however, raises another question. Thomas distinguishes between the natural and the artificial. But are not artifacts mobile too, and joined to principles of motion? A cellphone can fall as easily as a stone. A desk can be burned. And think of the very word *automobile*.

Thomas would say that, yes, in a sense such things are mobile, but not because of their being such things. A cellphone falls, not because it is a cellphone, but because it is made of heavy materials. A table can be burned, not because it is a table, but because it is wooden. And despite the name, even

12. *STh*, I, q. 18, a. 1, obj. 1 & ad 1; see *Physics*, VIII.1, 250b14–15.

an automobile is mobile only in virtue of its natural components: rubber, metal, gasoline, and so forth. These things do not act as they do because they are parts of an automobile. In short, when Thomas defines the natural as the mobile, he means mobile per se, in virtue of itself. Artifacts are not mobile in virtue of what is artificial about them, but only by association, in virtue of what is natural in them. However, he does distinguish between artifacts and natural things produced under artificial conditions. For instance, he considers bread a natural substance. The baker only prepares for its production. What really produces it is the natural action of fire.[13]

What about the artifact-maker's own skill? Is that not the source of a motion, namely, the very process of making the artifact? Yet, even though the maker is himself a natural being, it is not in view of this skill that we call him natural. Why not? Because the skill is not joined to what *undergoes* the process. The baker does not bake himself. Or at least that is true for most skills. The process, the being made, is usually not in the maker. At most, it only happens to be so in a particular case, as when a health-maker, a physician, makes himself healthy. Aristotle says that nature is like this: a physician who heals himself.[14] If a thing is moved by skill, the skill may be, and usually is, in another subject. But if it is moved by nature, the nature is and must be in it.

These considerations bring us close to Aristotle's famous definition: "nature is a principle and a cause of being moved and of being at rest in the thing to which it belongs primarily and in virtue of that thing and not incidentally."[15] This is rather a mouthful. Thomas offers some helpful remarks about it.[16] The first is that the word *principle* here (and presumably also *cause*) serves to prevent us from thinking of nature as what Thomas calls an "absolute" item. The principles of different things differ.[17] What nature is, in a given thing, is relative to that thing. Nature is not a single, uniform "force instilled in things" (*vis insita rebus*). There is no Mother Nature. Instead of speaking simply of nature, we should speak of natures, the nature of this or the nature of that.

Thomas says that the definition's phrase, "in the thing to which it belongs," serves to set aside artificial things, to which motion (the referent of

13 *STh*, III, q. 75, a. 6, ad 1.

14. *Physics*, II.8, 199b31–32.

15. *Physics*, II.1, 192b21–23.

16. *In Phys.*, II, lect. 1, §145.

17. Cf. *Metaph.*, VII.16, 1040b19–21; XII.4–5, 1070a31–1071b2.

"it") belongs only by association with what is natural about them. Again, a table is not burned on account of any nature of table, there being no such thing (in this sense of *nature*), but on account of the nature of wood. As for the word "primarily," Thomas explains that it serves to ensure that the motion in question is understood to be the effect of the nature in question. For instance, an animal is a natural thing, and falling is a natural motion; but falling does not belong primarily to animals, i.e., because of their properly animal nature. If it did, only animals would fall. Of course, animals do fall. But Thomas says this is because of the "dominant element" in them, which I suppose would be earth or water. Thomas in fact follows Aristotle in positing four elements—earth, water, air, and fire—as the simplest of the bodily natures existing below the heavens. All the others, inanimate and animate, are in some way formed out of them. Falling is primarily due to the natures of earth and water. We would perhaps say that it is due to the nature of body itself. In any case, it is not due to something proper to animals.

As for the definition's phrase, "in virtue of itself and not incidentally," Aristotle himself says that this serves to set aside cases like that of the doctor who heals himself. The medical art is a principle of healing that merely happens, occasionally, to be in that which is healed. It might just as well cause something else to be healed. It is not the nature of what is healed.

The definition speaks not only of motion, but also of rest. Rest is the absence of motion in something mobile.[18] But rest too be may be natural to a thing. This is related to the thesis that natural things, as such, tend toward goals. A goal is something that is fit both to move toward and to rest in. When a heavy thing reaches the earth's center, it tends to stay there.

Aristotle declares that nature, as so defined, is something whose existence is too obvious to be demonstrated; he likens those who seek proof for it to someone blind from birth arguing about colors.[19] Thomas says that this is true of nature considered in a general way. The particular nature or principle of motion in a given thing, he says, might not be manifest. But things having in themselves some principle of motion or other are manifest to the senses, and so the existence of nature generally is immediately evident to us; that is, evident without any process of reasoning. It has the status of a first principle of knowledge. Natural science takes nature

18. *Physics*, III.2, 202a3–5; IV.12, 221b12–14; VI.2, 226b12–16; *Metaph.*, XI.12, 1068b22–25.

19. *Physics*, II.1, 193a3–9.

entirely for granted, and not even metaphysics proves it. Thomas does think, however, that we can get confused even about such obvious truths, and that metaphysics has a role in clearing up the confusion.[20] Right now there does seem to be some confusion about nature.

But we have not yet finished with the question of the meaning of the word—far from it. Despite its care and rigor, the above definition of nature does not yet give us its most strict and proper sense. This is because the definition is rather too general, even ambiguous. There is more than one sense in which something can be an intrinsic principle and cause of motion and rest. It might be so in the sense of *matter*, or it might be so in the sense of *form*.

In order to understand how these—matter and form—are senses of nature, we need to stand back and take an even wider perspective. Not all instances of matter and form are natures. Following Aristotle, Thomas holds that absolutely all motions—natural, or artificial, or any other sort, if there is any other—depend on factors that function as matter and as form. What follows, then, is a sketch of Thomas's general account of motion.[21]

Motion, Its Definition and Its Principles

Motions do not exist by themselves. There is always some thing—some body—that is moved. There is also always some respect in which it is moved. We may tend to think of only one respect, namely, place. We tend to identify motion with locomotion, a body's going from here to there. But for Thomas, there is motion not only in place, but also in size—growing and shrinking—and in shape and certain other qualities.[22] He calls qualitative motion *alteration*. Other examples of it would be getting warm or cool, soft or hard, angry or calm. We might prefer to call these processes rather than motions—although the results of the last ones cited are called *emotions*.

A motion or a process has termini. It has a starting-point and an end-point. Each terminus consists in a form, or something functioning like a

20. See below, 101–3, 166–71.

21. See *De princ. nat.*, cap. 1–2; *In Phys.*, I, lect. 11–13. On Thomas's reading of Aristotle's account of motion in terms of matter and form—in Greek, *hulē* and *morphē*, whence the name *hylomorphism*—see McInerny and O'Callaghan, "Saint Thomas Aquinas," sections 6 and 8. For a presentation of Thomas's hylomorphism from a contemporary perspective, see Brower, *Aquinas's Ontology of the Material World*.

22. See *In Phys.*, V, lect. 3–4. *In Meta.*, XI, lect. 12. Shape is a quality pertaining to quantity: *In Phys.*, VII, lect. 5, §917[5].

form: a quality, a size, a place.[23] Reaching one terminus implies having left the other. This is because each implies the negation or lack of the other: being hot implies not being cold, being indoors implies not being outdoors, etc. Between the termini there is an intermediate zone. The termini are its extremes, and as such they are called contraries, either absolutely (if the zone between them is not part of a larger zone), or with respect to that zone. The motion is through the zone. If it is truly one motion and not a series of motions, it is continuous or uninterrupted across the zone.

Of course one terminus does not become the other. Heat does not become cold. Forms are not transformed. Motion needs a third factor, a subject that can have now one form, now the other. A subject of motion is a body. The motion can be one and continuous because the body is.[24]

As that to which one form or the other belongs and which undergoes the motion, the body is called a *subject*. As having in itself the capacity or the potential for either form and for the motion between them, it is called *matter*. Materiality, and potentiality for a form, are not to be confused with the very privation or lack of that form. There must be privation, of course, if there is to be motion; what becomes hot cannot already be hot, but must first lack heat and then obtain it. But whereas its lack of heat ceases once it is hot, its potential for heat certainly does not cease then. Otherwise it would be hot when it no longer can be so, which is absurd.

However, usually Thomas will say that something is *in* potency to a given form only when it does not actually have the form. When it actually has the form, he says that it is, in that respect, not in potency, but in act. Here the word *act*—Latin *actus*—does not mean action or activity. Thomas says that the word originally referred to activity, but form can also be called act, inasmuch as it is both a source and a completion of activity.[25] Heat, which for him is a form, can function both as a source of the activity of heating and as its completion. In a later chapter we will see that there is also a more fundamental sense in which form is act.

The form to which a thing is moved, the endpoint, completes the motion. However, the motion itself exists only so long as the completion has not been reached. Likewise, the motion only exists once its other

23. A place is not properly a form, because it does not inhere in that which has it. But, like a form, it does make that which has it to be in a certain way. Just as having a shape makes a thing be so shaped, e.g., be round, so having a place makes a thing be so placed, e.g., be indoors.

24. See *Physics*, IV.11, 219a10–13.

25. *De pot.*, q. 1, a. 1.

terminus, its starting-point, has been left behind. When the subject is at either terminus, it is not moving from one or to the other.

During the motion, then, its subject is *in* potency with respect to the termini. On the other hand, we do regard motion itself as a kind of being in act, an activity. To what potential in the subject does this act, the motion itself, correspond? To its potential for the endpoint. Its potential for the starting-point is in a way incidental to the motion. If, having exited the starting-point, the subject happens now to have lost its potential for the starting-point, the motion can still go on; for instance, if what is aging no longer has the potential to be as youthful as it was, it can still be aging. But if it loses its potential for the endpoint, it cannot move to that point; what cannot *be* decrepit cannot *become* so. Usually, in fact, motions are named by their endpoints, not their starting-points.[26] A thing's being heated is a process toward heat in the thing, not from it. So a motion is essentially an actualization of its matter's potential for the motion's endpoint.

But it is an incomplete actualization. As long as the motion is going on, the endpoint has not been reached. When it is reached, the motion stops. In fact, so long as the motion is going on, there must be more of it still to come. Otherwise it has already stopped. A motion is both an incomplete act and act of something incomplete, something with a potential that is not yet fully actualized. And so Aristotle's definition of motion, which Thomas fully endorses, is this: "the act of that which is in potency, insofar as it is in potency."[27] The phrase "insofar as it is in potency" means with respect to the very act toward which the thing is moving and to which it is in potency as long as it is moving. This sets the motion off from any act, complete or not, that is merely incidental to it. For instance, if what is being heated is white, then it has both the act of being heated and the act of being white. But it has the being heated insofar as it is in potency to more heat. Its being white does not, as such, entail its being in potency to anything.

That definition of motion is not easy to understand. Some of the anti-Scholastic thinkers of early modernity found it simply unintelligible. But even if we can understand it, we might wonder why we need it. Can we not distinguish what is moved from what is at rest quite well without it? Probably so. But Aristotle and the Scholastics used it to distinguish motion not only from rest, but also from two other things: activity that is not motion,

---

26. *Physics*, V.1, 224b7–8. See *STh*, I, q. 23, a. 1, ad 3.
27. *Physics*, III.1, 201a10–11.

which will be treated in the next chapter, and immediate change, about which something must be said here.

By immediate change, I mean change with no zone between its termini. Such change is therefore instantaneous. The change from being at rest to being moved is of this sort. It is not an act distinct from its termini. It is nothing but the sequence or succession of them. In modern thought, the distinction between motion and immediate change has come to look rather insignificant, because of the practice of treating the continuous as a synthesis of indivisible units (e.g., of treating lines as sets of points). On this view, a motion can be treated as a series of immediate changes. Aristotle, however, had judged that such a view cannot be strictly true.[28] Dividing a continuous thing, he saw, does yield indivisible boundaries of the divided parts, as dividing a line yields endpoints. But, he insisted, if the continuous thing is not actually divided, the boundaries are only potential and do not actually exist. We do not start with indivisible units and build up a continuous thing out of them. Points, for example, have no size. How could the mere multiplication of points, by itself, yield something with any size?

This is not to say that immediate changes are not important. One reason why they are important for Thomas is that motions only exist in bodies, but immediate changes can occur in incorporeal beings too. Earlier it was mentioned that not only God but also angels stand outside natural philosophy, because they are not mobile. But only God, for Thomas, is absolutely changeless. Angels can undergo immediate changes, of a spiritual sort; e.g., from not understanding or willing something to understanding or willing it. Of course, we too can undergo such changes. And immediate changes are important in the philosophy of nature itself, because they include substantial change. We shall begin to address that notion shortly.

But returning to the general account of motion, we saw that what is moved, as such, is always on the way toward something. It is ordered to some form or act that it does not yet have. As Thomas sees it, this is unintelligible unless there is also something else in the picture: an origin of the motion, and of the form or act reached through it. A motion needs an agent, a mover.[29] Nothing is brought from being in potency to being in act except by something already in act, as water is heated by something already hot. We first conceive of action or agency, Thomas says, in encountering motion. And this conditions all our action-concepts, even those that

---

28. See *Physics*, VI.1, 231a21–232a22.
29. See *In Phys.*, III, lect. 5, §324[17]; *STh*, I, q. 2, a. 3, *Prima via*.

exclude motion and potentiality, such as the concepts of the Trinitarian *processions*.[30]

Thomas is not saying that the mover must literally possess the very same kind of act as that toward which the motion's subject is moved. Heating your coffee with a cool microwave does not refute him. He is saying that the mover must have an act sufficient to produce the motion. We would probably rather say that it must have sufficient energy. But then, *energy* comes from Aristotle's *energeia*, which passed into Thomas's Latin precisely as *actus*.[31]

Also, Thomas does not think that the mover must be acting throughout the motion's duration. It may only deposit a kind of determination or impulse, as it were a kinetic germ, out of which the motion later unfolds. This is how Thomas conceives the heaviness of a heavy body. It was received along with and through the body's nature, from the body's producer or generator. The motion that follows on it may only occur later on. If there is an agent acting right then when the body falls, it is only an indirect one, removing some obstacle to the fall, as when you let go of a stone that you are holding. And even that sort of agent operates only at the start of the fall.

Finally, not even the presence of an agent is enough to make a motion fully intelligible. We could at least imagine the agent's being able to move the thing, having the sufficient energy, but not actually doing so. The agent must also have some inclination or tendency toward ordering the thing to an endpoint and producing the motion to it. If it had no such tendency, it would not act in this way rather than that. It would do nothing.[32] The endpoint must engage its energy, so that it move the thing in that direction. The endpoint, although it does not yet exist, is already making a difference to what is going on. The agent acts because of it, for its sake. The endpoint is an end—*finis*—not only as a stop, but also as a goal.

Thus, in very broad terms, the general account of motion invokes the famous doctrine of the four kinds of cause: material, formal, agent or efficient, and final.[33] Later we will see how the kinds of cause can be traced

---

30. *STh*, I, q. 41, a. 1, ad 2.

31. See the very interesting paper by Thomas McLaughlin, "Act, Potency, and Energy."

32. See *STh*, I–II, q. 1, a. 2, and *In Meta.*, VI, lect. 2, §1183.

33. A full treatment of the causes would involve several distinctions under each kind. See, e.g., Aristotle, *Physics*, II.3–9; Thomas, *De princ. nat.*, cap. 3–6 (which also reflects *Metaph.*, XII.1–4, 1069a18–1070b35). Of particular importance is the distinction between direct and indirect movers, as in the example of falling. Thomas also uses this distinction in moral matters; see, e.g., *STh*, I–II, q. 6, a. 3, and I–II, q. 76, a. 1.

back to matter and form themselves, at least in natural things. But first we must identify the matter and the form that constitute senses of *natura*.

Substance and Accidents

Motions, we said, are with respect to a body's place, size, or quality. These are categories of what Aristotle calls *accidents*. Bodies are in the category of *substance*. For us, neither term is very felicitous. *Accident* can sound like a mistake or a coincidence, something unintended. Aristotle too uses it in that sense sometimes.[34] But when he applies it to certain categories, he simply means an accompaniment or an addition, a further modification of something (viz., of a substance). It may very well be intended, and it may be very important. Thus, as Thomas explains, no substance is complete or perfect merely by being the substance that it is. Its full perfection, its unqualified goodness, needs additional being, which is through accidents: size and shape, qualities, relations.[35] Virtue, for example, is a quality.[36] Friendship is a relation.[37]

Still, no matter how important accidents may be for the perfection of a thing, they are not the thing. The thing is a substance. Accident and substance differ radically, so radically that in a sense only substances exist. Calling a thing a substance means that it is a genuine subject of being. A substance is something that truly *is*. We do *speak* of accidents as though they were subjects of being, for instance when we say that courage *is* a virtue. But really it only confers some being on a substance.[38] What *is* courageous is not the soldier's courage; it is the soldier. Accidents do not even exist in the sense in which parts of a substance do. A part, for instance a nose, is a true subject of being, albeit only partial. It shares in the being of the whole. So parts too are substances.[39] Thomas says that accidents "inhere" in substances, but it is not as parts do. For accidents inhere in

34. For instance, in *Metaph.*, VI.2, 1026a33–1027a28.

35. *STh*, I, q. 5, a. 1, ad 1; I–II, q. 18, a. 1.

36. *STh*, I–II, q. 55, a. 4.

37. *STh*, I–II, q. 49, a. 1.

38. See, e.g., *STh*, I, q. 9, a. 2, ad 3; q. 45, a. 4; q. 90, a. 2; I–II, q. 110, a. 2, ad 3.

39. *Categories*, 2, 1a24–25, and 5, 3a29–32; *Metaph.*, VII.2, 1028b8–13. Ultimately this requires some qualifying; see below, 112n9.

parts too, as snubness inheres in noses. But whereas parts can have parts, accidents cannot have accidents.[40]

As for the term *substance*, it sounds like what stands under the rest. And since motion is with respect to accidents, it also sounds like something static or inert. One imagines a stage or a platform, with everything happening above it. Aristotle, however, says the most proper mark of a substance is that, "while remaining numerically one and the same, it is capable of admitting contrary qualities through a change in itself."[41] Notice that he does not say simply "while remaining one and the same," without qualification, as though it stayed unvaried in all respects; that would indeed make it inert, and also changeless. He says "numerically" one and the same—that is, the same individual. Socrates changes from fat to thin, vicious to virtuous, bearded to clean-shaven, etc., only if he remain Socrates. Fatness, vice, beardedness—these do not change while they remain; they simply appear or disappear. Notice too "a change in itself." Again, heat does not change into cold. A hot substance changes into a cold substance. Also statements and opinions, which can change from being true to being false, do so only through changes in what they are about, not in themselves.[42] Aristotle is saying that if there were no substance, there would be no motion. Of course he does posit an unmoved substance. But it makes all the others move. It is pure activity. In general, the substances are the things that act or are acted upon, or both. A nose can grow, bleed, be punched. Its snubness cannot. Not even its growing or bleeding or being punched can. Motions do not undergo motion.[43]

Substantial Change and Protomatter

Aristotle's unmoved substance is everlasting. Unlike many of his predecessors, however, he holds that a large number of substances come into being and pass away. Plants and animals, for instance, are born and die. Obviously his predecessors knew that. But on their views, these things were not substances. They thought the substances, the real beings, were the underlying components or materials. Those were the primary subjects of change, and they did not come into being or pass away. According to Aristotle,

40. See *Metaph.*, IV.4, 1007b2–16.
41. *Categories*, 5, 4b17–19.
42. Ibid., 4a21–b13.
43. *Physics*, V.2, 225b13–226a18; *Metaph.*, XI.12, 1068a13–b15.

Thales attributed this function to water; Heraclitus, to fire; Empedocles, to the four elements of earth, water, air, and fire.[44] Similarly, Democritus posited a huge multitude of tiny, highly mobile bodies that were indivisible—*atomic*, in the original sense—as the first and permanent subjects of change. All else was made out of them.[45]

For Aristotle, even the simplest earthly bodies, the four elements, come into being and pass away. Fires are lit and extinguished. Water condenses and evaporates. Minerals dissolve. Also in support of this view, he judged, is that simpler bodies can be blended into new kinds, such as living kinds—plants or animals. The blends have their own natures. They do not act in the way that mere combinations would act. They may show some of the properties of the elements, and when they corrupt, the elements may be regenerated out of them; but while they exist, the elements are in them only potentially, not actually. We will return to this idea.[46]

Our present concern is the very idea of substances coming into being and passing away. It is not an easy idea. A major difficulty arises from Aristotle's own hylomorphic analysis of motion and change. Substantial generation and corruption, if they exist, consist in the conversion of one substance into another. They are supposed to be quite commonplace occurrences. They are not a substance's sheer popping into or out of existence, out of or into nothing. They allegedly happen when you eat and digest an apple. They happen when an animal dies. Thomas, I suppose, would say that they happen when hydrogen and oxygen are made into water. The problem then is, what is it that underlies the conversion of one substance into another? What functions as the matter?

We must not forget that *matter*, in this philosophy, is just like *nature*: it is a relative term, not absolute. It does not at all mean *stuff*. Relative to a statue or to the process of making it, marble or wood is matter. Relative to a syllable, letters are matter. What is matter for one thing may have another as its matter. Bricks are matter for a house, and (say) earth is matter for bricks. The Presocratics were saying, in effect, that there is some kind of thing, or set of kinds, having nothing else as matter, and functioning as the first matter for everything else.[47]

---

44. *Metaph.*, I.3, 983b6–984a12; also *Physics*, II.1, 193a9–28.

45. *Metaph.*, VII.13, 1039a7–11.

46. See below, 48, 56–57.

47. Aristotle, *Metaph.*, IX.7, 1049a24–26.

We may find their physics crude, but with respect to the doctrine of matter, similar views have also appeared much more recently. Descartes, for instance, held that what underlies all bodily changes was what he called *res extensa*, extended reality. (It sounds just like substance as subject to quantity—Thomas's description of the field of mathematics.) The *res extensa* is ingenerable and incorruptible, never turned into anything else nor what anything else ever turns into. It is the first matter, and substance, of all physical things. It receives all motion and all kinetic properties. It differs from the Presocratics' substance only in being utterly inert and passive.

But returning to Aristotle and Thomas: if there is substantial change, there has to be a subject or a matter underlying it. Substances function as matter for accidental changes. But this matter will be prior to them and will have no matter of its own. It will be the first matter. Thomists writing in English commonly call it prime matter, though William Wallace calls it protomatter.[48] Here too, however, matter is only a relative term. That which is called prime matter or protomatter is called matter relative to those substantial changes. But what is it just in itself?

Nothing. That is, nothing actual, nothing definite. If it were something, it would already be a substance. What is something just in itself, with its own being and own intelligibility, existing separately and not just relative to something else, is precisely a substance. Of course, matter is not an accident either, added on to a substance. But accidents are essentially only modifications of substances, and prime matter is essentially only potency for substances. If we want to distinguish prime matter from accidents, we can call it substance in a qualified sense or substance in potency. But if we remove all reference to substance in the unqualified sense, which is actual substance, both accidents and prime matter simply disappear. And especially matter does. Accidents are at least forms and bring some actual being with them, even if what has the being is a substance. But prime matter is only potency, and it has no form of its own. This is why Thomas holds that not even God can make it exist by itself, apart from any kind of substance. In that case it would actually be, but there would be nothing that it actually is, which is absurd. "It is the same to say that matter is in act and that

---

48. In *The Modeling of Nature*, the word first appears on p. xi, then on pp. 8 ff. This book is an interesting attempt at a synthesis of modern science and the Aristotelian conception of natural things.

matter has form. So, to say that matter is in act without form is to say that contradictories hold together. Hence, it cannot be made by God."[49]

If there is nothing that prime matter is in itself, is it only a being of reason, not real at all? That might be the verdict if we reached it by mere logical analysis, stripping away whatever is predicated of a subject and leaving something that seems to be totally indeterminate and unidentifiable. This would perhaps not show that there is any such thing in reality. But Thomas insists that prime matter is only fully brought to light through the analysis of change.[50] The reality of prime matter stands or falls with the reality of substantial change. If substantial change is real, then so is prime matter; and, unlike what is nowadays called dark matter, it is no mere conjecture.[51] However, in speaking of it as we do, we do give it more being than it really has. We give it a name, an identity, and things are named and identified according to their forms.[52] But matter does not have a form of its own. It only has an order toward form, *habitudo ad formam*.[53] We treat this as a sort of form in its own right. That is how we can make matter a subject of propositions. In reality it is not a full-fledged subject, but only potency for a subject.

We should not think of prime matter as immediately ready to be just anything you please. A sow's ear cannot become a silk purse at once. This is so even though generation and corruption, in themselves, are immediate changes, not motions.[54] An example is an animal's death. Between a cow and its carcass there is no middle zone. Nevertheless, a substance has accidents that are characteristic of it, and its corruption occurs as the terminus of a process (or processes) of accidental change; e.g., aging or cooling or being cut up. And its generation must be preceded by processes disposing for its characteristic accidents. So there are orders regularly followed in the sequences of generations and corruptions. As Aristotle observes, by a series of processes water can become wine, and wine can immediately become

---

49. *Quodl.*, III, q. 1, a. 1. Cf. *De princ. nat.*, cap. 2; *STh*, I, q. 66, a. 1.

50. See *In Meta.*, VII, lect. 2, §1285–87; also VIII, lect. 1, §1689.

51. On prime matter and modern science, in addition to Wallace's book see also Gilson, "In Quest of Matter."

52. *STh*, I, q. 13, a. 11.

53. *In De Trin.*, q. 5, a. 3; *De ver.*, q. 10, a. 5.

54. See *In Phys.*, V, lect. 3, §662[3]–665[6]; *In Meta.*, XI, lect. 12, §2376–84.

vinegar, but vinegar cannot immediately become wine; it must go back to water first.[55]

Substantial Form and the Meanings of *natura*

Now, just as substantial change implies an underlying matter that is substance in potency, so too it implies acts by which the substances serving as its termini are successively in act. Aristotle calls such acts substance as form. Thomas calls them substantial forms. It would be hard to overstate the importance of substantial form in Thomas's philosophy.

Earlier, in discussing motion, we remarked that an accident or accidental form confers a certain being on the substance to which it belongs. It makes the subject be in a certain way, as heat makes water be hot. However, accidents do not give what Thomas calls *esse simpliciter*, unqualified being, the being according to which a substance simply is or exists. Accidents presuppose the substance and its unqualified being, and they add further, qualified being: being hot, being so large, etc. What makes a substance simply be, however, is its substantial form. Exactly how a thing's substantial form relates to its being is a topic for metaphysics, and we will take it up in detail later. But we must at least say something about substantial form as a principle of being here, because it bears directly on the notion of nature.

Aristotle says that what has a nature is always a substance, and that what exists *by* nature includes substances and their accidents and their motions.[56] The nature of a thing, then, is not solely a principle of the thing's motion. That may be why it is called a nature, but in fact it is also a principle by which the thing exists. Now, the analysis of the generation and corruption of natural substances shows that their existence does indeed have principles: their matter and their form. However, the matter is only potential for a substance. A substance exists without qualification, not when it is merely in potency, but when it is in act. It is in act in virtue of its form. So the form is more truly and properly a principle of its being than the matter is.

And the form is also more truly its nature. With it, in fact, we have finally reached what Thomas considers the primary sense of the word *natura*.[57] This fits with the fact that the nature of a thing is intrinsic to it. We do not say that something has the nature of a tree, for example, until

---

55. *Metaph.*, VIII.5, 1044b29–1045a6.

56. *Physics*, II.1, 192b32–193a1.

57. *In Meta.*, V, lect. 5, §826; *In Phys.*, II, lect. 153[5]–155[7].

it has in it the form of a tree—until it actually *is* a tree. Moreover, nature is an intrinsic principle of motion and rest, and things of different kinds have very different ways of moving and resting. So they have very different natures. But what decides a thing's kind is its form.

Here, however, lies an important distinction, and also still another sense of *nature*. The distinction is between a thing's substantial form and its kind. They are close, but Thomas will not quite identify them. A sign of their closeness is the fact that, to the chagrin of his readers, Aristotle uses the same word for both: *eidos*. Thomas uses *forma* for form; for kind, he uses *species*. Our *aspect* is related to this, and both *eidos* and *species* refer to a look or an aspect. In this case, though, it is not visible but intelligible. In fact, one way to explain the notion of kind is with reference to intellect. We understand a thing insofar as we know what it is. But knowing what it is is tantamount to knowing its kind. What is Lassie? A dog; her kind is dog.

Her substantial form, however, is not dog. It is only a principle of her being a dog. And at least on Thomas's view, it is not the only principle. It is only part of what makes Lassie a dog, though indeed, it is the really decisive part. To show how it is the decisive part, Aristotle offers a helpful comparison, using the syllable *ba*.[58] He likens the letters *a* and *b* to the elements out of which a natural thing is generated. Then he observes that what makes the letters be the syllable *ba* is not at all another element. It is rather the order of the letters. This is a sort of form. (Notice that, unlike shape or color or other typical examples of form, this one cannot be pictured in itself. Neither can a substantial form.) And this form cannot even be thought of apart from the letters or from *ba*. But it can be distinguished from them, and whereas *b* and *a* are indeterminate as between *ba* and *ab* (and as between them and no syllable at all), it is quite determinate, and determining. Its presence or absence is what immediately decides the existence or the non-existence of *ba*.

Nevertheless the letters are clearly principles of *ba* too. If we were to define the syllable *ba*, we would certainly have to mention *a* and *b*. And certain bodily parts are essential to being a dog. This is precisely because a dog is essentially something natural and mobile. The definition of a natural thing's kind expresses not only its form but also its matter; not the matter by itself, of course, since (unlike the letters) prime matter is nothing determinate by itself, but the matter as subject to the quantitative and qualitative conditions necessary for moving and acting as that kind of thing does:

58. *Metaph.*, VII.17, 1041b11–33.

having flesh or nerves or DNA or protons. So both form and matter are in a thing's *essence*. This is the whole set of factors constituting its kind.[59]

And this, for Thomas, is yet another meaning of *natura*: the essence of a natural thing, as expressed by the definition of its kind. He will often even treat it as a sort of form in its own right. (Again, not everything that the mind treats as a form really is one, or is even thought to be one.) A definition, after all, is a *formula*—a "little form." When we put the kind's name abstractly, as in *dogness*, we treat the essence as a simple unit. And we use this as the formal principle, the distinguishing factor, for judging between what is and what is not of that kind.

Finally, since the essence of a natural thing is called nature, any and every essence can be called a nature, "by a certain metaphor and extension of the name."[60] This is that very broad sense of nature that applies to just about everything, whether or not it is physical or mobile. But the chief and most proper sense of nature is the substantial form of a mobile substance.

Taking a bird's-eye view of the meanings of *natura*, Thomas says that generation or birth is what we first call nature, and form is last, because we know the forms of things by their acts. But really nothing has nature except insofar as it has form; and so, "chiefly and properly what is called nature is . . . the form of things having in themselves a principle of motion, as such. For matter is said to be nature because it is receptive of form. And generations have the name of nature because they are motions proceeding from form and also toward forms."[61]

Substantial Form as Unitive Energy

Now let us return to the idea mentioned at the start of this chapter, the idea of a thing's makeup being a source of its active properties. Perhaps we can make sense of this idea, if we focus on the role of substantial form. It is analogous to the role played by the form of *ba*. The form of *ba* is what unites the letters and makes one syllable of them. What we need to see is

59. On matter in the definitions of natural kinds, see *Physics*, II.2, 193b31–194a15; *Metaph.*, VI.1, 1025b28–1026a7. On the essences of natural things as including matter, see *In Meta.*, VII, lect. 9, §1467–69; here Thomas takes issue with Averroes for equating substantial form and essence. He insists on the point in *STh*, I, q. 75, a. 4.

60. *In Meta.*, V, lect. 5, §823. Yet another extended sense of *nature*, close to essence, is differentia; see below, 79–80. Thomas rehearses the senses of nature in his discussion of the definition of *person*: *STh*, I, q. 29, a. 1, ad 4.

61. *In Meta.*, V, lect. 5, §826.

that a body needs a form, simply in order to be a body; in order, that is, to be *one* body.

Quite generally, Aristotle insists, a continuous thing—a line, a motion, an extension, a body—must have something indivisible in it that makes it one.[62] This seems undeniable. What is continuous, as such, is divisible into continuous parts; why then are it and they not divided, in any of the indefinitely many ways in which they might be, but rather are one? This question is not asking for an agent or an origin of the unity, an outside cause putting the thing together. It is asking about the togetherness itself, asking what the thing's unity consists in. A body is something continuous. Continuity entails infinite divisibility, and hence potency. So a body's unity entails some act, one that is distinct from the body itself.[63]

Now, when we call a body *one*, what do we mean? We do not mean only that its surface looks or feels continuous. We also mean that it moves and acts as a unit. The whole rises or rolls or runs together.[64] Of course, what moves as a unit may turn out to be many bodies somehow joined—by nails or glue or hooks or whatever. Many artifacts are like that. But not all bodies can be like that. A nail is not nailed together. And even if particle-forces hold larger bodies together, what holds a particle together? There have to be bodies that are not smaller bodies held together by something else. They may be generable and corruptible, but while they exist, they hold together by . . . nature. Running through each is a unifying factor that is not a body and not divisible, but simple—all or none. This is a substantial form.[65]

These bodies are what qualify as the truly natural ones. Aristotle thinks that they come in many kinds. Some of them are quite large; e.g., you. And the same form making a body be of the kind that it is also makes

---

62. *De an.*, III.6, 430b17–20.

63. *STh*, I, q. 3, a. 1.

64. See *Metaph.*, V.6, 1015b35–1016a15.

65. As mentioned above, 43, there is no motion, but only instantaneous change, with respect to substance. Substantial kinds are not on a continuum; see *Categories*, 5, 2b15–28, 3b33–4a9. This may help to explain why substance and substantial form seem to have little place in modern science: they cannot be directly quantified. (Cf. *De an.*, III.6, 430b14-17; *STh*, I, q. 76, a. 8.) Modern science generally treats causality in terms of correlations among quantities. Thomas does say that "cause and effect are proportioned to each other" (*In Meta.*, 6, lect. 2, §1185), but what he means by "proportion" is not exclusively quantitative. Is modern science then incompatible with his thought? Perhaps not, if it can be seen as taking only a partial or abstract view. As Aristotle says about mathematics, abstracting does not yield falsehood: *Physics*, II.2, 193b35.

it be what he calls a *this*: a determinate and separate entity, an undivided whole, united in itself and distinct from others. A thing's being of a given kind is tied to its having a specific way of moving and acting, and so a specific way of being one whole subject of motion and action. There is no such thing as being one and whole but in no specific way. A substance is a *this something*: this stone, this dog, this human being.

Once all this is grasped, there should be less mystery in Thomas's claim that the human soul—a substantial form—is in every part of the body, and whole in each. It unifies every part, and it is whole in each because in itself it is all or none, simple. Otherwise it would need a unifier. Of course he knows that a human body's parts also differ greatly. He thinks the soul is responsible for the diversity too. But this is a peculiarity of soul.[66] Common to all substantial forms is to be whole in every part of what they inform. We must not think of a substance's parts as having distinct unifying principles of their own, like those of an automobile. An automobile does have a form. Its form is like that of *ba*, the order among its parts. But this is an accidental form. Substantial form runs through all the parts as well, giving them unity too. In whatever it is found, it is the very first form. This is why Thomas insisted that a given substance can only have one substantial form. If a water-molecule is a substance, then the form of water is also the form of its parts. Even if it was produced by combining hydrogen and oxygen, it cannot actually contain such substances or have parts that behave exactly as they do. This does seem to be the case. For instance, hydrogen is immediately combustible, but no part of water is.

So a good way to think of substantial form is as a body's chief inner cause of unity: unity of its extended parts, of its attributes, and also of its motions and actions over time. The term *inner* is important; again, the form is not a unifying agent, which would be extrinsic. There is only one *this*. And most substantial forms cannot exist separately from what they inform at all.[67]

Matter and form are often said to be "components" of a bodily substance, and Thomas too speaks this way, but it can be misleading. It would at least be better to say that the body's matter is composed—that is, unified—according to or through its form. Matter and form are distinct, and they are real, but neither is an unqualified *this*. They are not two kinds of

66. See below, 57, 114.

67. Cf. *De anima*, III.6, 430b18. The exception, for Thomas, would be the human soul (see below, 114–16).

thing needing to be unified by yet a third kind. They are the potency and the act of one entity. Their unity is immediate.[68] For the same reason, however, they are not at all on an equal footing. Form is by far the dominant partner. Aristotle even says it is more of a being than matter is.[69]

This then is how a thing's makeup can be a source of its active properties. What is a subject of motion or activity must already be an actual unit.[70] It must already have a kind of strength or energy, not yet for motion or action, but first of all for its unity, and hence for its being. Thomas in fact calls substantial form *virtus essendi*, strength to be.[71] He also thinks of it as *inclination* toward being: form "holds a thing in being."[72] Whether a thing is in motion or at rest, it is enduring in its own identity, which is its substantial unity.[73] As Thomas sees it, this is itself a sort of event. Even at this level, a thing's nature is *at work*.[74] And even kinds that do not reproduce or beget—rocks, water, stars—display such energy and tendency. Is it not easy to see how form, so conceived, can also be a source of motion and action?

Perhaps we even catch a glimpse here of why he says that the order of nature is instituted by divine wisdom, and that other principles such as reason, virtue, and even grace, imitate it. Wisdom orders all things to the good, and Thomas understand the good of each thing to be nothing other than the fullness of its being according to its nature. A substantial form is nothing if not an ordering in that direction. And since it is a thing's very first form, all other good principles must presuppose it and in some way conform to it.

And of course the motions and actions that flow directly from a thing's substantial form must conform to it. They must be in the direction

---

68. *Metaph.*, VIII.6, 1045a7–1045b23.

69. *Metaph.*, VII.2, 1029a5–6; see *In Meta.*, VII, lect. 2, §1278. This does mean that there just might be forms that are able to exist separately from matter. That is a topic for metaphysics; see below, 109–14.

70. See *STh*, I, q. 76, a. 4. obj. 2.

71. See *Scg*, I, cap. 20, §174, and II, cap. 30, §1073; *In De caelo*, I, lect. 6, §62[5].

72. *STh*, I, q. 59, a. 2.

73. See *Metaph.*, V.15, 1021a11.

74. See *STh*, I, q. 10, a. 1, ad 2: just as time regards motion (and rest: *STh*, I, q. 10, a. 4, ad 3), so the "stretching forth" (*protensio*) of duration in being seems to regard activity (*operatio*, "being at work"). Also *STh*, I, q. 66, a. 1: "if unformed matter preceded [its formation] in duration, then it was already in act, since duration implies this; . . . but this very thing, act, is form. So, to speak of matter preceding form is to speak of a being in act without act."

of the fullness of its being according to its kind. Thomas holds this even in the case of such apparently indifferent motions as the falling of heavy things. The places to which things naturally tend, he argues, must have some power to conserve those things; that must be why they tend there. It is their motion's final cause.[75]

Interestingly, in the same passage, he insists that this does not mean that the place aimed at has some "attractive power" (*virtutem attractivam*), "unless this be understood in the way that an end attracts." In other words, the place is not acting upon the thing. Heavy things tend to the earth's center, but the tendency is not produced by the earth's center. To repeat, its only producer is their generator. Would Thomas have to retract this judgment in view of the mere universality of gravitation? I doubt it. He would only need to modify (and not much) the account of the good that gravitational motion favors. Just as each thing naturally tends toward its own being according to its kind, each also naturally tends toward others of the kind. It is almost the same tendency: toward the fullness of being of the kind. Thomas finds the old proverb, that birds of a feather flock together, expressing a very general truth. He formulates it thus: "Speaking per se, the similar is naturally desirable and lovable."[76]

This is not to say that there is no such thing, for Thomas, as acting upon something so as to attract it. Even in his day there was, for example, such a thing as advertising. That sort of action, however, cannot be exercised upon all bodies, or even all natural bodies, but only upon some of those whose forms are what Thomas calls souls.

---

75. *In Phys.*, IV, lect. 1, §412[7].

76. *In Eth.*, VIII, lect. 1, §1547; the proverb is mentioned in §1545. He grants that, *per accidens*, what is similar may be undesirable, and what is dissimilar, desirable. Of course things that are of the same general kind, such as body, may be of different specific kinds. Even though birds, as heavy things, naturally tend downward, Thomas would not at all deny that flying is natural for them, as birds. The point goes back to the general definition of *nature*; see above, 32–33.

3

Souls

Form as a Principle of Life, Kinds of Soul, and Grades of Immateriality

Soul as a Topic for Natural Science

IF THOMAS'S CONCEPT OF nature is strange to us, his concept of soul is, if anything, even stranger. Here, for example, is Oxford's first (and only relevant) online definition of *soul*: "the spiritual or immaterial part of a human being or animal, regarded as immortal."[1] With that in mind, look at how Thomas begins his treatment of the human soul in the *Summa theologiae*.[2] The first thing he asks is whether a soul is a body. Does he not know what the word means?

Our own first question about soul, I suppose, would be whether there even is any such thing. Thomas takes soul entirely for granted. You may say it is because he is a Christian theologian. But then you must explain why, earlier in the *Summa*, and certainly speaking as theologian, he did ask whether there is any such thing as a God.[3] You must also explain how here, after arguing that a soul is in fact not a body, he can go on to ask, in effect,

---

1. https://www.oxforddictionaries.com/definition/english/soul.
2. *STh*, I, q. 75, a. 1.
3. *STh*, I, q. 2, a. 3.

whether or not a human soul is spiritual.[4] That too, Oxford says, is part of the word's very meaning. Then, after answering this question affirmatively, Thomas asks whether the souls of beasts are spiritual too. He says no; but he is taking it quite for granted that there are such things as beast-souls. And three articles later he asks whether or not the human soul is immortal.

Most of Thomas's contemporaries would not have found any of the above strange. As mentioned in the first chapter, however, another position of his regarding the soul was indeed problematic for many of them, and it too is hard to square with our usual conception.[5] On his view, a soul is not a body, but it is quite thoroughly *of* a body. It does not have matter in it, but it is immediately united to matter. It is a body's one and only substantial form. It is thus the very nature of a certain bodily substance, in the strictest sense of the word *nature*. It is something quite *physical*. Even the human soul is so—despite its being spiritual and its making us be in the image of God.

Now, Thomas would surely push back against the word *despite* in the previous sentence. The spiritual soul's being the body's substantial form is the very thing that accounts for those uniquely human aspects of the image of God that we noted earlier.[6] That man is from man, as God is from God, rests on the soul's function as nature and as principle of generation; and that the soul is whole in the whole body and whole in every part, as God is in the world, rests directly on the soul's function as substantial form. But Thomas is insisting that these are not, as it were, optional functions of the human soul. They flow from its very essence. The human soul is not really an angel that happens to have assumed a body. It is not even in the same genus as angels. It really is a soul, that is, an *anima*, and it is "in the genus of animals." Of course it is not an animal in its own right. It is in that genus "as a formal principle."[7] But this is exactly how the souls of beasts are in that genus.

If nothing else, it should be clear that, for Thomas, the word *soul* does not refer to just one kind of thing. Souls come in several different kinds. If we want to make any sense of his conception, then despite the special interest of the human kind, we cannot treat it alone. In fact we must broaden

4. On the question and argument of *STh*, I, q. 75, a. 2, see below, 111–13.

5. See above, 12.

6. See above, 28.

7. *STh*, I, q. 90, a. 4, ad 2. See my "The Physical Status of the Spiritual Soul in Thomas Aquinas."

our scope beyond the genus of animals. We must include plants. I hope that eventually it will be clear why Thomas sees no tension between being a substantial form and being spiritual. But first we must get clear about the soul's being a substantial form.

The Substantial Form of an Organism

Let us go back to that first *Summa* article, on whether the soul is a body. Thomas begins his answer by telling us what the word means for him. Let us take it as given, he says, that the word *soul* means "the first principle of life in the living things around us." If we use his word, *anima*, the point may be clearer. *Anima* is what makes the difference between the *animate* and the *inanimate*.[8] Since the difference between them is life, *anima* means the first principle of life in a living thing.

To say this, however, is to leave wide open the question of what an *anima* consists in. And in fact, as Aristotle reports, there were thinkers who held that it is some kind of body or other: fire, air (breath), highly mobile atoms, etc. But precisely because the mere word says so little about the soul's constitution, it leaves little or no doubt about its existence. One could doubt its existence only if one doubted the distinction between animate and inanimate things. Thomas sees no reason to doubt that.

His next step is to grant that a body can be some sort of principle of life. Most animal life, for example, depends on heart, blood, brain, and so on. Today some might say that the principle of life generally is DNA. But Thomas then argues that no body can be the very *first* inner principle of life (remember that he put *first* in the word's very definition). For any such body will need an inner principle of its own. Why? Because a body's being alive, or a principle of life, means more than just being a body. It means being a body of a certain type or quality, being *such* a body (a heart, a brain, an animal). What is the root, within it, of its being *such*? The fundamental answer cannot be yet another body. That too would be *such* a body, and the question would still stand.

At this point Thomas introduces the word act, *actus*. We are talking about what makes a body be such—be alive—*in act*. The term *act* is especially suitable in this context, because the very notion of life is tied to activity.

8. Robert Sokolowski, in "Soul and the Transcendence of the Human Person," suggests using the word *animation* instead of *soul*. It is a very helpful essay, both on the notion of soul and on that of spirit.

In the first place, living things are natural things, and as we have seen, all natural things tend to move and act in some way or other. But living things are especially active. They somehow move themselves or engage themselves in their activity, as its very agents. We judge that a living thing has died when it stops doing that. Living things are more self-sufficient for their activity than non-living things are.[9]

A soul, then, is not a vital activity, but it is the *act* underlying such activity. Thomas likens it to heat. Heat is a principle by which a body performs the activity of heating. It is not a body, but an act of that body. Thomas thought heat was a sort of form. Nowadays that view is rejected. But no one says that heat is body. It is some kind of energy in a body. And that is at least quite close to what Thomas is saying about it here—and about soul as well.

In effect, Thomas is simply spelling out Aristotle's reasoning, at the start of Book II of *De anima*, for the thesis that a soul is not a body. Of natural bodies, Aristotle says, some have life and some do not. So a body that has life is *such* a body or a body of a certain type; hence a soul cannot be a body. Rather, a body is its subject or matter, and it is a form and an act.[10]

Now it should be clear why Thomas can still ask whether the human soul is spiritual. He is not already saying that it is so, any more than he is saying that heat is so. In fact, here he is saying even less than Aristotle does in that place. Aristotle says a soul is "substance as form," substantial form. Thomas has not yet said that; but he will. He fully endorses Aristotle's general definition of soul: "substance, as form, of a natural body having life potentially."

A Principle of Activity and of Substantial Unity

By this last phrase, "having life potentially," Aristotle means having capacity for vital activity. In this passage, he defines life simply as self-nutrition, growth, and withering. Later he also identifies other kinds of vital activity. But these three, along with reproduction, are the kinds that all living bodies have and that coincide with their being alive at all.[11]

9. On the meaning of *life*, see *STh*, I, q. 18, aa. 1 & 2.

10. *De anima*, II.1, 412a13–21. Here the word that *act* translates is *entelecheia*, meaning a perfection or a completion. Aristotle connects *entelecheia* and *energeia* in *Metaph.*, IX.3, 1047a30–b2; IX.8, 1050a23; cf. *Physics*, III.1, 201a3–202b29 and *Metaph.*, XI.9, 1065b5–1066a34.

11. *De anima*, II.4, 415a23–25.

However, Aristotle does not always identify life with vital activity. He also calls life the very being (*einai*—Thomas's *esse*) of a living thing. He appeals to this meaning to confirm the notion of soul as a substantial form. Substantial form causes a thing to be (as the order of the letters causes *ba* to be); and soul causes a living thing to live; and for a living thing, to live is to be; and so soul is a substantial form.[12] Thomas says that *life* means both vital activity and the being of a living thing, but the latter is its primary meaning.

Later we will look at the relation between being and form more closely. These are highly abstract notions, and it will help to have on hand this concrete example: life as being, and soul as form. But the distinction between being and activity is also important as regards the nature of soul itself. Actual being, or being alive, follows immediately and inseparably upon the possession of soul. But not all vital activity follows upon it in that way. Whatever has a soul is actually alive, not just potentially so; but it is not always performing all the kinds of vital activity that it is capable of. This seems inevitable, given that it is a self-mover. Some of its activities are brought about by way of others, and at least some of these are motions and so take time to complete. Normally, for instance, a new organism has to grow for a while before it is ready to reproduce. With respect to the vital activities, then, what follows immediately upon the possession of soul is only a determinate potential or capacity for them. Aristotle in fact stresses that the phrase "having life potentially" in his definition does not refer to what does not yet have soul, as though soul were the act of that potential; the act of that potential is vital activity. The phrase, he says, refers to what does have soul and is thereby both actually alive and in potency to vital activity. In other words, soul is what he calls a "first act." Vital activity is a further act, the potential for which accompanies that first act.[13]

Another way to see the distinction between being alive and vital activity is to consider that an individual living thing's vital activities are of many kinds, but the thing itself is one thing, with one being and one life. And the form, the soul, is first of all the very principle of its unity. It makes the living body be one body. So it is not added to the body, but rather is constitutive of it. What it is added to is matter, which is only potency for a body. To be sure, both Aristotle and Thomas often follow the common practice of

---

12. *De anima*, II.4, 415b11–14. See *In De an.*, II, lect. 7, §319.

13. *De anima*, II.1, 412a22–28 & 412b25–26. See *STh*, I, q. 77, a. 1. Thomas calls activity "second act."

speaking of soul and body as the components of a living thing. But Thomas justifies this practice by saying that although the same form that makes the thing a substance and a body also makes it be alive, we can consider being a body as a merely imperfect effect of this form, one that it has in common with forms that are not souls, and as merely potential or material relative to the effect of being alive, which is proper to it as soul.[14] Our habit of speaking of soul and body, then, merely reflects our way of getting at the natures of things, which involves comparison and contrast. This procedure gives rise to conceptual or logical distinctions that do not always line up exactly with the real makeup of things.[15] They are not therefore bad or false, but they must not be confused with real distinctions, such as the distinction between form and matter.

However, we can still ask whether it is really true that the form proper to a living thing is a substantial form. This amounts to asking whether the thing itself is really a substance. Right after defining soul as the first act of a natural body having life potentially, Aristotle observes that such a body is organic. This means that it has bodily parts serving as tools or instruments (*organa*) of vital activities. The parts have very diverse qualities and operative tendencies. Might the living thing not really be just a combination of bodies of different natures, like a machine?

The question may sound rather modern, but Aristotle faced it squarely.[16] He tells us that Empedocles explained the downward growth of plant-roots by their containing earth, which naturally tends in that direction, and the upward growth of other parts of the plant by their containing fire. Aristotle retorts: there must at least be something that holds the earth and fire together so that the plant is not torn apart. And what is more, the movements involved in the growth of a plant (or an animal) are intrinsically regulated and limited, toward a fairly definite size and shape and disposition. Growth is not a combination of unrelated motions, but a distinct kind of motion in its own right. Qualities of elementary bodies may very well be contributing to it somehow.[17] But its primary source is a principle proper

14. See *In De an.*, II, lect. 1, §225.

15. See *STh*, I, q. 76, a. 3, ad 4; a. 6, ad 1 & ad 2; below, 100–101.

16. *De anima*, II.4, 415b28–416a18. The doctrine of the elements in this discussion is, of course, obsolete. But that need not affect the essential points much, at least not if hylomorphism in general is valid. See below, 81–82.

17. Interpreters of Aristotle have offered different accounts of how the elements remain present in what he calls "mixed" bodies and in organisms. For Thomas's view, see *STh*, I, q. 76, a. 4, ad 4; *q. D. De anima*, a. 9, ad 10.

to the living thing, a principle running through all the thing's parts. Its parts are essentially just that, parts, defined by their function in and order to the whole. They do not exist outside the whole, at least not in a stable way; it is unnatural for them. The thing is a single substance, with a nature and a form proper to it. There is no form or set of forms in it that is more basic than the form by which it is alive, its soul.[18] Our machines imitate living things. It is a kind of anthropomorphism to suppose that living things are constituted in the manner of machines.

Thomas's notion of soul and body, then, is hardly a specimen of "Greek dualism." Nor is Aristotle's. It makes no sense, Aristotle says, to ask whether soul and body are one, any more than to ask whether wax and the shape impressed in it are one. Matter and form are potency and act, and what is one in the primary sense is what is one in act.[19] Again, instead of saying that a thing is composed of matter and form, we would do better to say that its matter is composed—unified—according to its form. An organism is not two kinds of things somehow joined. It is one kind, now in potency, now in act. The whole point, we might almost say, of Aristotle's hylomorphism—of which the doctrine of soul is the very centerpiece—is to uphold the substantial unity of natural bodies.[20] And substantial unity is the primary type of unity.[21]

Grades of Substantial Form and Kinds of Soul

We might wonder why, if soul is nothing but a particular kind of substantial form, it has this special name, soul. Thomas would surely answer that not all substantial forms are equal. Souls are more perfect than the forms of inanimate bodies. They are more perfect precisely as substantial forms, that is, as principles of being, unity, and activity. With respect to activity, their greater perfection is shown by the living thing's self-movement or self-engagement. With respect to unity, it is shown by the generally greater definiteness and distinctness of living bodies, and also by the very diversity of the organism's parts; to effect substantial unity in such diversity requires more, not less, unitive energy. It is also shown by the living thing's aptitude for producing and repairing its own parts and organs and thereby

18. See *STh*, I, q. 76, aa. 3 & 4.
19. *De anima*, II.1, 412b6–9.
20. See *Metaph.*, VIII.6, 1045a7–b23.
21. See *Metaph.*, V.6, 1016b1–11.

preserving the thing's integrity.[22] With respect to being itself, their perfection is shown by the nutritive and reproductive operations, through which the organism preserves both its own being and that of its kind. Indeed, it is especially in living things that the nature of the kind, as founded on the form, is seen to function as its own promoter and its own end.[23] The causal roles that form is apt to exercise—formal, efficient, and final—are on full display.[24]

Plants have only nutrition, growth and withering, and reproduction. Animals of course also have sensation and (usually) movement from place to place, and, in the case of man, intellect or understanding. Do animals then have a plant-like soul together with one or more others? Thomas says no, each is one substance with just one form. But those with different and ampler sets of vital activities have different, more perfect kinds of soul.[25] Thomas takes on board an ingenious comparison proposed by Aristotle.[26] The different kinds of soul are like different rectilinear figures: triangle, quadrilateral, pentagon. Each is a single figure or form, but every successive one contains "in potency" whatever is in the prior, plus more. It has more vital powers. The powers that even plants have are called vegetative powers. Animals also have sensation. But the vegetative powers of an animal are obviously very different from those of a plant. They are reconfigured and integrated with the animal's other powers. Similarly, man's vegetative and sensitive powers differ from those of plants and beasts. They are integrated with reason.

As mentioned in the first chapter, Thomas's insistence on man's having just one soul troubled the theologians, who saw it as a threat to the spirituality and immortality of the properly human, rational soul. After all, the idea of sub-rational powers existing apart from the body makes little sense. Can souls metabolize, or walk, or thirst? Thomas, however, simply distinguishes between the soul just in itself, or in its essence, which is to be

22. See Sokolowski, "Soul and the Transcendence of the Human Person," 155–57. The soul belongs primarily to the whole organism and secondarily to the parts, by reason of their order to the whole: *STh*, I, q. 76, a. 8. In general, parts are more on the side of matter, and whole is more on the side of form: *STh*, I, q. 7, a. 3, ad 3.

23. See *Physics*, II.1, 193b8–18; II.8, 199a23–32.

24. See *STh*, I, q. 5, a. 4.

25. The theme of grades of life in Thomas extends beyond the idea of soul (which applies only to organisms) and reaches all the way to God; see John Boyle's elegant and rich essay, *Master Thomas Aquinas and the Fullness of Life*.

26. *De anima*, II.3, 414b19–415a13; *STh*, I, q. 76, a. 3 (toward the end of the corpus).

a certain form and act, and its powers. If the human soul can exist apart from the body, then it can also exist without those powers that are seated in bodily organs. It can do so even though it remains a principle of such powers, just as it remains a form apt to inform an organism.[27]

The question of the human soul's unity also bears on current issues. For instance, does the irreversible cessation of cognitive functions imply that a person is dead? Does it imply the loss of the soul itself, or only of certain organs or powers? On Thomas's account of the soul, death cannot be without the loss of the body's integrative vegetative functions.[28]

The Distinction and Distribution of Powers of Soul

Different kinds of soul bring different sets of vital powers, but not every distinct power implies a distinct kind of soul. And although the living thing need not always be exercising its vital powers, and some powers can be exercised independently of others, the possibility of separate or independent exercise is not the basis upon which Thomas distinguishes the powers. In fact, he considers the exercise of certain powers inseparable from that of certain others, and yet the powers remain distinct. For instance, sense-appetite cannot be exercised without sensation, nor (in this life) intellect without imagination, nor will without intellect; and none of the properly animal or human powers can function if the vegetative powers are inactive. But the proper basis upon which Thomas distinguishes the powers is the nature of their activities. These, in turn, are distinguished by what he calls their proper objects.

This is a complicated topic, and a full treatment would require a book of its own. Here I would simply stress that the word *object*, in this context, is not synonymous with *thing*. A thing may very well be an object, but in calling it an object, we are seeing it as related to an activity or a power—as

27. See *STh*, I, q. 77, a. 8. On the unnatural condition of the separate soul, see below, 116.

28. See Eberl, *Thomistic Principles and Bioethics*, 43–61 (though I demur on whether whole-brain death entails the loss of integrative functions). Notice too that what Thomas himself posits, both in the process of generation and in the phases following death, is a series of *incomplete, unstable* forms (*In De generatione et corruptione*, I, lect. 8, §60[3]). So if the integrative vegetative functions are stable and going on indefinitely, then on his view, the body cannot have lost its human soul; it is not only still alive but also still a person. (Regarding generation, however, I am not suggesting that today Thomas would hold to the idea of a succession of forms. I do not think he would. See Eberl, 23–42.)

something with which the power or activity somehow engages. The idea is reflected in the grammatical notion of the object of a verb. Thus the objects of many different activities may be one and the same thing. Charlie pitched the ball, Jimmy hit the ball, Tommy caught the ball, etc. Conversely, a single kind of activity or power can engage with a variety of things or have many things for its object. However, if it is really a single kind, then there is always some single feature of the things, by virtue of which it engages with them. There is something that constitutes the thing's interface with the power. This is what Thomas means by the activity's or the power's proper object. For instance, eyesight can bear on many different things, but it bears on them by virtue of their having color (or more precisely, illuminated color). Color is the proper object of eyesight. And if different powers can engage with the same thing, it is because the thing has different features, corresponding to them. Sight grasps a thing according to its color. Intellect may grasp the same thing according to the feature that engages intellect or functions as its proper object, namely *what the thing is*.[29] To understand a thing is to know what it is; the better that is known, the better the thing is understood.

Thomas's broadest distinction of vital powers is into five broad classes or genera. The distinction proceeds according to two criteria.[30] The first, which yields a threefold set, is the range or the extension of the powers' proper objects. The most limited are the objects of the vegetative powers, those that even plants have: nutrition, growth, reproduction. The objects of these powers are always within the organism itself: its own conservation through the assimilation of nutrients, its due size and shape, its offspring (which at least begins within the organism). Then there are powers whose objects belong also to other sensible bodies. Finally, there are powers whose objects extend even beyond bodily things to absolutely all beings.

Thomas does not give these last two groups, those with broader objects, names of their own. Instead he subdivides each of them into two and names the four results. It is here that he uses the other criterion of distinction. It applies only to these broader powers, because it supposes the possibility of bearing on things entirely outside the organism. The criterion is the direction of the relation that the power establishes between the soul

29. Thomas often uses the Scholastic term for this, *quiddity*, which literally just means *whatness*. The words *quiddity, nature,* and *essence* all refer to the same reality, but they have different connotations. *Quiddity* indicates its answering the question, "what is it?" *Essence* expresses its functioning as that in and through which the thing has being. *Nature* points to its role as principle of activity. See the beginning of chapter 1 of *De ente*.

30. See *STh*, I, q. 78, a. 1.

and the things that have the power's object. First of all, there are powers by which the soul can, as it were, take things into itself—not in their own being, of course, but according to some likeness of them. These are the cognitive powers, sensitive (bearing on physical bodies) and intellectual (bearing on all beings). Then there are powers by which the soul, having the cognitive likenesses of things, can incline or tend toward them according to their own being. These are of two sorts. The primary sort are the appetitive powers, by which the soul relates to things as ends that it is apt to desire and cling to.[31] And then there are the motor powers, which are instrumental to the appetites, enabling the animal to move from place to place in pursuit of the end: power to walk, or swim, or fly, and so forth.

It is important not to think of the powers as little agents inside the organism. Properly speaking, what performs the activities pertaining to a given power is not the power itself, but the power's subject—the organism that has the power. The power is only a principle in virtue of which the subject acts. Thomas will sometimes speak of the senses sensing, the intellect understanding, and so forth, but this is mere economy of language. On the other hand, organisms do have parts, which are distinguished precisely by their powers, and Thomas judges that it is indeed proper, in a secondary way, to say that the part performs the activity in question. For instance, it is not proper to say that hearing itself hears; and what is most proper is to say that the animal hears with its ear, by virtue of its hearing; but, assuming that hearing is seated in the ear, it is not improper to say that the ear itself hears. This fits with the fact that for Thomas, as for Aristotle, the parts of substances—roots, ears, brains—can be considered substances too, albeit partial ones.[32] They may not be able to exist separately from the whole, or to operate independently of other parts, but they are still partial subjects of the living thing's activity, just as they are partial subjects of its life and its being.

The aforementioned powers are distributed among living things in such a way as to constitute four "modes of life." The simplest mode is occupied by plants, which have only vegetative powers. Then there are animals (relatively few) such as oysters, that have sensation and appetite but no motor powers. Then come the animals that also have motor powers. The

---

31. There are appetitive powers that bear on things apprehended by the senses, which are capacities for feelings or emotions, such as hunger or sexual desire or fear; and there is one that bears on things apprehended by intellect, namely the will: *STh*, I, q. 80, a. 2.

32. See above, 39.

most complex mode, of course, is man's, who also has intellect and will. Appetitive powers do not constitute a mode of their own, since everything that has cognition also has appetite.

The Elevation of Soul above Matter:
Metabolism and Reproduction

But let us go back to the various kinds of soul. Thomas ranks them in more than one way. The most obvious way is according to the number of powers that they bring with them. That is how the four modes of life are ranked. But it should also be clear that the powers can be ranked among themselves, according to the extension of their objects. The vegetative powers are more limited than, and as such are less perfect than, the sensitive, and the sensitive are more limited and so less perfect than the intellectual. (In this ranking, the sense-appetite and the motor power can be grouped with the senses, and the will with the intellectual powers.) Now, Thomas takes this threefold ranking of powers to reflect a threefold ranking in the essential perfection of souls themselves; that is, their perfection as first acts of natural bodies. Putting it more concretely, he holds that the greater breadth of a power's object indicates an activity that "rises above" mere bodily nature to a higher degree. And this in turn indicates a soul that "exceeds" or stands out from bodily matter to a higher degree.[33] *Every* form, Thomas says, considered as act, stands far from matter, which is a being merely in potency.[34] Standing out from matter pertains to act as act and form as form. And so a form that stands out more from matter is a more perfect act, and a more perfect form.

This is not an easy topic. But we can hardly set it aside. It will prove crucial for Thomas's conception of spiritual reality, and of reality simply. I shall approach it quite gradually.

First, let us see briefly how even the vegetative soul stands out from matter more than non-vital forms do. Earlier we remarked on how, even at the vegetative level, soul is a more perfect principle of being, unity, and

33. For "rises above" (*supergreditur*), see *STh*, I, q. 78, a. 1. For "exceeds" (*superexcedit, excedit*), see *Scg*, II, cap. 68, §1454–59; *STh*, I, q. 76, a. 1, and q. 78, a. 1.

34. *STh*, I, q. 76, a. 7, ad 3. The notion of act as standing out from potency reflects Aristotle's language in his account of *energeia* in *Metaph*. IX.6. He speaks of a statue or a half-line being potentially in a block of wood or in a whole line because they can be "pulled out" (*aphairethein*, 1048a33); and he says the infinite can exist potentially but not actually because it cannot exist "separately" (*chōriston*, 1048b15; *chōrizesthai*, 1048b17).

activity than other substantial forms are. Thomas traces this to a greater degree of self-sufficiency vis-à-vis matter. Obviously it is not that a plant's soul can exist without matter; that would be absurd. Nor is it that a plant has features or activities that are not somehow conditioned by matter. But two phenomena show a certain transcendence of matter. One is metabolism. By it, an organism's matter undergoes constant changeover, and yet the organism retains its identity.[35] This is because the form through which it lives and exists continues. So long as it has the same life and existence, it is the same being. The form always needs some portion of matter or other, but it needs the portion that it is in now only for a time, and it is what guides the renewal process.[36]

The other phenomenon is reproduction. The soul transmits something of itself, its own *ratio* or formula, to other portions of matter.[37] Of course a non-living kind may have many instances, but they are seldom self-multiplying. Non-living things are not born, properly speaking, and do not have offspring; rocks do not reproduce. Vital form, soul, is fully self-communicating and self-multiplying, and in this way it stands out more than other forms from the matter in which it inheres. Thomas says the reproductive power in a way approaches the dignity of the sensitive soul, inasmuch as its operation within the living thing extends to exterior things as well.[38]

The Elevation of Soul above Matter: Cognitive Likeness

But the sensitive soul, he goes on to say, regards exterior things in a more excellent way. And this way, he holds, involves an even greater elevation above matter. The intellectual soul's excellence and elevation are greater still. To some extent, however, the two can be treated together, under the general heading of cognition. In what follows I shall first consider how Thomas thinks cognition generally involves a more perfect soul and one

35. Thomas insists on this point: *STh*, I, q. 119, a. 1.

36. See *In De gen.*, I, lect. 17, §118.

37. On reproduction as essentially communication of form, it being incidental whether any matter passes from generator to offspring, see *STh*, I, q. 119, a. 2. How living things are properly classified, and the ontological status of their species, are matters of much dispute now, and applying Thomas's thought to the issues would be very complex. But all do agree, I take it, that living things tend to generate things quite similar to themselves.

38. *STh*, I. q, 78, a. 2.

more elevated above matter. This will take several steps. Then I shall discuss the superiority of intellect over sense. Along the way, key elements of his philosophy of cognition and knowledge should emerge.

As we saw, cognitive operation extends to exterior things by virtue of likenesses of them received in the operation's subject. Right here, Thomas argues, we see the greater perfection of the cognitive soul. It is, as it were, so big as to contain the forms of other things too.[39] At the start of the *Summa's* first article on knowledge (God's), we read: "Cognizers differ from non-cognizers in this, that the latter have none but their own form, whereas a cognizer is apt to have the form of some other thing as well; for the cognitive likeness of the thing cognized is in the cognizer. Hence it is clear that the nature of a non-cognizer is more contracted and limited, while the nature of cognizers has a greater amplitude and extension."[40]

Cognoscens is the Latin word that I have rendered with the admittedly ugly *cognizer*. It is supposed to cover both what has only sensation and what has intellect. Perhaps *knower* would do, but I prefer to reserve *know* and its cognates for Thomas's *scire* (whence *scientia*, which, like *knowledge*, is broader than what is usually meant now by *science*, yet narrower than *cognition*). As for *cognitive likeness*, the original term is *species*, which in Latin is ambiguous. It can mean what it does in English—a kind of thing (especially living thing)—but it can also mean an aspect, a look, a likeness, and other things as well. But in the context of discussions of cognition, Thomas uses it to refer to that likeness of a thing which a cognitive power enables the cognizer to take into itself. In the above passage he presents it as a type or a mode of form. This is simply because likeness is agreement in form.[41] Not all likeness, however, is in the cognitive mode. In a moment we will consider what Thomas thinks is special (pun intended) about this mode.

Why does a cognizer have to have a likeness of the thing cognized? The reason is simple: the activity of cognizing, even when it bears upon an external thing, is in the cognizer. If the thing itself is not in the cognizer, as obviously it often is not, then at least its likeness or its form must be so. The form need not be the thing's substantial form; Thomas thinks only

---

39. On the perfection of form as a sort of quantity, see *STh*, I, q. 42, a. 1, ad 1 (discussed below, 134–35).

40. *STh*, I, q. 14, a. 1.

41. *STh*, I, q. 4, a. 3.

intellect can assimilate that. But the senses can assimilate accidental forms of various sorts.

Now, as Aristotle presents them, most of his predecessors held that what cognizes has a likeness of what is cognized.[42] He agrees. Nearly all of them, however, were thinking that "it takes one to know one"—that the cognizer's own nature was actually like that of the thing cognized. Aristotle finds this untenable. If it were true, he says, then the cognizer should always be actually cognizing the thing. It should also always be cognizing itself, since it is like itself. And indeed all things, being like themselves and like others, should be cognizing. So he concludes that what the cognizer's nature has is not an actual likeness of what is cognized, but only potency for such likeness. The cognitive powers are just such potencies. But they are actualized—actual cognition occurs—only through the action of the things themselves. The things must impress their likenesses upon the cognizer, according to its potency to receive them.

This, however, is by no means Aristotle's whole account of cognition. It hardly could be, since it applies to any sort of change (on his account of change). When fire heats something, it impresses a likeness of itself on what has potency to receive it. Yet being heated by fire is by no means the same thing as perceiving or knowing fire. What is the difference? Thomas's passage indicated it, very briefly. The cognizer, he said, not only has its own form, but also is apt to have the form of some other thing. He is not saying that the cognizer is apt to lose its own form and take on one like that of another thing. That is what happens when cool water is heated by fire. It loses its coolness and takes on heat. And the heat that it takes on is its own, not the fire's; it is only like the fire's. By contrast, the form which the cognizer is apt to take on is not just like a form of the thing cognized. It also *is* a form of the thing cognized. When you put your cold hand in warm water, you feel the water's warmth well before your hand becomes equally warm. This means that your hand already has a likeness of the water's warmth—a likeness that is *not* your hand's warmth, because your hand is not yet warm. The likeness of the water's warmth is a form in your hand, but it is also somehow the water's form. It must be, if by it, what you feel the warmth of is the water, not your hand. Of course, eventually your hand does take on its own warmth. But in many other cases of sensation, you never do take on a similar form of your own. With your blue eyes you are seeing the black and white page. Nothing in you thereby is, or is even in the process

42. *De anima*, I.2, 404b8–18, 405b12–23; I.5, 409b23–410b10.

of becoming, black and white. The blue in your eyes is only the blue of your eyes. But the forms of black and white in them are also the page's forms. They are the page's inasmuch as by them, the page itself is being seen.

So when Thomas says that the nature of cognizers has a greater amplitude and extension than that of non-cognizers, the notions of amplitude and extension go together. After all, anything that has a substantial nature, whether or not it has cognition, can also take on additional, accidental forms. But the nature of what has cognition is more ample, because it can take on additional forms that, while being in it, are also of other things. In other words, the forms that it can take on are themselves ampler forms, because they extend to other things. They do so in this sense: the form by which the cognizer actually knows, and the form by which the thing cognized is actually cognized, is one and the same form. I mean one and the same individual form. It is in the cognizer, but it is not contracted or confined to him.

Clearly it is crucial not to think that the cognitive likeness itself is what is being cognized.[43] The likeness is nothing but the formal principle, in the cognizer, by which it (he/she) cognizes the thing. Thomas's very point of departure in the treatment of cognition is that, through it, the soul's activity extends to other things. The soul, or the animal, is not perceiving or knowing itself and then somehow taking itself as a representation of other things. Quite the contrary: what is first cognized is something else, and then that act of cognizing makes the cognizer cognizable to itself (himself/ herself), *as* cognizing something else. This is what nowadays is called consciousness. For Aristotle and Thomas, it exists at both the sensitive and the intellectual levels.[44] But it is not the defining or most characteristic feature of cognition.

---

43. See *STh*, I, q. 85, a. 2. As he points out there, if the likeness itself were what is cognized, then all appearances would be true. There could be no disagreement or dialogue. We would never be talking about the same things.

44. Sensitive consciousness is one of the functions of the so-called "common sense": See *STh*, I, q. 78, a. 4, ad 2. On why the cognition of the cognitive act is secondary, see my "Intentional Being, Natural Being, and the First-Person Perspective," 113. This is not to say that self-knowledge is of little significance in Thomas's thought; quite the contrary. See the excellent study by T. Cory, *Aquinas on Human Self-Knowledge*.

The Elevation of the Cognitive Soul:
One Act of Diverse Potencies

This may all sound very odd. From the standpoint of Aristotelian natural philosophy, the oddness can be somewhat mitigated, if we recall an observation of Aristotle's about physical activity: the activity of the agent, its action, and the activity of what is acted upon, its passion, are one and the same motion, taking place in what is acted upon.[45] A fire's action of heating, for example, is not a process that the fire itself undergoes. The process is in the thing heated. Yet it is still of the fire too, inasmuch as it is still the fire's action. Similarly, a thing that is cognized impresses its likeness on the cognizer, and although the impressing is the action of the thing, it takes place in the cognizer. In short, heating and being heated are one and the same activity, and so are the cognizer's cognizing the thing and the thing's being cognized.[46]

However, there are also large differences. The form by which the fire heats is in the fire and not in the thing heated. Once the thing heated becomes as hot as the fire, or has an equal form of heat, the heating stops.[47] And the form in the thing heated is only its form, not the fire's too; what the thing does because of that form does not regard the fire at all. By contrast, the activity of cognition takes place precisely as a result of the cognizer's having the likeness of the thing cognized. The impressing of the likeness upon the cognizer is only the origin of this activity, not the activity itself. You are seeing the banana's yellow because you have already received the form of its yellow. And whereas the form by which the fire heats is only a form of the fire and not of the thing being heated, the very form by which the cognizer cognizes is a form of the thing cognized too. Cognizer in act and cognized in act are one and the same.[48] That is, one and the same form is the act of both.

What are not the same are the forms by which cognizer and cognized are in potency to this activity.[49] The cognizer's potency is its cognitive power: touch, eyesight, intellect, etc. The cognized's potency is simply the form inhering it, whose likeness it is apt to impress on the cognizer: its heat,

---

45. *Physics*, III.3, 202a13–b22.

46. See *In De an.*, III, lect. 2, §592–93.

47. Cf. *De anima*, II.5, 417a19–21.

48. *De anima*, III.7, 431a1–2. See *In De an.*, II, lect. 12, §377.

49. See *In De an.*, III, lect. 13, §788.

its color, its substantial nature, etc. Color and eyesight are very different things. Indeed the chief contrast that Thomas wants to draw in the above passage is right here. He is pointing mainly to the amplitude and the extension of cognitive powers and of the natures that underlie them, as compared with non-cognitive forms and natures. The passage thus goes on: "For this reason the Philosopher says in *De anima* III [8, 431b21] that the soul is in a way all things." He is talking about the soul that has sensation and intellect. It is in a way all things insofar as it has potency for the cognitive likenesses or forms of all things.

How exactly is this to be all the things themselves? Of course, it is to be them only in potency, but that is not the main point. Indeed, the same could be said of prime matter, which is in potency to all forms. But matter, as we said, has no actuality or identity of its own at all. It simply *is* all things, though only in potency. By contrast, the point here is that we have a single form and act, the soul, which is quite distinct in its own nature from the forms of other things, and which in that sense is only itself and not all things, even in potency; but which is also in a way a form of all things, insofar as it has potency for the forms by which all things are actually cognized. It is the "place of forms."[50] Or better, as Aristotle says in the course of spelling out the thesis that the soul is in a way all things: just as the hand is the "tool (organ) of tools," i.e., the tool in or by which all tools are used, so the soul is the "form of forms," i.e., the form through which the forms of all cognizable things, as such, can be in act and render the things actually cognized.[51]

We should be struck, I think, by the extent to which Aristotle and Thomas regard being cognizable as a genuine feature of things, despite its being actualized only in a few special kinds of things (partially in the beasts, and fully in man). And we should be even more struck by the fact that this actualization is itself attributed to things, even though it does not inhere in them. It is their act of being cognized. To be sure, their own existence, and even their being as they are cognized to be, does not at all depend on this act. In that sense it is merely accidental to them. But it is still theirs. It is so as their effect; and, unlike other effects, it is an effect that in a way contains them. For in it, they manifest themselves or present themselves.

50. *De anima*, III.4, 429a27–28.
51. *De anima*, III.8, 432a1–3.

The Perfection of the Cognitive Soul:
Cognition and Immateriality

But why are the cognitive likenesses themselves not in the things? If all things have forms, why is that not sufficient for their having at least some measure of cognition? Why is cognition actualized only in or through this special form, soul? Or rather—since plants have souls too—through certain special souls? Thomas's article on God's knowledge continues:

> Now the contraction of a form comes from matter. Hence, as said above, forms, according as they are more immaterial, approach to a kind of infinity. So it is clear that a thing's immateriality is the reason why it is cognitive; and the mode of cognition is according to the mode of immateriality. Thus it is said in *De anima* II [12, 424a32–b3] that plants do not cognize because of their materiality.[52]

Cognition and materiality are inversely proportional.[53]

Earlier we remarked that plant-soul enjoys a certain transcendence with respect to matter, insofar as it is not absolutely tied to the portion of matter that it actualizes now. But this is not the immateriality that Thomas is talking about. He is talking about being in some way or in some respect free of, or not conditioned by, any matter. I suspect that for most of us the initial reaction to this is simply to wonder what in the world matter has to do with it. If we recall the specifically Aristotelian doctrine of matter, however, we should be able to see the point.

In that doctrine, as we saw, matter's primary role is that of a subject of change; and more precisely, a subject of the sort of change that is either itself a motion or at least (as in the case of substantial change) connected with motion. Such change involves a succession of mutually exclusive or contrary forms. In the matter, then, the forms are incompatible with each other. This point is not confined to prime matter and the substantial forms received therein; it applies to anything that functions properly as matter for any sort of forms. What is matter for heat and cold cannot have the forms of heat and cold together (in the same part), any more than a thing can *be* hot and cold together (in the same part). And if it is hot, the form of heat that it has is strictly its own form, not anything else's, just as its being hot is not anything else's being hot. But as we saw, what perceives or knows by a

---

52. *STh*, I, q. 14, a. 1.
53. *STh*, I, q. 84, a. 2.

form of heat is not thereby hot; and the form that it has it not solely its own, but is also of what is perceived or known as hot through it. So the form of heat is in it, not according to the sort of potency that characterizes matter, but according to potency of a different sort. It is a potency that follows the cognizer's specific nature as cognizer, and it is the result of the cognizer's substantial form. The substantial form does of course inhere in some matter, but with respect to this potency, it is in some respect free of matter or not conditioned by it.

This thesis can be confirmed through other points of comparison and contrast between forms in matter and cognitive likenesses. For example, in acquiring the cognitive likeness of something, the cognizer passes from potency to act; but such passage does not strictly entail the loss of anything, even of another likeness. One can see red and green at the same time. Nor is the red seen with one part of the eye, and the green with another; the whole eye is seeing them both. As fashion designers know, one sees the combination. Again, taking on a cognitive likeness does not require a continuous passage from one's original condition through an intermediate zone. One may pass at once from feeling something hot to feeling something cold without feeling anything lukewarm, or from seeing white to seeing black without seeing gray. This is to say that the cognitive power is equally, immediately ready for all the likenesses that it can take on; it is a kind of mean with respect to them.[54] Matter is not equally ready for all the forms, accidental or substantial, that it might have. The form in it now makes it more ready for some than for others. Recall the example of wine and vinegar.

Moreover, the cognitive power's capacity for various forms positively excludes their material presence in at least some part of the cognizer. For instance, a part of the eye must be colorless; the ear must be silent; the nasal passage, odorless; the tongue, tasteless. It is true that the organ of touch is not entirely without tangible properties. That is impossible. But the organ is in a mean or middling condition—neither very hot nor very cold, neither very hard nor very soft—so that it is at least free of the extremes and hence open to their cognitive likenesses.

There is also a significant difference between the activity to which matter is subject and cognitive activity. Not all cognitive activity is a change or a motion. The simplest sort is not. To be sure, the acquisition of the cognitive likeness of something is a change. But properly speaking, that change is not the very act of cognizing (perceiving or knowing) the thing.

54. *De anima*, II.11, 424a2–10; II.12, 424b1–3; III.13, 435a21–22.

It is only that act's origin. Seeing something is not a process of acquiring the visual likeness of it. Rather, one sees it in virtue of already having acquired that likeness. Of course, the thing seen may be changing, and one sees the change. But the seeing does not constitute another change.

Acts of this sort—seeing something, understanding something, and also appetitive acts such as desiring or wanting or being pleased at something—are what Aristotle calls perfect or complete activities. He is contrasting them with motions, which are imperfect activities.[55] A motion is a process toward a form not yet had, an act of something in potency, as such. A perfect activity is simply the exercise of a form already had, remaining in that which has it. To be sure, even a motion proceeds from a form, in its agent. But the motion is not *in* the agent. It is in what is acted upon and moved. This is what is called transitive action, passing from the agent into what is acted upon and moved. And what is moved undergoes the motion just so long as it does not yet have the form that defines or specifies the motion. In some cases, of course, the agent and what is moved or acted upon are parts of one whole. The whole is then said to move itself. This sort of activity is what plants have. They develop themselves or transform themselves through the mutual interactions of their parts. But a perfect act remains in the very agent, and (in the case of a thing with parts) in the very part, from which the act proceeds.[56] It does so even if the form that defines it is the form of something else. For (to repeat), in cognition, the form of the cognizer and the form of the object cognized are one and the same. It is the likeness of the object cognized, in the cognizer. Action remaining in the agent, as such, is called immanent action.

This notion of immanent action helps us see that the substantial form of the cognizer is a more perfect form—a more perfect principle of activity. Thomas writes,

> In things that share in cognition, [substantial] form is found in a higher way than in those that lack cognition. For in things lacking cognition, there is found only a form determining each to one proper being (*esse*), which is the natural being of each . . . . But in things that have cognition, each is determined to its proper natural being, through its natural form, in such a way that it is

55. *De anima*, III.7, 431a3–8; *Metaph.*, IX.6, 1048b18–36; cf. *EN*, X.3, 1174a13–b14. See *STh*, I, q. 18, a. 1 and a. 3, ad 1. Of course, there can be a progressive series of such acts, which resembles a motion; e.g., learning or reasoning.

56. *Metaph.*, IX.8, 1050a23–b6. Cf. *STh*, I, q. 18, a. 3, ad 1; q. 54, a. 1, ad 3, & a. 2; q. 56, a. 1; I–II, q. 74, a. 1.

nevertheless receptive of the cognitive likenesses (*species*) of other things . . . and thereby, those things that have knowledge approach in a way a resemblance of God, "in Whom all things pre-exist," as Dionysius says.[57]

From here Thomas goes on to argue that what has cognition, having a more perfect substantial form than what does not, also has a more perfect mode of appetite. It has not only fixed physical tendencies but also the capacity to incline to things that it apprehends, insofar as these pertain to its own good.[58] It is, in short, a more perfect *nature*.

The Qualified Immateriality of Sensation

Now, Thomas does regard sensation and intellect as two levels, quite distinct. In a passage quoted earlier, from the article on God's knowledge, Thomas said, "the mode of cognition is according to the mode of immateriality." Both cognition and immateriality, then, come in various modes. In fact, there are varying degrees of immateriality. The same passage goes on: "but sense is cognitive because it can receive cognitive likenesses without matter, and the intellect is still further cognitive, because it is more separated from matter and unmixed, as is said in *De Anima* III [4, 429a18, b5]." Intellect is "unmixed," by which he means, not intrinsically conditioned by matter at all; we will consider this shortly. But sensation has only a qualified mode of immateriality. Against what he takes to be Plato's view, Thomas insists that, for Aristotle and in truth, sensation is exercised by a bodily organ.

But let us go back to where Aristotle says that plants do not have sensation on account of their materiality. He also says there that all the senses receive forms without matter. Yet he illustrates this idea by comparing the

---

57. *STh*, I, q. 80, a. 1. The cognitive likenesses that the senses and human intellect get from bodily things do not give natural being; nor do they give natural operation. "The heat in the fire, not in the soul, heats" (*De ver.*, q. 22, a. 12). The greater extension of these cognitive likenesses, as opposed to that of the soul itself, is bought at the cost of a certain weakening or denaturing. Thomas calls this weak mode of forms "intentional being" (*esse intentionale*). This mode, however, is not essential for all cognition; some natural forms, such as the angels' and God's, are naturally immaterial, and so they are per se principles of actual knowledge. Thomas's *esse intentionale* is thus related to, but not the same as, the modern notion of intentionality; I discuss this at length in "Intentional Being, Natural Being, and the First-Person Perspective."

58. That is why the likenesses of other things exist in it without the inclinations or active tendencies that are proper to them in the things themselves. In that case it would tend toward their good, not its own.

senses with wax that receives the imprint of a signet-ring without the iron or the gold. And he goes on to say that what does the sensing is an extended thing, a body—a sense-organ.[59] Is this even coherent? How can a body receive anything without matter? And is immateriality not all or none? How are there degrees of it?

Here again it is crucial not to forget that, in Aristotle's lexicon, *matter* is a relative term. It does not refer only to prime matter. Wax contains prime matter. But his point here is that it is not, and does not contain, the matter of a signet-ring. A signet-ring must be made out of something hard, something that keeps its shape, such as iron or gold. The wax gets the ring's shape without thereby becoming another ring. The nature or the essence of a signet-ring (in the sense in which an artificial thing has a nature or essence) includes not only the form but also a determinate type of matter, the type needed for being a signet-ring. It is just what we saw earlier: the cognitive likeness of a thing does not make the cognizer be a thing of the same sort.[60] The eye receives the form of yellow, but without the type of matter that the form of yellow must inform in order to make something be yellow. And so the eye seeing yellow is not thereby yellow itself.

The wax has the form of the ring without being a ring. For that very reason, it can be a sign of the ring. If the form were impressed in another piece of iron or gold, that would not be a sign of the ring; it would be a counterfeit ring. Moreover, the ring has the power to signify the king's authorization, but the ring by itself does not actualize this power. The power is actualized in the wax, because of its capacity to receive the ring's form without its matter. Likewise, a sensible thing's power to be sensed is actualized in the sense-organ, because of a similar capacity in it.

So understood, the "immaterial reception of form" is an utterly commonplace affair. It is how the images and the music are on your hard disk. Your hard disk neither looks like the images nor sounds like the music at all. It has the forms, or as we say, the information, of them, but not in the sort of matter in which these forms make images to see or sounds to hear.

Of course, the wax does not perceive the king's authorization. Nor does the hard disk see the images. Why not? Because they do not have soul! This is not sudden mystification. It is just the general point that we are considering: the gradation of substantial forms. Some are more perfect than others, and this means, less conditioned by matter, in their own being

---

59. *De anima*, II.12, 424a17–28.

60. It does not give the cognizer "natural being": see above, 71–72.

and in their operations. The wax and the hard disk do not have substantial forms that are perfect enough to make any use of the forms-without-the-matter of rings or of images or of sounds. The wax and the hard disk can only function in the way the media of the senses do, transmitting such forms to what can use them to perform the vital activity of cognizing. What can use them in that way must be alive and have a form that is a soul, one even more perfect than a plant's.

But how can Aristotle be so sure that the sense-powers are still forms inhering in bodily organs, and that the organs themselves are not just media by which the likenesses of things reach the powers? He is sure because he finds that the powers themselves show the traits of forms-in-matter: involvement in contrariety and process. A sense-power can be weakened, taking time to recover; and it can even be destroyed. What shows that it is really the power itself which is weakened or destroyed is that what weakens or destroys it is its very own activity, as initiated by its very own object.[61] Seeing a bright light dazzles, so that for a while one cannot see dimmer things, and it may even blind; hearing a very loud sound deafens; etc. There is then, a material dimension that is essential to these powers. Their activities are not primarily bodily motions, but bodily motions are inseparably, essentially joined with them, as instrumental to them.

So the senses have a certain immateriality, but it is qualified. Thomas also finds diverse grades of immateriality among the various senses. Touch is the most material; even though it gets the form of the tangible body without the matter, as when your cold hand feels the water's warmth, this is accompanied by the material reception: your hand does gradually get warmer. Touch is also the most limited as to the distance of its possible objects from it. At the other extreme is sight, whose activity involves a minimum of material change and which extends very far indeed. Then there are the so-called interior senses, such as memory, which other animals also have; these serve to combine, preserve, and evaluate the data of the external senses. They do not even need the object's material presence outside the soul. They extend to past and future (perhaps merely potential future, never actualized). But they too, Thomas holds, are in an organ. Today, I assume, he would say it is the brain.

61. *De anima*, II.12, 424a28–32; III.4, 429a29–b5.

The Total (Intrinsic) Immateriality of Intellect

Only intellectual activity, then, is "separate and unmixed," not seated in a bodily organ at all. A sign of this is that strong objects do not affect it in the way strong objects of a sense affect the sense.[62] There is no such thing as something's being so intelligible as to render its knower dull-witted or stupid. Grasping highly intelligible things does not make grasping lesser ones harder, but if anything, easier.

Thomas's fundamental proof of the total immateriality of intellect, however, invokes once again the notion of a power's amplitude and extension. By intellect, he says, we can know the natures of all bodies.[63] But if it had any bodily nature of its own, or an organ with such a nature, that would obstruct the knowledge of others, just as the pupil's having some color would obstruct the vision of other colors. He is saying that, in matter, the forms of bodily things are opposed or contrary to one another. But none of them is opposed to intellect. Nor, as they are in intellect, are they opposed to each other. Grasping one is perfectly compatible with grasping others. Intellect's proper seat, then, is not a body.

A further argument rests on the way in which intellect knows the natures of things.[64] It knows them "absolutely." This does not mean that it knows them perfectly or exhaustively, but that it knows them in a pure way, unconditioned by factors extraneous to them. For instance, it knows stone absolutely, just as stone. It grasps the nature of stone just in itself, according to its own formula or *ratio*—the nature common to all stones, anywhere, anytime. It is not grasping only this stone here and now, in the way the eye is seeing only this patch of blue. But this means that intellect itself must be an "absolute form," not inhering in matter. Otherwise its cognitive likenesses of the natures of things would be under the conditions of its own matter, and it would grasp the natures in a correspondingly conditioned and individual way.

---

62. *De anima*, III.4, 429a29–b5. See *STh*, I, q. 75, a. 3, ad 2.

63. Here I follow the argument as given in *STh*, I, q. 75, a. 2. Nowhere, as far as I know, does Thomas argue for the thesis that we can know all bodily natures. How can he be sure of this? I do not think he assumes that we have actually known them all. He is only saying that our minds are open to them all. Perhaps the point is simply that we already do grasp the general nature of body. That casts a net over the whole field. All specific bodily natures must fall under it. Notice that the senses cannot do anything like this; one cannot see color in general.

64. *STh*, I, q. 75, a. 5.

Intellect, then, enjoys a kind of infinity. It embraces all natures, without limit, and it bears on each in the unlimited, universal extension of the nature's own absolute formula. Earlier in the article on God's knowledge, Thomas had in fact said that "the contraction of a form comes from matter. Hence, as we said above, forms, according as they are more immaterial, approach more to a kind of infinity." The reference is to *STh*, I, q. 7, a. 1, which is on God's essential infinity. There Thomas presents God's infinity as that of a form not contracted by matter. His argument turns on the thesis that "form, considered in itself, is common to many, but by being received in matter, it becomes determinately the form of this thing."

It may sound as though he is speaking only of forms that are abstract and universal—i.e., commonly predicable of many things—and that are individuated by being applied to matter. That is indeed an example of what he is talking about, but it can hardly be the only one. I say this because his aim here is to show that God is infinite, and he certainly does not think that God is a universal. But besides universality or common predicability, there are also other ways of being common to many; and some of these ways can belong to individual forms.[65] A form can be one, or in one thing, without being "determinately of" that thing, i.e., of it and of nothing else. Thus, a cognitive likeness is an individual form in the cognizer, but it is an act of both cognizer and cognized. And a cognitive power is an individual form in the cognizer, but it is a potential of the things that are its objects, a potential for their being cognized. This is exactly how the intellect is in a way "all things." In the case of God, Thomas will say that His intellect, which is identical with Him, is itself the *act* of all the intelligibles, the act of the whole of universal being.[66] This is because, as he says in *STh*, I, q. 7, a. 1, God is an act of being, *esse*, that is not received in any subject, and because *esse* is what is "most formal of all." And so, as Thomas concludes in our article on God's knowledge, existing at the summit of immateriality, God is at the summit of cognition.

These assertions about God are highly metaphysical and involve notions that we will try to clarify in the next two chapters. But for the moment what I wish to stress is that Thomas is saying that an individual

65. Very explicit on this point, and very much in line with *STh*, I, q. 7, a. 1, is *In De an.*, II, lect. 5, §282–83.

66. *STh*, I, q. 79, a. 2; I–II, q. 51, a. 1, ad 2. Elsewhere he says that God is "act and likeness of all things" (*De ver.*, q. 20, a. 2). And he says that, whereas our intellect is in potency to the forms of all things, God's form naturally contains them all in act, as the perfect contains the imperfect: *STh*, I, q. 4, a. 2, and I, q. 14, a. 6.

intellect is a form not received in matter, and that this is why it is common to many, "in a way all things." Your intellect is so. It is so despite its being in you and your being corporeal and material. This is what the Averroists found unintelligible: that a form which does not and cannot inhere in matter should belong to a material being.

Thomas knows that his position is delicate. But he thinks he can avoid sheer incoherence, again by distinguishing between this power of the soul, intellect, and the essence of the soul itself as a substantial form. The intellect is not a substantial form; it is an accident, a quality. But the substantial entity that it properly inheres in is not a body. It is the soul itself. The soul, in its turn, does inhere in matter, thereby constituting a human being. In fact the whole soul inheres in matter. There cannot be part of it in matter and part outside. It is simple, all or none. It does not even have distinct substantial parts. If it did, it would need another soul to hold them together. Nevertheless, its intellect is not in matter, in the sense that it is not at all intrinsically conditioned by matter. This cannot be imagined! But we can at least see that it is not a merely ad hoc solution. The intellectual soul stands at the peak of a whole hierarchy of forms, each higher one being less conditioned by matter. The senses have a qualified immateriality. Plant-souls are not tied to *this* matter. Every substantial form overcomes the divisibility of matter and makes a body an unqualified unity, a substance in act.

The immateriality of intellect is crucial in Thomas's understanding of the being of the human soul and its destiny after a person's death. This too is a metaphysical topic that we will look at later. There we will see how Thomas ties the human soul's possession of intellect to an especially high grade of perfection as a substantial form.

That you have your own intellect and are exercising your own understanding is also crucial, on Thomas's view, for ethics. Otherwise you would not be making any free choices. Freedom of choice is rooted in the enormous amplitude and extension of the properly intellectual appetite, the will. This is the most perfect of appetites, inclining toward the good in an absolute way, as good, in all its multiform universality.[67]

67. See, *inter alia*, *STh*, I, q. 59, a. 3; q. 82, a. 2, ad 1; q. 83, a. 1; I–II, q. 9, a. 6, ad 3; q. 10, a. 1, ad 3; q. 13, a. 6. Generally on Thomas's conception of the will, see the excellent study by David M. Gallagher, "Thomas Aquinas on Will as Rational Appetite."

The Intellect of an Animal

But we must not lose sight of the fact that what is doing the understanding (and willing) is, for Thomas, in the genus of animals. It is—you are—a natural, physical being. This has serious consequences for the intellect itself. Even if it is not intrinsically conditioned by matter, matter does condition it in an extrinsic way, and the conditioning is quite pervasive, because it regards the intellect's very object. Intellectual activity is not performed by a bodily organ, but ours is inseparable from the activity of a bodily organ. This is because it has to have an object. There is no such thing as understanding without understanding something. But our intellect finds its object in something presented by the senses; in particular, in what he calls a *phantasma*, an image, produced by the interior senses. This is why, if the brain is injured, understanding may be hampered or suspended. It is not that intellect itself is damaged, as by an object that is too strong. It is that its contact with its object is rendered faulty.

Notice that even if the external senses are operating, without a *phantasma* the intellect cannot work. Thomas often speaks of the intellect "abstracting" its object, which is a nature taken absolutely and universally, from the *phantasmata*. This might sound as though it is a question of stripping away a thing's particular sensible features and pulling out the nature underlying them—almost as though those features conceal the nature. In that case, it would be hard to see how a *phantasma* is of much help. But instead of stripping away or pulling out, a better metaphor would be compressing and unifying. (To be sure, in the process something does get squeezed out; but it is only matter.) We are talking about the nature of a bodily thing, and about a grasp of that nature that has its origin in the nature itself, in its self-presentation. This is through the body's sensible features, of course. But a mere photograph will not do. What is needed is more like a video-clip, or several of them, capable of running at extremely high speed. A bodily nature is strictly a *nature*, a principle of motion and rest. It shows itself through the motion and rest that it is principle of, and we grasp it by discerning the unity in that motion and rest. Even the nature of a stone presents itself piecemeal. In order to grasp it, we need to put the features and parts and episodes together, in such a way that the unifying *logos* or *ratio* or proportioning that runs through them stands out. This work of synthesis, this "spiritualizing" of a bodily nature, is prepared by the interior senses. But it is brought to completion by the intellect itself, and it is only the intellect that directly grasps that *logos*. The unity of a subject of change, substantial unity—which is seen above all in identity through change[68]—is a strictly intelligible object.

Thomas is not saying that we can only think about sensible things. We are now thinking about intellect and soul, which are not sensible. But the natures of sensible things, he says, are the first and most fully proportionate or adequate objects of our intellect.[69] Thinking about anything else requires some sort of connection or comparison with such natures. For instance, we can think about God only because we have *phantasmata* of His effects— and only to the extent that He can be thought of in terms of those effects.[70]

As Thomas sees it, our intellect's dependence on the senses explains many features of its activity; in particular, the fact that it does not grasp everything all at once. As befits the power of a natural being—a growing being—it proceeds towards its due perfection or maturity gradually.[71] It starts with a general and confused knowledge of things and works toward more proper, distinct knowledge of them.[72] Thomas even likens it to prime matter, since it is by nature merely in potency to intelligible forms, as prime matter to natural forms.[73] Its discursiveness even serves to sum up the difference between it and the other intellects, divine and angelic. It, and it alone, is the reasoning intellect.[74]

To say *rational*, then, is already, implicitly, to say *animal*. According to Aristotle, this is one of the features of a good definition: the ultimate differentia implies all the others. In that way it captures the whole form, and everything entailed by the form, of what is being defined.[75] Rationality is a mode of intellect—of the quality of being, in a way, all things—and hence it implies a dimension of pure immateriality. But it is the mode that is intrinsically connected to the life of the senses, and therefore to the sense-organs; and to the vegetative functions and the physical ingredients that constitute the organs; and to matter itself. That there is such a differentia is itself proof

---

68. See above, 40.

69. *STh*, I, q. 87, aa. 4 & 7.

70. *STh*, I, q. 12, a. 12, ad 2. This is true even of the knowledge of God that comes through grace: *STh*, q. 12, a. 13.

71. See *STh*, I, q. 79, aa. 4 & 8; cf. I, q. 14, a. 7, and I, q. 58, aa. 1, 3, & 4.

72. See *STh*, I, q. 85, aa. 3, 5.

73. *STh*, I, q. 87, a. 1; see *STh*, I, q. 56, a. 1. And thus Thomas can explain spiritual changes without having to posit spiritual matter to make them possible. See above, 13.

74. *STh*, I, q. 79, a. 8.

75. *Metaph.* VII.12, 1037b8–1038a35; cf. *In Meta.*, VII, lect. 12, esp. §1555–65.

that what is defined—in this case, man—is indeed of one nature, not a mere combination. Thomas calls this a "wonderful connection of things."[76]

At the same time, he also thinks that we should not be too surprised to find that what is highest in the corporeal order, namely the so finely tuned human body, should be joined to what is lowest in the spiritual order, namely that intellectual substance which is the human soul.[77] Of course, as we have seen, the body exists thanks to the soul itself, which is its formal principle. That is why the nature is one: it has one form. And thus,

> the intellectual soul is said to be a sort of horizon and border of corporeal and incorporeal things, inasmuch as it is an incorporeal substance and yet the form of a body. For something made out of intellectual substance and bodily matter is not less one than is something made of the form of fire and its matter, but, if anything, more so; because the more a form dominates matter, the more what is made from it and matter is one.[78]

In the ensuing lines, Thomas takes the reader by the hand through the various grades of form that we have already surveyed.

In calling the human soul a substance, Thomas does not just mean that it is a substantial form. He really means a substance, in the sense given earlier: a subject of being, at least a partial one.[79] This is a very metaphysical point, and I shall put off discussing it until chapter 5. But before closing this one, let me briefly address a strictly physical concern.

The concern, in a word, is neuroscience. Thomas knew that the human body was finely tuned, but really he had no idea how fine the tuning is. For that matter, he had no idea how finely tuned, or at least how complex, a mineral body is. Can his account of human cognition, and with it, of human nature, or really of any physical nature, still be taken seriously? Would even he think it could? After all, as we saw, he holds that the complete definition of a natural thing's kind expresses not only its form but also its specific matter or material dispositions. If, as it seems, he is wrong about the matter of things, can he have gotten their forms right?

I can only venture a guess at what his own answer would be. I think he would say that it depends. In some cases, indeed, the sheer possibilities

---

76. *Scg*, II, cap. 68, §1453.

77. *Scg*, II, cap. 68, §1453. On the suitability and dignity of the human body, see *STh*, I, q. 76, a. 5; q. 91, *passim*.

78. *Scg*, II, cap. 68, §1453.

79. See above, 39–40.

of observation that he had available were so limited that he got both the matter and the form wrong. I am thinking of his account of the heavenly bodies. But there the main problem was the inability (now overcome only in part) to observe the bodies themselves, as the whole beings and subjects of activity that they are. He was wrong about what they were actually doing. The situation is different with the things that he had under his nose (and behind it). No amount of experimenting, for instance, will overturn the thesis that we can think about things in a universal way.

People sometimes say that neuroscience has rendered the idea of the mind's immateriality obsolete. But surely, if Thomas's argument for that is invalid now, then it was invalid in the thirteenth century too; and if it was valid then, it still is. For his argument is to the effect that *no matter what* the brain (or any other body) is doing, it cannot be understanding. More mere evidence about what it is doing is therefore simply irrelevant. But in fact, when people say that, they hardly ever have in mind Thomas's argument for the immateriality of intellect. They almost always take the issue to be the status of consciousness. But for Thomas, some consciousness, the sensitive sort, is indeed in an organ. Ever since Descartes, the deep distinction between intellect and sense that Aristotle urged against his predecessors has been obliterated. And even regarding the qualified immateriality of the senses: more evidence about (say) the eyes is irrelevant to Thomas's main thesis, which regards the amplitude and extension of sensation, and which pretty much boils down to the claim that your eyes (or whatever you see with) are in your head, while that which you are directly seeing is not in your head but on the page in front of you.[80]

If we have a clear grasp of what something as a whole is doing, then we can have a valid conception of its form, even if we are in a good deal of ignorance or even error about its parts and matter. And the conception of the form should precede and guide the inquiry into the matter. If we lose sight of the whole, we cannot grasp how the parts function as parts, as we cannot grasp the potency apart from the act. Wholes and forms are naturally prior in intelligibility. According to Thomas, this is how Aristotle proceeded with organisms.[81] Among Aristotle's biological works, Thomas says, the one that comes first (doctrinally, not chronologically) is the *De*

80. A similar point also holds regarding Aristotle's response to Empedocles's account of plants (see above, 56–57). The doctrine of the four bodily elements is obsolete, but it is also beside the point as regards the question whether a plant functions as a single nature or a mere combination.

81. *Sentencia Libri De sensu et sensato*, Proem.

anima. It treats the soul—the form—in a certain abstraction from the body and the matter. The subsequent works involve "concretion" or application to the body, first in general ways—for instance in the treatise on the senses, which are common to all animals—and then with respect to each particular kind of animal or plant. Thus, being prior, the abstract treatment can be valid even if there are problems in the subsequent "concretion." The form allows for a certain amount of free play in the matter. How could it be otherwise, if the thing is mobile?

This could explain why, while many of Aristotle's biological works are ignored today, the *De anima* is still taken very seriously. It can be, *if* hylomorphism in general is valid. And experimental science can hardly be what decides that.[82]

Thomas also remarks that there is no such "concrete" treatment of the intellect, because it has no organ. Its greatest "concretion" is in the soul itself (which is not a body, but is still of a body), while the most abstract treatment would regard the separate, totally immaterial substances. They are the ones that are by nature absolutely first in intelligibility. Their consideration, however, pertains not to natural science, but to metaphysics.

---

82. On Thomas's hylomorphism in relation to contemporary philosophy of mind, see Madden, *Mind, Matter, and Nature.*

4

Firsts

Logic, Truth, and the Science that Determines First Principles

The First Science to Learn

PHILOSOPHY, AS THOMAS CONCEIVES it, is not a single body of knowledge with a single subject matter, but an ordered set of them. They can be ordered in various ways. One is the sequence in which they are suitably learned. In this sequence, what Thomas puts first is logic, because it teaches the general philosophical way or method.

> Boys should first be instructed in logical matters, since logic teaches the way of all philosophy. Secondly, they should be instructed in mathematics, which neither requires experience, nor transcends the imagination. Thirdly, in natural things, which, though not exceeding sense and imagination, do require experience. Fourthly, in moral matters, which require experience and a mind free from passions . . . . And fifthly, in sapiential and divine things, which transcend the imagination and take a strong intellect.[1]

Logic is the mind directing its own activity, reason reasoning about reasoning, in order to reason well.[2] But even though Thomas puts it first, I am only bringing it up now, because this book is not a course in Thomistic

---

1. *In Eth.*, VI, lect. 7, §1211.
2. *In Post. an.*, I, Proem., §1[1].

philosophy, but only a sketch of it, and because some of the (few) things that I want to say about his views on logic are easier to explain in light of things seen in the previous two chapters. (For similar reasons, I have put the discussion of Thomas's moral thought in the final chapter.)

Like most Scholastics, Thomas takes logic quite seriously. He regards Aristotle's logical writings as a systematic and fairly complete treatment of the discipline, and he has left us a finished commentary on the *Posterior Analytics* and an unfinished one on the *De interpretatione*. He also makes use of earlier medieval work in logic, for instance on the roles that words can play within statements or propositions, and on the various ways in which the same name might apply to many different things.[3]

Logic is about the operations of reason.[4] Those that directly pertain to science and philosophy are of three basic types. The first is what Thomas sometimes calls the understanding of indivisibles, and sometimes simple apprehension. This operation results in a conception that is typically signified by a single word; it expresses the understanding of what some kind of thing is, some nature or form (or an object grasped in the manner of a nature or form). Such understanding may be more or less perfect. Not all natures are equally intelligible to us, and some of us may grasp a given nature better than others do.

Then there is what Thomas usually calls composition and division. By this he does not mean just any combination or separation of concepts. He means affirmative and negative judgment. From here on I shall call it affirmation and denial. It is the kind of judgment that is expressed in a proposition and is typically signified by a declarative sentence, in which a predicate is either applied to a subject or withheld from it.[5]

---

3. Under the latter heading belongs the doctrine of analogical names. Thomas wrote no treatise on this topic, and squaring the many passages of his that touch upon it is not easy. They are usually framed with a view to some particular application, the most important being language about God. Their interpretation has been heavily conditioned by Cardinal Cajetan's *De nominum analogia* (1498), even though this work was not intended as a synthesis of them (see Hochschild, *The Semantics of Analogy*). Helpful sources of information are J. Ashworth's "Analogy and Equivocation in Thirteenth-Century Logic: Aquinas in Context" and "Medieval Theories of Analogy." The difficulties of interpretation make me shy away from attempting a synopsis. Below I shall say just a few things about Thomas on names common to God and creatures (141–42).

4. *In Post. an.*, I, Proem., §2. Here and in the proem of the commentary on the *De interpretatione* Thomas offers interesting, complementary discussions of the tasks and divisions of logic. For a full discussion, see Schmidt, *The Domain of Logic*.

5. Declarative sentences signify, in an absolute way, a conception that is either true

The third type of operation is reasoning. This is a process. It starts from things taken as known, and it ends in something taken as hitherto unknown and as now known in light of them. It consists in gathering up propositions already formed and combining them in some way, such that a new one results. A combination of this sort is called a syllogism. Scientific knowledge, in the strict sense, consists of syllogisms that possess a number of specific characteristics; these are treated in the *Posterior Analytics*. Scientific syllogisms are called demonstrations.

Truth

Of the three types of operation just listed, in a way the principal one is the second, affirmation and denial. Simple apprehension, by itself, is incomplete. It is like someone's saying "Snow" and nothing more, so that we are left wondering, what about snow? What do you mean to affirm or deny of it? On the whole, knowledge that is fully actual is not the mere apprehension of the nature of a kind, but the judgment of something in accordance with such apprehension; for instance, a grammarian's judgment that *this A is an A*.[6] As for reasoning, it can certainly be a complete operation, but what completes or concludes it is precisely an affirmation or a denial.

Why does completion lie in affirmation and denial? The reason is that this is the proper seat of the intellect's intrinsic perfection and end, which is truth.[7] Thomas insists that truth, in the proper sense of the word, is "in the mind."[8] This is because, as we saw, cognitive activity terminates in the soul itself, through a likeness of the thing cognized. Of course, not all cognition is true. The likeness can be defective, distorting how the thing is cognized. So falsehood is in the mind as well, and most properly, in affirmation and denial.[9] Thomas therefore says that it belongs properly to logic

---

or false. There are also other complete utterances, but they are more or less incidental to reason's intrinsic perfection. They signify orders by which reason directs others according to its conception: *In Peryerm.*, I, lect. 7, §85[4]–86[5].

6. See *De anima*, II.5, 417a28–29; *Metaph.*, XIII.10, 1087a15–25.

7. See *In Peryerm.*, I, lect. 7, §85[4]; *STh*, I, q. 16, a. 1.

8. Thomas's *mens* (mind) includes both *intellectus* (intellect) and *voluntas* (will, which is intellectual appetite). Occasionally he uses either *mens* or *intellectus* to refer to the human soul, as in *STh*, I, q. 75, a. 2. But taken strictly, they signify powers of the soul, not its very essence: *STh*, I, q. 79, a. 1.

9. *STh*, I, q. 17, a. 3.

to consider both the true and the false.[10] But simple apprehension cannot be either true or false, in the proper sense. This is because truth cannot be in it in the way that a cognitive power's end must be in the power, namely, *as* something cognized. Simple apprehension does not include cognition of how the thing cognized compares with what is cognized about it. Such cognition, Thomas says, is found primarily in the judgment that a thing is (or, in the case of a denial, is not) such as is a form that it apprehends about the thing.[11] This sounds abstruse, but he is speaking of very ordinary judgments, for instance *Snow is white*. To make this judgment is to have grasped the form called whiteness, compared snow with it, and found a match. Such a judgment, then, involves cognition of truth. Of course, the judgment itself might not be true cognition; it might only seem so to the one making it. It is true if the thing really is such—if snow is indeed white. If not, it is false.

This is Thomas's notion of truth as the conformity or agreement (*adaequatio*) of intellect and thing. Obviously the idea is not that a true judgment about a thing is one that looks like the thing.[12] The judgment that snow is white does not look like snow at all. Still, on Thomas's account, the very nature of judgment—whether true or false—does present a certain analogy or proportion to the makeup of sensible things. He thinks that the relation between subject and predicate in a judgment reflects somewhat the composition of matter and form in things. To say that snow is white is, in effect, to assert the inherence of whiteness in snow, after the fashion of the inherence of a form in matter.[13]

However, this is only an analogy, not a strict isomorphism. Whereas the matter and form of a thing differ, an affirmative judgment asserts a kind of identity between its subject and its predicate. To judge that snow is white is to judge that snow is identical with something having whiteness.[14] Moreover, the judgment does not imply that the thing judged possesses material and formal components that are directly signified by the subject and the predicate. For instance, the judgment that a man is an animal does not mean that man is matter for the form of animality. Thomas is only saying

10. *In Meta.*, IV, lect. 17, §736.

11. *STh*, I, q. 16, a. 2. See *In Peryerm.*, I, lect. 3, §24[2]–31[9]. As he explains in these passages, sensation is like simple apprehension and cannot be true or false, properly speaking.

12. On this see *Scg*, I, cap. 59, §495.

13. See *In Meta.*, IX, lect. 11, §1898–1900.

14. *STh*, I, q. 85, a. 5, ad 3.

that subject and predicate play material and formal roles in the constitution of the judgment itself. Nor does a judgment have to mean that what the predicate signifies is a real form of any sort. We can give the status of forms to items that we understand not really to be forms. For instance, we can understand blindness to be a mere lack of the form of eyesight, not a real form in its own right; yet we give it the status of a form in judging that Milton was blind. In fact, on Thomas's view, something can even be predicated of itself. In that case, the same thing plays a material role as subject, and a formal role as predicate. *Blindness is blindness* is a genuine predication, and a true one, even though blindness is certainly not matter for the form of blindness.[15] Thomas goes so far as to hold that a concrete individual can be predicated of itself. *Socrates is Socrates* means, in effect, that Socrates is identical with something having the form of Socrates. We could call this form Socrateity. But the statement does not imply that there really is any such form in Socrates.[16]

Truth itself is a sort of form, and Thomas thinks there are as many instances of it as there are true judgments. But there is also a primary instance, which all others reflect; this is God.[17] A true judgment can become false, and vice-versa, if the thing judged can change with respect to the feature that is affirmed or denied of it.[18] Of future events not predetermined by present causes, our present judgments are proportionally indeterminate with respect to truth and falsehood.[19] Yet there is always truth about such events in God. This is not because He predetermines them, but because His grasp of temporal things, unlike ours, is not successive or temporal.[20] This point, however, involves issues that go beyond the science of logic.[21]

Why does truth consist in conformity with things? That is, why is such conformity the mind's proper good or end? "The human intellect's knowledge is somehow caused by things; whence it is that knowable things are a measure of human knowledge. For what is judged by the intellect is true

---

15. See *STh*, I, q. 13, a. 12.

16. Thomas speaks once, in another context, of *socrateitas*: *De pot.*, q. 8, a. 3.

17. *STh*, I, q. 16, a. 6.

18. *STh*, I, q. 16, a. 8.

19. *In Peryerm.*, I, lect. 13, §169[6]–175[12]; lect. 15, §201[2]–203[4].

20. *In Peryerm.*, I, lect. 14, §191[16]–196[21]. See also *Epistola ad Bernardum abbatem casinensem*. On this and related topics, very helpful is Harm Goris, *Free Creatures of an Eternal God*.

21. *In Peryerm.*, I, lect. 14, §199[24].

by the fact that the thing is so, and not vice-versa."[22] The perfection and goodness of an effect is measured by its cause. Our knowledge is caused by things inasmuch as they are the objects that initiate its actualization.

Notice, however, that being measured by things in this way is not the same as being dominated or mastered by them. Although things initiate the mind's actualization, the mind itself has a very active role too. It abstracts the natures of things from matter and thereby makes them actually able to function as intelligible objects, and it is what produces the affirmation or the denial in which the truth is properly found. Moreover, the truth is in us, not in things, and it is our good and end, not theirs. And there are truths that are not just means to something else, but for their own sake. These are theoretical or speculative truths. A free being, Aristotle says, is one that is for its own sake and not just for another's.[23] What is only for another's sake is a tool or a slave. And of all speculative knowledge, the freest is wisdom, because it is not even a means to other truth.[24] Rather, all other truth serves it. The wise man is his own master to the highest degree. On the other hand, he is not the "master of nature." He does not determine the natures of things or decide how things shall naturally be and act.

This account of truth, of course, regards us. God's knowledge is not actualized by "things." It is God Himself, and its truth is His very being.[25] Things—the very natures of things—are its effects, and it measures them.

Still, we do after all have knowledge that causes and measures a few things, such as artifacts. Both in relation to God's knowledge and in relation to this knowledge of ours, things themselves can, in a sense, be called true.[26] They are true if how they are is how the knowledge that causes them says they should be. This is only a qualified sense of truth, however, since the conformity to the knowledge is not in the thing *as* something known. It is merely the thing's being so.

Knowledge that causes things and thereby measures them is called practical knowledge. This is opposed to theoretical or speculative knowledge, which simply beholds things and does not cause them. Thomas insists, however, that practical and speculative knowledge are works of one

22. *Scg*, I, cap. 61, §512. Cf. *Categories*, 5, 4b8–9; *Metaph.*, IX.10, 1051b6–9; *STh*, I, q. 16, a 5, ad 2.

23. *Metaph.*, I.2, 982b25–26.

24. *Metaph.*, I.2, 982b27–28; see *In Meta.*, I, lect. 3, §56.

25. *STh*, I, q. 16, a. 5.

26. *STh*, I, q. 16, a. 1; see *In Peryerm.*, I, lect. 3, §29[7]–30[8].

and the same power of intellect.[27] The power is the same because the formal object is the same. The difference between them is accidental to the object's nature. They differ only in the goals to which they order their objects. Intellect working speculatively aims only to consider the truth; working practically, it orders and applies the truth that it knows to action. Nevertheless, "practical intellect cognizes truth just as speculative intellect does."[28] Clearly, *what truth is* in the two cases, the *ratio veri*, must be the same. Otherwise the parallel would be specious. Thomas is explicit about this.[29]

This means that practical knowledge too is measured by things. How so, if it measures things? The answer, I believe, is that it measures and is measured in different respects.[30] If you judge truly that you need to go to bed, and if you go to bed on account of that judgment, then your action of going to bed is true (in a qualified sense) by its conformity to your judgment. But your judgment is true (in the proper sense) because it conforms to your going to bed. I do not mean that it is true because going to bed is something that you actually do; indeed, you may be prevented from going to bed, and yet the judgment may still be true. But the judgment is true because your going to bed is something that you need—this being what the judgment both asserts and conforms to. If it were not something that you needed, the judgment would be false. And in that case, your action's conforming to it would not make your action true in any sense.

Thomas and the Critique of Knowledge

From a modern point of view, or at least a nineteenth- or twentieth-century one, Thomas's account of human cognition may seem naïve. It simply takes for granted that we can grasp real things, as they really are, and that we can thereby measure against them our own thoughts about them. Thomas even assumes that we can reach the perfection of cognition that is called *knowledge*, which constitutes a vantage-point from which to make judgments that cannot but be, and cannot but seem to be, true of things. Thomas does not think that, in order to be rigorous, philosophy must begin with a general critique of knowledge and only subsequently determine its content. He is aware of radical forms of skepticism, but he does not pay much attention

27. *STh*, I, q. 79, a. 11.
28. Ibid., ad 2.
29. *STh*, I-II, q. 64, a. 3.
30. I discuss this matter at some length in "Practical Truth and its First Principles."

to them. This is partly because he thinks no one can genuinely believe them (though some may think they can). He thinks there are many things that we all know and cannot reasonably doubt that we know, even if no formulations of them can preempt all questions.

But perhaps the real issue is not how seriously to take skepticism. If Thomas's account of cognition now looks naïve (or at least did so until recently), it is largely, I think, because he does not share the modern tendency to think of cognition as bearing primarily on representations of things; i.e., ideas, impressions, or what have you. It may indeed be naïve to assume that a representation of a thing presents the thing as it is, or even that the thing exists at all. But while Thomas is perfectly aware that much of our mental life involves working with representations, he consciously rejects the view that these are what it originally or chiefly feeds upon.[31] To put it in his terms, and to repeat a point already made, but worth stressing, he denies that the form inhering in a cognitive power, by which the power is first actualized, is that which is primarily known.[32] The form is only that *by which* the thing from which it originates is known.

The heart of the matter, I think, is the very notion that external things themselves can be the proper determinants of our cognition of them. The modern tendency is to suppose that they cannot. In the thirteenth century it was not so hard to think that they can, because there was current a notion of something enabling them to do so, something in them that is intrinsically self-communicative: the very notion of form. (I mean, the Aristotelian notion.) With the overthrow of Scholasticism, that notion fell into virtual oblivion. Things became inert, not only physically but also cognitively. The mind has had to look mainly to itself for the constitution of its objects.

Today many cognitive theorists regard knowledge itself as something material, and so as quite similar in nature to the material things known. A minority regard it as immaterial or spiritual. But the latter tend to think of spirit as something no less closed in on itself than a body is—as a "sort of stuff, as it were immaterial matter, a refined ethereal medium."[33] Theorists in either group may grant that cognition does presuppose some sort of influence of the things to be cognized upon the cognizer. But my point is that hardly anyone conceives of cognition as a kind of union with the things, a

---

31. On this topic see O'Callaghan, *Thomist Realism and the Linguistic Turn*.

32. See above, 66.

33. Anscombe, "Analytical Philosophy and the Spirituality of Man," 9. She is talking about Descartes.

joint activity of subject and object. Thomas's view, as we saw, is that even though actual knowledge of material things is not in the things but in the knower, it is nevertheless an actuality of the things too, as knowable (even though this is rather accidental to the things). And the cognitive likenesses, or forms, from which our knowledge originally proceeds are essentially the effects of the things, and in a way they are the same as forms inhering in the things—the same in formula.[34]

It is for this very reason that not all our cognition is necessarily true, but can, in some cases, be either true or false. If our primary objects were in our minds, we could hardly err about them at all.[35] And there would be no strong grounds for saying that our mind's end, truth, consists in judging about external things as they are. The evaluation of the representations might very well have other criteria. And in that case, we might indeed want a critique of any claim to know, or even to need to know, external things as they are. But the modern tendency has been simply to assume, without argument, that our primary objects are in our minds. This too seems somewhat naïve.

First for Us versus First Simply

Logic is the first philosophical science to study. But what Aristotle and the tradition after him call first philosophy is another science, namely metaphysics.[36] And even if logic is about the things that properly have truth and falsehood, it is metaphysics that he calls the science of truth.[37] Metaphysics is the science of truth in the sense that it achieves truth to the highest degree. And it is in just that sense that it is first philosophy. It is the dominant philosophical science, because it aspires to and reaches the dominant truths, those that explain all the others, and because the whole aim of philosophy is truth. Yet the true is not the proper subject matter of

34. That is, the primary cognitive forms are of this sort. From these we go on to make others, such as those by which we grasp negations or privations (darkness, death, evil), or those that reflect reason's own activity about things (species and genus, subject and predicate, universal and particular, etc.).

35. See *STh*, I, q. 85, a. 2.

36. The secondary literature on Thomas's metaphysics is vast. See Villagrassa, *Bibliografia sulla metafisica*. The most comprehensive single presentation is Wippel, *The Metaphysical Thought of Thomas Aquinas*. On many metaphysical themes I have found the writings of Lawrence Dewan, O.P., especially illuminating.

37. *Metaph.* II.1, 993b20; *Scg*, I, cap. 1, §5.

metaphysics, but of logic. The highest science is not mainly *about* truth. Most truths are not about truth. Truth is in the mind, but the mind is not mainly about itself, and most truths, including the primary or dominant truths, are about things not in the mind. They are about real things, things *in rerum natura*. The subject of metaphysics is not what is true, but simply what *is*. Thomas's term for it is *ens*. I shall use the word *being*, taking it as in the expression, *a human being*. I shall also want to use that word occasionally for what Thomas calls *esse*, to be. English does not always allow using the infinitive as he does. But I shall try to avoid ambiguity, and often I shall simply leave *esse* untranslated.

Metaphysics does, of course, have things to say about truth. It may even have the last word (I mean, the last philosophical word). But the nature of truth is not a major factor in the nature of being.[38] The nature of being is found mostly *in rerum natura*. And the primary truths are those that are about the primary beings, the ones that account for all the others—the primary causes. This is because "each thing is in respect of truth as it is in respect of being."[39] A truth is true to a higher degree inasmuch as it is about a being that *is* to a higher degree.[40] So metaphysics aims at truth about the primary, highest beings, and about how they explain or account for the rest. Aristotle is sure that these beings are everlasting.[41]

It would be a little more accurate, however, to say that the aim of metaphysics is to know as much truth about those beings as human reason can, given its point of departure. The distinction between the first science to learn and that which is simply primary is an illustration and an application of Aristotle's observation, at the beginning of the *Physics*, that the things that are first and more knowable to us are not the same as those that are first and more knowable by nature or in themselves.[42] Much of our learning consists in going from the former to the latter. Things more familiar to us stand in need of explanation, and we need to find out about the things that explain or account for them. We experience this need every time we wonder why something is, or happens, in the way that it is or does. Continuing

---

38. See *In Meta.*, VI, lect. 4, §1243.

39. *Metaph.*, II.1, 993b30–31.

40. See *In Meta.*, II, lect. 2, §291–98.

41. *Metaph.*, II.1, 993b28–30.

42. *Physics*, I.1, 184a16–21. See also *Prior Analytics*, 23, 68b35–7; *Posterior Analytics*, I.2, 71b33–72a5; *Topics* VI.4, 141b3–142a13; *Metaph.*, VII.3, 1029b3–12.

the pursuit, we may eventually reach things needing no further explanation at all. They will be the primary things.

Thomas explains:

> Those things are more knowable in themselves that have more of the nature of being (*plus habent de entitate*); for each thing is cognizable insofar as it is a being. But those are more beings, which are more in act; and hence they are by nature cognizable to the highest degree. But with us it is the reverse, because we proceed in understanding from potency to act, and the starting point of our cognition is from sensible things, which are material, and intelligible [only] in potency; whence they are known to us prior to the separate [=immaterial] substances, which are better known by nature, as is clear in *Metaphysics* II.[43]

He is referring to that passage in which Aristotle says that our minds are related to the most evident things as the eyes of bats to the daylight; the passage is just a few lines prior to those cited earlier in this section.[44] Thomas's gloss on this passage is that we can know of immaterial things only what we can infer from the things that we abstract from sensible images—that is, the natures of bodily beings—and that from this starting-point it is not possible to form a proper notion of the natures of immaterial things. Such natures are out of proportion to sensible things.[45] They are not directly visible us, even intellectually.

First for Us *and* First Simply

The general rule just considered, that what is first for us differs from what is first simply, is not entirely without exceptions. Thomas calls attention to a most important exception in commenting on a passage in *Nicomachean Ethics* VI. This passage is yet another reminder of *Metaphysics* II. Aristotle says that wisdom (*sophia*), taken without qualification, must be the most certain form of knowledge.[46] Thomas explains that this is because

43. *In Phys.*, I, lect. 1, §7[7]. The reference is, again, to *Metaph.*, II.1, 993b28–31.

44. *Metaph.* II.1, 993b9–11.

45. *In Meta.*, II, lect. 1, §282–84. Thomas says many times that we cannot know what such things are, though we can know that they exist. He thinks this is Aristotle's view; see also *In Meta.*, IX, lect. 11, §1916.

46. Here he speaks of wisdom, whereas in *Metaphysics* II what he identifies with the science of truth is love of wisdom, *philosophia*. Perhaps it is because in *Metaphysics* II he is stressing the difficulty and limits of this science, whereas the *Ethics* passage is

wisdom reaches the things that are in themselves most knowable, namely the first principles of beings. These are most knowable in themselves, he observes, even though some of them are less known to us, namely the immaterial beings. And then he explains why he says *some* of them and not *all:* "extremely universal principles (*universalissima principia*) are also more known to us, such as those things that pertain to being (*ens*), inasmuch as it is being; the cognition of which pertains to unqualified wisdom, as is clear in *Metaphysics* IV."[47]

What principles is Thomas talking about? They are not immaterial substances. In fact they are not substances at all. They are the features or the attributes or (we can even say) the natures that belong most universally to things. What is most universal in this way is being itself, together with the features that it brings with it, insofar as it is being. These features are not agents or efficient principles. Rather they are formal principles of a certain sort.[48] They are principles of *distinctions*. Being is the basis of the absolutely most universal distinction. If being and non-being were not distinct, there would be no distinctions at all. For instance, if being white were not distinct from not being white, it would not be distinct from being black. It is distinct from being black only because being black implies not being white.

Thus, being is also the most universal principle of understanding. And it is principle of the most universal truth, that which is called the principle of non-contradiction. This truth is a principle relative to all the other, less abstract truths, and to the processes of reasoning by which the mind moves from one truth to another. One way of formulating it is even in terms of the opposition between affirmation and denial.[49] To consider or to formulate it in this way, and indeed to call it the principle of non-*contradiction*, is to see it from a logical point of view. Nevertheless, it is not a truth confined to logical matters. That is, it is not *about* reason or affirmation or denial, at least not solely or even primarily. It is about everything that affirmation and denial can be about, which is to say, everything—all being. It is founded on the simple apprehension of being. Affirming something's being white excludes denying it, because something's being white excludes its not being white.

---

presenting it simply as the most perfect intellectual habit or virtue. Thomas also calls the most perfect intellectual virtue wisdom: *STh*, I–II, q. 57, a. 2; q. 66, a. 5.

47. *In Eth.*, VI, lect. 5, §1181.

48. See *STh*, I–II, q. 9, a. 1.

49. *STh*, I–II, q. 94, a. 2.

And Thomas is saying that being and its companions are what are first known to us. Now, this thesis is not incompatible with the view that what a boy should first study is logic. Logic is only the first *science* to learn. There is understanding prior to science. Science is reasoned, teachable knowledge. It presupposes unteachable knowledge, sheer understanding of certain things. Obviously a boy comes to logic already having understood many things. And what he first understood was not thought itself, or even truth, but simply being.[50] He abstracted the notion of it from sensible things.[51] So the fact that our boy studies logic first does not at all entail that the first things he understands are logical things. The very first thing must be being. Other things, its proper attributes, come close on its heels.[52]

But what is striking is that this first thing understood, or this set of things—being and its entourage—is very definitely something metaphysical. The *Ethics* commentary passage could hardly be clearer about this. It speaks of those things that pertain to being, inasmuch as it is being, which is exactly what Thomas takes to be the subject of metaphysics. And it says, citing *Metaphysics* IV, that the cognition of them pertains to unqualified wisdom. The wisdom taught in *Metaphysics* IV, of course, pertains to metaphysics itself. And elsewhere Thomas says that metaphysics "regards the maximally universal principles, which indeed are being (*ens*) and the things that follow upon being, such as one and many, potency and act."[53]

How can these principles pertain to metaphysics, if a boy already knows them, and if he will not learn metaphysics until much later in his intellectual life (if ever)? I think the answer is fairly simple. Aristotle himself, in the *Ethics* VI passage that Thomas is glossing, even seems to hint at it. He argues that the wise man must not only know what follows from principles, but also "verify" (*aletheuein*) the principles themselves.[54] Perhaps he means that the wise man must not only grasp the principles, so that he can reason to conclusions in light of them, but also express them accurately in speech, defend them against objections, and determine their very role as principles.[55] He must see the priority that they enjoy, see how everything else depends on them. This is just what Aristotle does in *Metaphysics* IV,

---

50. See *STh*, I, q. 16, a. 3, ad 3; a. 4.

51. See *In De Trin.*, q. 1, a. 3, ad 3 (cf. q. 5, a. 4, ad 5); *De ver.*, q. 10, a. 11, ad 10.

52. See below, 170.

53. *In Meta.*, Proem.

54. *NE*, VI.7, 1141a17–18.

55. Cf. *STh*, I, q. 66, a. 5, ad 4.

especially with the principle of non-contradiction. He formulates it with precision; he explains why it must be the most certain truth of all, one about which error is impossible, and which is known to anyone who knows anything at all; and he disputes with arguments to the contrary.[56] Obviously our boy does not do these things. Yet he does know the truth of the principle of non-contradiction.

What Aristotle means by "the principles" in the *Ethics* VI passage seems to be the most universal and fundamental truths on which demonstrative or scientific knowledge depends.[57] Grasping the content of these principles would belong to the mental habit which he calls *nous*. Thomas calls it *intellectus principiorum*, the understanding of principles.[58] A child can very well have this habit. It is not wisdom or metaphysics. Thomas, in fact, holds that it develops spontaneously in the mind, immediately upon grasping the terms or notions from which the principles are formed.[59] However, Thomas also associates those very terms or notions with wisdom. The association serves to show why wisdom is even higher than the understanding of principles.

> The truth and cognition of indemonstrable principles depends on the notion (*ratio*) of the terms; for, once it is known what a whole is and what a part is, immediately it is known that every whole is greater than its part. But cognizing the notion of being and non-being, and of whole and part, and of the other things that follow upon being, out of which indemonstrable principles are constituted as out of their terms, pertains to wisdom . . . .[60]

Now, this same passage continues: ". . . for common being is a proper effect of the highest cause (*causae altissimae*), namely God." *Common being* is simply another way of referring to the subject of metaphysics. But metaphysics is called wisdom because it reaches the highest principles and causes. And the mention of God leaves no doubt that the highest of all are not the merely intrinsic, formal principles—being itself and its companions—but rather the separate, immaterial beings that are substances in their

56. *Metaph.*, IV.3–6, 1005b8–1009a38.

57. See *In Post. an.*, I, lect. 18, §154[6]–155[7]; lect. 20, §168[2]–170[4].

58. *EN* VI.6, 1140b31–1141a8, which immediately precedes the discussion of wisdom, is about this habit.

59. *STh*, I–II, q. 51, a. 1; q. 63, a. 1.

60. *STh*, I–II, q. 66, a. 5, ad 4. That he means metaphysics, not theology, is clear from *STh*, I, q. 1, a. 6, ad 2.

own right and are principles of the rest in the manner of extrinsic causes. They are principles upon which common being itself depends. Their type of universality is not that of a feature belonging to many things, but that of an origin or an end of many things.[61] And these principles are certainly not first for us. Our boy may not be aware of them at all.

Nevertheless, if indeed he has grasped being, and if this pertains to wisdom or to metaphysics, then what he has grasped somehow pertains to the science that considers those principles; it is precisely what they are principles of. In some way, then, his understanding of being must be able to extend to them, at least potentially, even if he has not yet actually made the extension.[62] If materiality were part of his very notion of being, then the very idea or the very question of immaterial beings would never be available to him. I do not mean that he can already judge that immaterial beings are really possible, in the sense of being truly compatible with the nature of being. Perhaps he does not yet know the nature of being well enough to form such a judgment. But his notion of being must in some way already orient his mind toward such things.

How Thomas thinks natural reason can rise to an actual grasp of immaterial beings and of God as the highest cause, cause of common being, will be considered in the next chapter. But there is something else that I think we should also notice about his view of the connection between the cognition of common being and the cognition of God. This is that its significance is not exclusively philosophical. "Only created rational nature," he writes, "has an immediate order to God. For other creatures do not attain to anything universal, but only to something particular, sharing in divine goodness either by merely existing, as inanimate things do, or also by living and cognizing, as plants and animals do; but rational nature, inasmuch as it cognizes the universal nature of good and being, has an immediate order to the universal principle of being."[63] And he goes on to argue that this imme-

61. See *In De Trin.*, q. 5, a. 4; *De ver.*, q. 10, a. 11, ad 10.

62. Interpreters dispute whether the *ens* that is the very first object of understanding coincides with the *ens* that is the subject of metaphysics. I cannot address the issue here. It seems to me, however, that the passage from the *Ethics* VI commentary leaves hardly any doubt about their coinciding. For a defense of this view, see Dewan, *Form and Being*, 47–60.

63. *STh*, II–II, q. 2, a. 3. I suppose he brings in the notion of good (which is certainly one of the associates of being—see, e.g., *STh*, I, q. 5, aa. 1 & 3) because he is talking about relating to God as principle or cause of being. The notion of the good involves the notion of the primary kind of cause, final cause (*STh*, I, q. 5, a. 4).

diate order is the reason why the rational creature, and no other, is apt for a supernatural share in the divine good. There is no such thing as relating to God—the true God—without in some way relating to Him as universal principle of being, "creator of heaven and earth."

Logic and Metaphysics

The relation between logic and metaphysics is not as simple as the foregoing remarks may make it seem. Thomas sees a certain kinship between the two sciences. It is something that the metaphysician can exploit, and it may also create pitfalls for him. Let me say a word or two about this.

A peculiarity of logic, among the sciences, is that the things that it is about, acts of reason, are themselves about things. In a sense, therefore, logic itself extends beyond reason's acts, to whatever things those acts themselves might be about. And this means that in a sense logic extends to everything, because there is nothing that reason's acts cannot be about. Other sciences deal with only a part of what there is. But we can see anything and everything from the logical point of view. This gives logic a special affinity with metaphysics.[64]

In another sense, however, logic is more remote from metaphysics than other sciences are. For although other sciences focus on more restricted features of things, as natural philosophy focuses on motion, the features that they focus on belong to the things themselves, in their own natures. Needless to say, being too, as considered by the metaphysician, is a feature that belongs to things themselves. Logic, however, extends to everything, not because its focus is a feature that belongs to the nature of everything, but only because its focus is something that relates to everything, namely reason. Even though things happen to have what it takes to be grasped by reason, this is rather incidental to the natures of the things themselves. A rock is not what it is because it is knowable in a certain way; it is knowable in that way partly because of what it is, and partly because of what our minds are.

Nevertheless, even though the way in which things relate to reason is incidental to them, it is still something that reason itself can consider about them. And this results in our attributing certain features to things themselves. For instance, when we say that *dog* is a universal, we are thinking of

64. See *In Post. an.*, I, lect. 20, §171[5]; *In Meta.*, IV, lect. 4, §574; VII, lect. 2, §1287; lect. 3, §1308.

it as the object of an operation of reason, the operation of predicating. We mean that dog is something predicated of many individuals. Or if we say that dog is a species of animal, we mean that in the definition of dog, the genus-term is animal. We are seeing dog as an object of reason's operation of defining. Thomas follows the usage of his day in calling such features—universal, species, genus, and other terms of logic applied to things—"logical intentions."[65] He even speaks of logic as the science of such intentions.[66] And he says that such intentions are "extraneous to the natures of things."[67]

This, however, does not mean that no other science treats them at all. Most do not, but there is one that does: metaphysics.[68] This is partly because, in some weak sense, even they are beings, "beings of reason." But it is also, and perhaps more importantly, because in certain ways such intentions reflect the being of things in themselves rather closely, and may even shed light on it; and in other ways they only reflect our ways of getting at things, and indicate little about the things themselves. The metaphysician needs to sort all this out.[69]

For example, Thomas holds that the most general ways or modes in which something is predicated of a subject—ways in which a subject is said to *be* somehow or other—correspond to the most general modes of being itself. These are the so-called *categories*, which is merely Greek for *predicates*. There are ten of them. The primary one is substance; the others are types of accidents, which affect or modify substances in different ways.[70] Thomas often speaks of the division into the categories as a division of being, inasmuch as it is being. Here the logical features are of very direct service to the metaphysician. On the other hand, Thomas does not at all mean that everything which is truly predicated in a certain mode really has the corresponding mode of being. Adjectives, for instance, are predicated

65. Here the word *intention* has nothing to do with a goal or purpose. *Intentio* was adopted to translate into Latin an Arabic word used by Avicenna to signify something like a meaning or a thought or a conception.

66. *In De an*, III, lect. 8, §718.

67. *In Meta.*, IV, lect. 4, §574.

68. *Scg*, II, cap. 75, §1550; cf. *In De Trin.*, q. 6, a. 1 (the first few lines of the corpus).

69. Much of the *De ente et essentia* is concerned with sorting out the relations between logical and real intentions about things, and between the components of a thing's definition and the components of the thing itself.

70. *In Phys.*, III, lect. 5, §322[15]. Thomas wrote no commentary on the *Categories*. He explains how the categories are distinguished in this passage of the *Physics* commentary and *In Meta.*, V, lect. 9, §889–94.

in the mode of accidents, but many things truly predicated as adjectives are not accidents.[71] We can truly say that Socrates is human, but humanity is not an accident of Socrates. It would be a serious mistake to think that what every adjective signifies is really an accident.

Another example appears in Thomas's commentary on Book VII of the *Metaphysics*, regarding Aristotle's inquiry into the nature of substance. Thomas says that Aristotle begins the inquiry from a logical point of view, considering substance as essence and as that which is captured in a definition.[72] It is only a preliminary treatment, sketchy, but it is useful nonetheless.[73] At the same time, Thomas is very insistent—and thinks Aristotle is too—that the components of a definition need not directly correspond to components in the thing defined. Even if man is truly defined as rational animal, human beings do not consist of instances of animality joined to instances of rationality. Rather, one and the same form, the human soul, actualizing prime matter, constitutes something that is both rational and animal (and also organic and bodily and substantial and existent).[74]

Thomas does find some thinkers taking merely logical features of things, or the relations among such features, for real features or real relations, and as a result, falling into no little confusion. The most conspicuous example, I suppose, would be that of Plato. In Thomas's judgment, Plato posited the Forms or Ideas chiefly because he simply assumed that what is abstract in thought must exist abstractly in reality.[75] But far worse, in Thomas's judgment, is the approach of the twelfth-century Jewish thinker Solomon Ibn Gabirol, or Avicebron to the Latins. As Thomas reads him, Avicebron took each differentiating term in the definition of a substantial kind to stand for a distinct form in the substance; and he took what the most general term stands for, substance itself, to be the substrate and matter of all things except God.[76] Thomas criticizes this procedure in many plac-

---

71. See, e.g., *STh*, I, q. 39, a. 3.

72. *In Meta.*, VII, lect. 3, §1306, 1308. Thomas thinks the logical approach runs throughout Book VII; see *In Meta.*, VIII, lect. 1, §1681.

73. On the "sketchiness" of the logical approach to real things, see *In Meta.*, VII, lect. 2, §1280; cf. lect. 11, §1536, and lect. 13, n. 1576. Generally on the ways in which logic is employed in the other sciences, see *In Post. an.*, I, lect. 20, §171[5]; *In Meta.*, IV, lect. 4, §576. Regarding logic and metaphysics, helpful is te Velde, "Metaphysics, Dialectics and the *Modus Logicus* according to Thomas Aquinas."

74. *STh*, I, q. 76, a. 6, ad 1; cf. a. 3, ad 4, and a. 6, ad 2.

75. See, e.g., *In Meta.*, XII, lect. 1, §2423; *STh*, I, q. 84, a. 1; q. 85, a. 1, ad 2.

76. This theory is set out in his best known work, *Fons vitae*. How influential this

es. In *De substantiis separatis*, where the criticism is especially detailed and severe, he contrasts it very unfavorably with Plato's approach. Plato rose to the highest beings by analyzing things into formal principles, whereas Avicebron analyzes things into material principles. This is "altogether repugnant to reason," Thomas says, because matter is to form as potency to act, and potency is "less of a being" than act.[77]

I wonder whether Thomas would not also find potential confusion of this sort in certain views that are fairly widespread in analytical philosophy. For instance, it is common to hold that identity statements and predications are distinct and even opposed types of proposition; one and the same proposition cannot be both. An individual can be said to be identical with itself, but it cannot be predicated of itself. Only something like what Frege calls concepts—meaning, very roughly, what Thomas calls forms—can be predicated of anything. I think Thomas would say that this view gives too much metaphysical weight to mere modes of thought. As we saw, he thinks that an individual can be predicated of something, because reason can give it a formal role, even vis-à-vis itself. The fact that the individual is not really a form is irrelevant.[78]

Metaphysics and the Other Speculative Sciences

Metaphysics is first philosophy, and even wisdom—as far as this is within the reach of mere animals—because it reaches the very first principles and causes of things. It is the most "intellectual" science.[79] This puts it at the extreme of the human mind's natural perfection and, as such, in a class by itself. However, its being in a class by itself does not mean that it has little or nothing to do with the other sciences. On the contrary, it has a unique and fundamental bearing on them all. This is because it considers the principles of them all. Calling it wisdom alludes to this function.

First, there are the common principles, those pertaining to being as being. All the sciences use these principles. No science sets aside being

---

work was on Latin thinkers, for instance regarding the idea that spiritual creatures contain matter, is disputed.

77. *De subst. sep.*, cap. 6.

78. On the lack of "ontological commitment" in Thomas's inherence theory of predication, see G. Klima's very illuminating "The Semantic Principles underlying Saint Thomas Aquinas's Metaphysics of Being," esp. 97–110.

79. *In Meta.*, Proem.

and its attributes, as though they were merely accidental to its subject. The mathematician can set aside the sensible and physical characteristics of bodies because they are accidental to his subject, which is quantity. The fact that something is so large or so many does not, by itself, say anything about how the thing affects the senses or how it moves. But the fact that something is a man or a star, or even so large or so many, does say something, immediately, about how it *is*, its status as a being. The other sciences do not filter out the notions of being and its attributes. They constantly use such notions in their own accounts. But they take them for granted and do not focus on them. This is the metaphysician's task. He tries to ascertain the exact meaning or meanings of each notion. Most, in fact, turn out to have several meanings. This enables him to give the truths based on these notions their most precise, rigorous formulation. These are the truths that apply to all things, the most common and hence very first principles, such as the principle of non-contradiction. By clarifying them, he is able to defend them against doubts or apparent objections, showing that these rest upon some kind of confusion and bringing to light the way in which the objector himself must willy-nilly be assuming them. In doing so, the metaphysician is clarifying and defending absolutely all scientific and philosophical activity.

But his consideration is not confined to the grand generalities. He also examines the proper subjects of the other sciences. That the other sciences take for granted their subjects' status as beings means that they take the very existence of their subjects for granted. If someone denies the subject's existence, the science of that subject has nothing to say in reply. To deny the subject is also to deny the science itself. Parmenides, for example, denies the existence of motion. In so doing he is silencing the physicist, whose discourses all take motion for granted. Answering Parmenides is a metaphysical task. He is saying, in effect, that the nature of being, "what exists," excludes motion. The metaphysician has to show that it does not, by showing how the nature of motion can be "resolved" or analyzed in terms of the nature of being. To do this is also to give motion itself its most definitive formulation. As we saw, Aristotle defines motion as the act of what is in potency, insofar as it is in potency.[80] In commenting on this, Thomas observes that potency and act are among the "first differences of being."[81] This means that they pertain to being as being. They are metaphysical. The metaphysi-

---

80. See above, 36.
81. *In Phys.*, III, lect. 2, §285[3].

cian has examined the nature of being and found within it the distinction between act and potency—a distinction that Parmenides overlooked—and he explains motion in terms of this distinction. In so doing he confirms the existence of motion. Casting the light of being on motion does not make it vanish after all.

Thomas holds generally that it belongs to metaphysics to confirm both the existence and the essential definition, the "what it is," of the subjects of the other sciences.[82] The geometer, for example, gets the definition of magnitude or size from metaphysics.[83] And although natural philosophy can obtain many definitions of physical things directly through sense-experience, it belongs to metaphysics to "determine" those definitions. Thomas gives the example of *animal*.[84] The natural philosopher can define animal simply by the observable characteristics of sensation and self-motion. But getting down to the essence of animal means sooner or later getting to its form, which is a kind of soul. And clearly the definition of soul—which is in terms of substance, form, and act—is quite metaphysical. These pertain to being as being. In short, Thomas's metaphysics not only overlaps with the other sciences but also penetrates them. In determining the principles proper to other sciences, it does not step down from its universal vantagepoint. It is analyzing those principles into the principles of being. This in turn is part of its effort to trace things back to the first, universal cause. And this most of all is what puts it in a class by itself.[85]

Being and Matter, Metaphysics and Physics

As wisdom, metaphysics is in a class by itself. But in another way it is simply one science among others. Like the others, it constitutes an organized body of demonstrative knowledge about a determinate subject matter. It identifies the subject's proper attributes and explains them in the light of the subject's own principles and causes. As mentioned earlier, Thomas agrees with Avicenna, against Averroes, that the subject of metaphysics is *ens commune*, common being. This subject has its own attributes.

Both common being and its attributes are features that are not confined to any particular category of beings. They are therefore termed

82. *In Meta.*, VI, lect. 1, §1147–51.

83. Ibid., §1149.

84. Ibid.

85. See *STh*, I–II, q. 57, a. 2.

transcendental.[86] This does not mean that they go beyond being, or even beyond the categories, but that they go beyond any single category and run through all of them. They are those things that "follow upon being, such as one and many, potency and act," as he says in the proem to the *Metaphysics* commentary. There are also others, such as true and good. But I suppose he mentions these, partly because they are the ones to which Aristotle devotes most attention in the *Metaphysics*, and partly because he himself thinks they stand especially close to the nature of being. As we saw, truth in the proper sense only pertains to being as it is in the mind; and good, although it is in things, involves a relation to appetite (especially intellectual appetite, will).[87] By contrast, *one* means undivided, and a thing's undividedness is in the thing itself—so much so that the being (*esse*) of a thing "consists in undividedness," and "as each thing guards its being, so it guards its unity."[88] Again, "each thing has unity in the way that it has being."[89] As for act and potency, they stand, if anything, even closer to the nature of being. Indeed, unlike one and many, act and potency are themselves senses of the word *being*. After all, indivision is only a negation (of division). But act, like being, is something positive. And Aristotle insists that even matter and potency are positive, not to be identified with negation or privation.[90]

Just how fundamental act and potency are in Thomas metaphysics comes out in what I consider to be an especially important passage, and an extraordinarily synthetic one, even by Thomas's standards, in which he explains what he regards as the most proper sense of the word *being*. In this passage he weaves together the two chief Aristotelian divisions of

---

86. See Aertsen, *Medieval Philosophy and the Transcendentals.*

87. Thomas thinks Aristotle's formula at the beginning of the *Nicomachean Ethics* comes as close as anything can to a definition of the good: "what all desire" (*NE*, I.1, 1094a3; see *In Eth.*, I, lect. 1, §9). The good's special relation to the will is owing to its transcendental character; see *De ver.*, q. 1, a. 1. Regarding the connection between good and being, a subtle but important point emerges in a passage to be examined below, *STh*, I, q. 5, a. 1, ad 1: even though good and being always go together, *unqualified* goodness and *unqualified* being do not. Something is unqualifiedly a being through its substantial act of being alone (on this see below, 105–6); but it is unqualifiedly good only when it is perfect and has the fullness being or actuality that is due to it according to its nature, which fullness includes not only its substantial act of being but also additional, accidental acts.

88. *STh*, I, q. 11, a. 1.

89. *STh*, I, q. 76, a. 2, ad 2.

90. See *In Phys.*, I, lect. 15; *STh*, I, q. 5, a. 2, ad 1.

being—the division into act and potency, and the division into the categories—in a remarkable way. I would like to reflect a little on this passage.[91]

The passage's first point is that *a being*, said properly, expresses something's being in act. But potency is very much in the picture as well, because
act "properly has order to potency." This does not mean that act is *for* potency; it is the other way round. Nor does it mean that what is in act comes
from what is in potency. Thomas thinks that some things are by nature in
act and were never in potency. But act is intrinsically referred to potency,
as what it is *divided from*. And so, he goes on, "something is called 'a being'
(*ens*) unqualifiedly, according to that by which it is first divided from what
is merely in potency."[92] This is rather obscure, but the next remark sheds
at least some light on it: ". . . and this is the substantial being (*esse*) of each
thing; whence, each is called 'a being' (*ens*), unqualifiedly, by virtue of its
substantial being."

What is substantial being? It is nothing mysterious. It is just the being,
the actuality, that a thing has through that principle which we have insisted
upon so much, its substantial form. Thus, the substantial being of a living
thing is the being that it has through its soul. It is the thing's life. And this,
he is saying, makes the thing a being, unqualifiedly. I think we can put it
this way: a living thing *is*, *period*, just because and so long as it is alive.[93] It
may also be other things—warm, white, strong—but to be these things is to
be only in qualified ways. And likewise, the living thing ceases to be, *period*,
not when it ceases to be warm or white or strong, but when it ceases to be
alive.[94] As Thomas says elsewhere, the ten categories are not an *equal* division of being. A being in the primary and unqualified sense is a substance
in act, on account of its substantial being. Accidents only confer qualified
modes of being: being warm, white, etc. These are only qualified, because
they presuppose the initial division of the substance from mere potency,
and only add some further actuality.[95]

We should also notice, however, that even these qualified acts have
the substance for their proper subject. That is, properly speaking, what *is*

91. *STh*, I, q. 5, a. 1, ad 1.

92. This is surely an allusion to the account of act in *Metaph*. IX.6. See above, 62n34.

93. Generally speaking, this is what Thomas means by speaking of what is *unqualifiedly* (*simpliciter*) this or that: what is this or that, *period*. It is opposed to being this or
that *only in some respect* (*secundum quid*).

94. See, e.g., *STh*, I, q. 76, a. 4 & a. 6; q. 77, a. 6.

95. Which, however, the thing needs in order to be unqualifiedly perfect and good;
see above, 104n87.

hot, or what has *being hot*, is not heat itself, but what it is the heat of—a hot body. A hot body is a substance, even though in calling it hot we are considering an accidental feature of it and not its substantial being. Accidents are not, properly speaking, subjects of being. They are called beings only by their connection with substance, their serving as that by which a substance somehow is, in some qualified way.[96] To be a subject of being is, in Thomas's language, to subsist. Only substances have natures strong enough to enable them to subsist, to be in themselves and not in another.[97]

But let us go back for a moment to how Thomas presents substantial being. He says it is that by which a thing is first divided from *what is merely in potency*. What is this? We are already quite familiar with it. It is prime matter. And this is really rather striking. Thomas is saying that to call something a being in the proper sense is to say that it is a substance in act, and he is suggesting that to say this is always, ultimately, to make reference to matter. To be sure, one need not be saying that the thing itself has matter in it. But one is saying that it is divided, distinct, from the pure potency of matter. Apparently even the consideration of immaterial beings will involve this reference to matter. To say that they are beings to a higher degree or have more of the "nature of being" will mean that they are "farther from matter." So even the metaphysician, concerned as he is with spiritual things, never entirely leaves behind the consideration of material things. This confirms once again that our mind's proportionate object is corporeal nature and that this object conditions all of our thinking.[98]

Thomas's metaphysician actually devotes a good deal of thought to material or physical things. His primary concern is with the nature of substance, as such.[99] But his first and only direct encounter with the nature of substance is in material or corporeal substances. His field thus overlaps in significant ways with that of the natural philosopher. There is nothing very peculiar about this. Distinct sciences may very well treat the same thing. They are distinct because they focus on different features of it or treat it from different perspectives.

---

96. See above, 39–40.

97. On the other modes of being as "weak" in comparison with substance, which has "firm and solid being," see *In Meta.*, IV, lect. 1, §540–43.

98. A good deal more can be said about *STh*, I, q. 5, a. 1, ad 1. I discuss it at some length in "How Many Acts of Being Can a Substance Have?"

99. See *In Meta.* VII, lect. 1, §1245–62.

Clearly the perspectives of physics and metaphysics differ. One sign of this is simply the more limited scope of physics. It thinks in terms of the features proper to material things. It identifies and explains the various kinds of movements found in things, their ways of influencing each other through their movements, and so forth. Motion in the strict sense—continuous change—is a feature that requires matter. It is not something that material things share with immaterial things. Physics does not consider the material things precisely insofar as they are beings; that is a feature they somehow share with immaterial things. If, at the limit of its inquiry, it does reach something immaterial, it considers even this in physical terms, as a mover, unmoved, powerful, etc.; and this consideration itself is aimed at explaining the motions of physical things. The intrinsic condition of immaterial things is just not the sort of thing the physicist, as such, wonders about. There is no such thing as the physics of angels. But there is such a thing as the metaphysics of bodies, matter, and motion, inasmuch as they are beings.

How does it differ from the physics of them? Here I am not talking about how metaphysics determines principles for physics, but how it considers physical things from its own point of view, that of being. One difference is the very fact that the metaphysician compares material things with immaterial things. Only he can do that. Moreover, his interest in what we might call the material side of material things is minimal. Physics looks as closely as it can at the sensible features and other material dispositions of a thing, because they have a decisive bearing on the thing's movements. But metaphysics can generally make do with a very summary treatment of such features.[100] They do not contribute much to the account of a thing's being.[101] What especially capture the metaphysician's interest are the forms of things. Of course, the physicist is interested in forms too, as principles of movement. But he is not so concerned with forms as principles of the very being of things, nor with their own status as beings. We will see an illustration of what this means in the next chapter.

It would be a mistake, however, to think that Thomas's metaphysician simply sets aside the sensible and kinetic features of material things and treats their being in isolation from these. His perspective is not like that of the mathematician, who does consider quantity in isolation from such features. For being, unlike quantity, is not just one more feature alongside

100. For an example, see *In Meta.*, VII, lect. 10, §1489.
101. See *In Meta.*, III, lect. 4, §384.

the others that things may have. All of the features of things are themselves beings. They somehow exist. Sensible qualities, motion, and matter itself are beings too, and the metaphysician will have something to say about their being. He will also have something to say about the being of mathematical objects, and, as we saw, even about the objects of logic, which are mere beings of reason.

But the metaphysician looks especially at physical things and their proper principles, because physical things are substances, which is the primary sense of being itself. At the same time, they are not the substances that primarily interest him. He considers them mainly for the help they can give him in understanding something about immaterial substances, and about the first principles and causes of being as a whole. His gaze moves, so to speak, in the opposite direction from that of the physicist. The physicist starts with a fairly general and abstract consideration of sensible things, and descends more and more into their material details.[102] The metaphysician starts in the same place, but he moves toward what is even more universal and immaterial.[103] Once again, Thomas sees the procedure as an example of philosophical *manuductio*. "We cannot rise to the incorporeal things that transcend the senses except to the extent that we are led by the hand through sensible things."[104] We have to discern, in the sensible things, the character of effects of things that cannot be sensible or bodily. And then we have to use the notions that we have gathered from sensible things to build up some conception of the others. The results cannot but be modest. Nevertheless, Thomas finds them far from negligible.

---

102. See above, 81–82. Notice that physics, for Thomas, is the only science that considers the material *cause*: *In Phys.*, I, lect. 1, §5[5]; *In Meta.*, III, lect. 4, §384.

103. See *In Meta.*, VII, lect. 11, §1526. Presumably both of them are moving, in different ways, from the confused sort of knowledge of things that we all begin with, toward knowledge that is more clear and distinct.

104. *In Meta.*, VII, lect. 16, §1643; cf. lect. 11, §1526.

5

Invisibles

Spirit as Subsistent Form, Angels in Philosophy, and Reason's Glimpse of God

Back to the Soul: Substantial Form, Subsistent Form

WHY IS IT THAT the metaphysician's consideration of material things from the point of view of being points him toward immaterial things? One reason, perhaps the crucial one, is that he finds the being of material things depending primarily on that immaterial factor *within* them to which we have already given so much attention: substantial form.[1] Although a material thing's being depends on both its matter and its form, it depends much more truly and properly on the form. This, again, is because a being, in the proper sense, is something in act, and because a thing is in act through and according to a form. "Every *esse* whatsoever is according to some form."[2] Matter is only potency. Perhaps not every actual being has matter, but every one must have a form. Physics considers form insofar as it is in matter; metaphysics considers form, certainly insofar as it is separate from matter, but also and first of all just *insofar as it is form*.[3] Form is itself

---

1. See, e.g., *In Meta.*, II, lect. 1, §296.
2. *STh*, I, q. 5, a. 5, ad 3.
3. *In Phys.*, II, lect. 4, §175[10].

a cause of being, inasmuch as it is being; so much so that Thomas says metaphysics "maximally" considers the formal cause.[4]

It is by considering form as *cause of being to matter* that we can discern the very possibility of beings that exist separately from matter. Thomas explains: between "any things which are so related that one is cause of being to the other, that which functions as cause can have being without the other, but not conversely."[5] And so matter cannot be without form, but form can be without matter. Of course, as he goes on to acknowledge, many specific kinds of form—and nearly all the kinds that we are familiar with—do depend on matter. But he is saying that the very nature of form, as form, does not depend on matter.

I would venture to say that, for Thomas, it is only this intellectual experience of form, as cause of being to matter—that is, substantial form—which gives us the possibility of framing some positive notion of immaterial reality. It is nothing other than the notion of form at an especially high grade of perfection. If we try to conceive immaterial reality without reference to form, we will almost certainly end up, despite ourselves, thinking of it as corporeal, a "refined ethereal medium."[6] If we are not actually thinking of a body—say, some kind of gas—it will still be something only able to be found in bodies, something that presupposes extension; electricity, radiation, or some other type of physical energy.[7] These things are at best additions. They do function as principles of motion and change, but they are not the most fundamental principles, giving a body its very unity and being. We get beyond extension only by getting underneath it.

It is also crucial that, in surveying the forms of bodily things, we find some depending on matter less than others. We saw this in chapter 3. Living form is not as tied to the matter that it is in as is non-living form. The souls of animals are principles of activity that rises above matter—cognitive and appetitive activity. Our soul's intellectual activity is not intrinsically material at all, although it is connected with sensation, which has a material dimension. What we must now consider is what the human soul's activity

4. *In Meta.*, III, lect. 4, §384. Cf. *In Phys.*, I, lect. 15, §140.

5. *De ente*, cap. 3; see *De subst. sep.*, cap. 8.

6. See above, 90.

7. St. Augustine tells us that, as a Manichean, he was calling spirit and divine what was really nothing but ordinary sensible light, and that he did not realize his confusion until he read the writings of the Platonists: *De beata vita*, 1,4; *Confessiones*, 4,24; 4,31; 5,19–20; 7,1; 7,16.

implies about its status as a being. This is, as it were, our precise point of entry into the purely immaterial domain.

First, let us go back for a moment to the notion of substance. A substance is a being in the primary and most proper sense. It is a being per se, in virtue of itself. This does not mean having no cause distinct from itself. It means being a true subject of existence or of being (*esse*). A substance subsists. Non-substances can be spoken of in the manner of subjects, but they are not really so. Rather, they only somehow attach or relate to substances. At most, they serve as principles by which the substance somehow is. Accidents make a substance be in some qualified way—be warm, be tall, be courageous. Substantial forms make substances be without qualification. This, however, means that a substantial form does not really *inhere* in its substance, as though it presupposed the substance already constituted and were merely added on. It is constitutive of the substance, and what it presupposes and inheres in is only prime matter.

Now, Thomas holds that, just as substances are what properly are or exist, so also they are what properly act or do things. Every substance has some activity that is typical of it; and every activity belongs to some substance as its proper subject. Just as what *is* hot, properly speaking, is not heat, but what has heat—a hot body, which is a substance—so too what heats is the hot body and not its heat. "Nothing operates in virtue of itself"—that is, nothing is a true subject of operation—"except what exists in virtue of itself. For operating only belongs to what is a being in act, and so something operates in the mode in which it is. On this account, we do not say that heat heats, but that a hot thing does."[8]

At the same time, Thomas does allow that the parts of a substance may be said to act or to do things. It is more proper to say that the whole acts, but it is not improper to say that the part does so. For instance, the subject performing the activity of seeing the screen in front of me is I. But I am doing it with my eyes and not (say) with my feet. Different parts are organs, instruments, of different activities, and each activity belong to the whole organism by way of its proper organ. We distinguish the organs by their distinct powers for activity. Ultimately my sight is in me, but most immediately it is in my eyes—and not in my feet. So, therefore, is the activity of seeing. Hence, in a secondary, but not improper sense, we can say that my eyes are seeing the screen. And by the same token, we can say that my

8. *STh*, I, q. 75, a. 2.

eyes are true subjects of being. They subsist, even if only as parts. Aristotle does acknowledge that the parts of substances are substances too.[9]

With these preliminaries, consider now the activity of human understanding. We have already seen Thomas's arguments to show that the power of understanding neither is a body nor is seated in a bodily organ.[10] But it cannot be free-floating. If it is not a substance in its own right, then there must be some substance to which it belongs. Of course, it belongs to a human being. But does it belong to the whole human being immediately, or does it do so by way of some part, as sight belongs to me by way of my eyes? If I am indeed corporeal, then understanding cannot belong to me immediately. It cannot have a body for its proper seat. So it must belong to me by way of some part. But that part cannot be corporeal either. The only possible candidate is my soul itself. Most properly, it is I who understand. But in a valid, proper sense, my soul understands, just as my eyes see.

And this means that my soul itself is a substance, in the sense in which my eyes are. It is a genuine subject of activity, albeit a partial one, and hence it is also a genuine, albeit partial, subject of being. It subsists. Thomas stresses that the soul only subsists and acts as a part does.[11] It is not the whole subject of one's being or one's life; that is, it is not one's whole self. Thomas famously says, "my soul is not I."[12] A human soul is not a human person.[13] But it does properly exist, and it properly lives, just as a person's bodily parts do.

Or rather, it does so even more truly than they do. For a person's bodily parts, and the whole person, exist and live by virtue of the soul, but the soul exists and lives in an immediate way, by virtue of itself. This is simply to say that it is at once a subsistent form and the first formal principle, the substantial form, of the person and of each of his or her bodily parts.[14]

9. See above, 39. Clearly it is in a somewhat qualified sense, since a substance cannot be composed of other unqualified substances, each with a distinct substantial being. See *Metaph.*, VII.16, 1040b5–16.

10. See above, 75.

11. *STh*, I, q. 75, a. 2, ad 1 & ad 2.

12. Thomas Aquinas, *Super I Epistolam B. Pauli ad Corinthios lectura*, cap. 15, lect. 2.

13. *STh*, I, q. 75, a. 4, ad 2.

14. Notice that I do not say that the soul is one part of the person and that the other is the body. For Thomas, the human person *is* a body. Again, we must not confuse body with matter. The soul is one part of the person, matter the other. By informing the matter, the soul makes the human person be an actual being, and a body, and an organism, and an animal, and a human being (*STh*, I, q. 76, a. 6, ad 1). It makes the human person be a

Now it is easy for us, I think, to feel a tension between saying that the soul subsists or is a substance, even a partial one, and saying that it is a form of the body, even the substantial form. One reason for the tension, I suppose, is that we tend to think of forms as accidents, added on to bodies that are already constituted. But even once we achieve some grasp of substantial form, there may still be a tension, because we still tend to think of subsistents and substances as bodies. One bodily part may help keep another part going, but it cannot be the other's formal principle. Either the two bodily parts have distinct formal principles and are not parts of a single substance with a single being, but rather two substances joined together in mechanical fashion; or else they share in a single formal principle that is distinct from both and that informs and gives being and unity to the whole. So it is hard for us to think of the soul as subsisting, having being in itself, without either thinking of it and the body as two substances, each with its own distinct being, or else imagining the need for yet some other formal principle giving being and unity to the whole. But the soul itself is the formal principle of the whole, and it shares the very being that it has in itself with the body's matter, so as to constitute the whole.[15]

Perhaps, however, what we most need to see is that the soul's subsistence is not merely an ad hoc answer to the question of what it is that intellectual activity and power are seated in. Here I think it helps to consider that, whether or not the soul is the intellect's seat, it is at least the intellect's immediate *source*, as it is of all the vital powers. This is not at all ad hoc; it is merely to say that the human soul is the human animal's *nature*—first inner principle, not only of being, but also of activity. Intellectual power is a proper effect of the human soul. But an effect cannot be more perfect or more noble than its proper cause. Intellect is an extremely noble power, an "absolute form," not intrinsically conditioned by matter. Its origin can only be a substantial form that is proportionally perfect. I mean, proportionally perfect as form, as principle of being. It must not be wholly conditioned by matter, even in its being.[16] It must be so strong, with respect to being, that it is not just a principle of the being to which the body is subject, but also and first of all a (partial) subject of that being in its own right. And this is as much as to say that only a subsistent form can fully account for the activity of understanding.

---

person, an individual substance of a rational nature.

15. *STh*, I, q. 76, a. 1, ad 5.
16. See *STh*, I, q. 76, a. 1, obj. 4 & ad 4.

Moreover, precisely because it is so perfect, the subsistent soul is an even stronger cause of bodily unity than are other forms and souls. A sign of this is the extraordinary complexity of the human body.[17] Its unifying principle must be especially potent.

Almost Separate Form

But of course the body does die and corrupt. The soul is not so strong as to be able to prevent that. The body's matter can take on a new form or forms incompatible with the soul. Now, if the human soul were not subsistent, as other forms of bodies and other souls are not, there would be no question of its fate at the corruption of the body. Such forms are never subjects of being in the first place; such souls are never properly alive in their own right. Strictly speaking they cannot even be said to have come into being. They only did so in an indirect way, as the endpoints of the processes by which the bodies that they inform came into being. With such a form, the action by which the body began *is* the action by which the form began to be. And the body's cessation *is* the form's cessation. By contrast, whether or not the human soul can ever cease to be, the body's cessation cannot be simply identified with its cessation. This again is because the soul subsists.[18]

Here the comparison with bodily parts is helpful. The necrosis of one part of the body cannot be simply identified with that of another. This is true even if the necrosis of one leads to that of another. Similarly, even if the human soul does cease to be, does die, perhaps as a result of the body's death, it must have its own death, either simultaneous with the body's or subsequent to it, but not identical with it.

But the soul cannot die, cannot corrupt. Thomas's mature argument for this is a banner text for the role of form in his metaphysics.[19] It is extremely simple. He declares:

17. *STh*, I, q. 76, a. 5, ad 3.

18. Thomas does think that the human soul begins to exist at the end of the process of human generation and not before (*STh*, I, q. 90, a. 4). Nevertheless it does not begin in the way other forms and souls do, as the effect of some physical agent's action upon matter. A physical agent cannot produce a spiritual effect. It must be created by God (*STh*, I, q. 90, aa. 2 & 3). It is created then because it is by nature meant to inform a body.

19. On the development of Thomas's thought on the soul's immortality, see Dewan, *Form and Being*, 175–87.

To corrupt is altogether impossible, not just for it [the human soul], but for any subsistent thing that is nothing but form. For it is evident that what belongs to something by virtue of itself is inseparable from it. But being (*esse*) belongs to form, which is act, by virtue of itself. Hence matter acquires being in act inasmuch as it acquires a form, and corruption occurs in it inasmuch as the form is separated from it. But it is impossible that a form be separated from itself. Hence it is impossible that a subsistent form cease to be.[20]

Notice how strongly he puts it: the soul's ceasing to be is impossible. That means that its being is necessary. He is saying that the human soul is not a contingent entity. We probably find this odd, at least at first, because at first we probably take it to mean that the soul's being is what we call a logical necessity, i.e., that its not being would entail a contradiction.[21] Thomas does not mean that. In this same article, he says that if God withdrew His conserving influence, the soul would be annihilated.[22] Yet this does not make it contingent. Rather, it means, in part, that the soul's necessity is a caused necessity.[23] It also means that logical necessity is not the only kind of necessity that Thomas recognizes. In fact, it is not the only kind of *absolute* necessity.[24] Absolute necessity is necessity rooted in the necessary thing's own nature, and Thomas also calls it *natural* necessity.[25] It means that the thing has no principle, no potency or "possibility" in itself, for being otherwise. But its being otherwise may not involve a sheer contradiction.

The necessity of the soul's being is of this sort. The soul's nature has nothing in it whereby the soul can corrupt, no potential for not being. Only a subsistent thing that has matter, with potential for a form that is incompatible with the thing's own form, has in its own nature a potential not to be. Such a thing can be destroyed by being acted upon in such a way that its form is replaced with another. A soul cannot be acted upon in this way. It cannot be *killed*, even by God. There can be no such thing as a dead soul

---

20. *STh*, I, q. 75, a. 6. He gives a very similar argument for the incorruptibility of angels in *STh*, I, q. 50, a. 5.

21. For the use of the term *logical* in this connection, see *In Meta.*, IX, lect. 1, §1775.

22. *STh*, I, q. 75, a. 6, ad 2; cf. I, q. 50, a. 5, ad 3.

23. For this notion, see *STh*, I, q. 50, a. 5, ad 3; cf. I, q. 2, a. 3, *Tertia via*.

24. See *De pot.*, q. 5, a. 3, ad 12; *Scg*, II, cap. 30.

25. See *In II Phys.*, lect. 15, §270; *Scg*, II, cap. 28, §1061; *STh*, I, q. 82, a. 1; *In Meta.*, V, lect. 6, §833–5; *In De caelo*, I, lect. 25, §248[3].

or a soul-cadaver. It is only a creature, and God was free to make it or not. But He made it to last.

Thomas's treatment of the soul's condition after its separation from the body is extremely interesting, but here I will only sum up very quickly what he seems to think that mere natural reason can determine about it. Perhaps the most important thing is simply that the soul never was, and never becomes, an angel. That is, it remains a naturally partial entity. When separate, it can exercise some intellectual activity, not unlike that of angels, but only in a confused way.[26] In order to have clear and distinct knowledge, it needs the help of the senses. It always has the nature of a form that is apt and inclined to inform and give being to matter.[27] Separation is unnatural for it.

Separate souls also always remain distinct from each other. Each soul informs a distinct body, and at separation each retains the same distinct existence—the same individual life—that it enjoyed in the body. This means that the existence and life of the person to whom it belonged is not altogether extinguished at death. And this in turn means that the whole person's coming back to life is not inconceivable.[28] This would not happen by the soul's rejoining just any body whatsoever; Thomas argues that the idea of reincarnation in a non-human body, or in any body other than that of the person to whom the soul originally belonged, erroneously implies that the union of soul and body is merely accidental rather than substantial.[29] A person comes back to life only by his or her soul's being reunited to his or her same body—however different in quality the body may then be.[30]

This is all very abstract and remote from our experience. For Thomas, that is as it should be. The experiential condition of a separate soul must be so utterly different from our present condition that any attempt to convey it would be merely misleading. If there is a future that we can in any way imagine, it is the resurrection. And only then will *we* be alive again.

The resurrection is suitable, but supernatural, miraculous.[31] Thomas does believe such a miracle will occur. But unlike the soul's immortality,

26. *STh*, I, q. 89, a. 1.

27. *STh*, I, q. 76, a. 1, ad 6.

28. *STh, Supplementum*, q. 79, a. 2, ad 1.

29. *STh, Supplementum*, q. 79, a. 1.

30. *STh, Supplementum*, q. 79, a. 2, ad 1. More generally on the resurrection, see *Scg*, IV, cap. 81-89.

31. *STh, Supplementum*, q. 75, a. 3.

he does not think the future resurrection can be proved philosophically.[32] Philosophy can prove that all things depend on God's will and that He can work miracles, but not that His will is determined to a miracle of a given sort.

Angels

The human soul, even after death, is by nature the form of a body, although it does not then actually inform one. But now we must talk about forms that are not by nature forms of bodies and that always exist separately, by themselves. This may sound odd. How can there be a form that is not the form of anything? Thomas, however, would reject that question. A form that is not the form of a body can still be the form of *something*; namely, of itself. "Nothing is its own matter, nor is anything its own active principle. But something is its own form, as is clear in all immaterial things."[33] He is talking about the Persons of the Trinity and the suitability of saying that they are "of one essence." In this expression, he says, essence is signified in its function of form.

A thing's form is that by which it is in act. An immaterial thing is already, immediately in act, by virtue of itself, not by any formal principle distinct from itself.[34] So it is its own form. This is not, after all, so odd, if we keep in mind that even a form of a body is at least *part* of that which is in act by virtue of it. For that which is in act is not the matter alone, but the composite, the whole body. The form is part of the body that it informs and actualizes. In this sense, the form of the body is its own form too.

Now of course, on Thomas's view, the highest principle and cause of all, and that about which the metaphysician chiefly seeks to know the truth, is a single being, God. And we have already heard him locating God at the summit of immateriality.[35] In Thomas's metaphysical vision, however, God is by no means the only being that naturally exists apart from matter. There are other so-called separate substances. Sometimes, especially in philosophical contexts, he will call them *intelligences* or *intellects* or *minds*.[36] But he identifies them with what Scripture calls angels.

32. Ibid.
33. *STh*, I, q. 39, a. 2, ad 5.
34. See *Metaph.*, VIII.6, 1045a36–b7; *STh*, I, q. 75, a. 5, ad 3.
35. See above, 76; and below, 135.
36. See, e.g., *In Meta.*, Proem.

What is more, Thomas often follows Aristotle in saying that metaphysics reaches to the highest and most universal *causes*, in the plural. In some cases, we might conjecture that what he has in mind is that, although God is one being, He exercises several types of causality: efficient, exemplar, and final.[37] Sometimes, however, it is clear that among the "universal and primary causes of being," he means to include not only God but also the angels. Yet, as is obvious, angels are supposed to be caused beings, creatures. Thomas may seem to be minimizing the difference between creature and creator and to be making the one God, as it were, a mere first among equals.

As it turns out, however, the universality of the causality that Thomas ascribes to angels is only qualified. Angels are not causes of common being as a whole. In that case, they would be causes of themselves, since they exist by sharing in common being. No creature can be a cause of the very nature of being, nor can it cause everything that pertains to the being of a thing. It cannot produce something ex nihilo or create.[38] Nor can it produce prime matter.[39] But angels would have a certain universal causality with respect to material things, at least as to their motions. Thomas follows Aristotle in positing a multitude of separate substances as the immediate causes of the perpetual rotations of the celestial bodies. The very first cause is God, but Thomas thinks that the rotations are probably executed by lower separate substances acting under God's command. He finds this view in Aristotle, and he also gives reasons of his own for it.[40] All movement on earth depends on the influence of the celestial bodies, and the terrestrial movements include the cyclical processes to which all generable and corruptible things—all earthly things—are subject. Thus, by governing all earthly movements, angels cooperate with God in conserving the very being of all the generable and corruptible kinds of things. So they have a qualified sort of universal causality even with respect to being.

Why does a cause of this sort have to be immaterial? Once again, the study of the soul helps. As was stressed in the discussion of cognition, the more immaterial a form is, the greater its amplitude and extension. A form naturally subsisting apart from matter is by that very fact intellectual. And its intellectuality is nobler than ours. It does not depend on sense-cognition.

37. See *STh*, I, q. 44, especially a. 4, ad 4.

38. See *STh*, I, q. 45, a. 5, esp. ad 1. Even the angels only participate in *esse* and in the good; see *In De caelo*, II, lect. 18, §463[6].

39. *STh*, I, q. 65, a. 3.

40. I discuss this in "The Causality of the Unmoved Mover."

The angelic knowledge of corporeal things is not caused by or abstracted from the things. And unlike our intellects, theirs can know material individuals directly, through likenesses infused in them by the creator of matter. For that very reason, they can have a much fuller and extensive share in causing material things than we can.[41]

Obviously Thomas's cosmology is outdated. Many twentieth-century interpreters, however, held that even in his own purely philosophical thought, angels have, at best, a tenuous place. The only firm basis for affirming their existence would be revelation. This would be chiefly because Thomas's philosophy arrives at a first cause that is omnipotent and all-embracing, able to effect anything that can be a being.[42] As a result, any visible phenomena, such as the celestial rotations, that might be adduced in proof of angelic causes, could instead be caused immediately by God. The interpreters did notice that Thomas also offers arguments based on what he takes to be an end that God can be assumed to intend in the world and that would require angels as part of its realization.[43] But such arguments were judged merely probable, showing only the suitability of the existence of angels, not strictly proving it. A recent study, however, has shown persuasively that Thomas takes those arguments to be solid proofs.[44] Moreover, we should notice what Thomas himself takes to be the implications of God's all-embracing causality. Far from rendering other causes unnecessary or dubious, it actually offers a further motive for supposing them; and all the more so, the more their causality resembles His—which is to say, the more universal it is, less confined to "here and now."[45]

Thomas says, and by now it should come as no surprise, that whereas metaphysics considers material substances only insofar as they are substances and beings, not insofar as they are material, it considers immaterial

41. See *STh*, I, q. 57, aa. 1 & 2 (and cf. I, q. 55, a. 3, esp. ad 3); *In De Caelo*, II, lect. 13, §417[7]–418[8]. On how our intellect knows material individuals, see *STh*, I, q. 86, a. 1.

42. *STh*, I, q. 25, a. 3.

43. *STh*, I. q, 50, a. 1; *De spir. creat.*, q. un., a. 5.

44. Doolan, "Aquinas on the Demonstrability of Angels."

45. This is the whole drift of *STh*, I, q. 50, a. 1. Notice too that, in this respect, there is a sense in which angels might be said to play an even more important or more distinctive role in metaphysics than in theology. In theology, Thomas says, angels are considered for the same reason that any other creature is, namely, to manifest God (who is theology's subject); but in metaphysics, they are considered for the same reason that *God* is, namely to account for being (which is metaphysics' subject) as principles of it, albeit merely secondary ones, e.g., through the movement of the celestial spheres: *In De Trin.*, q. 5, a. 4, ad 3.

substances insofar as they are immaterial.[46] What he means by *immaterial* is not a mere negation, not just absence of matter. Although he does not judge matter positively bad, he does see it as limiting or contracting the forms that inhere in it, in themselves and in their efficacy. Immateriality stands for a high grade of perfection of form, and hence of being and of causality. It pertains to the very notion of the causes that the metaphysician is primarily seeking.

We still have to consider how Thomas distinguishes angelic form from the form of the very highest cause. I shall especially want to stress that Thomas thinks there really is such a thing as the form of the highest cause. Why I do so will emerge as we proceed.

That a God Exists

This book is called a sketch of Thomas's philosophy. What I shall be able to say about his philosophy of God is more like a sketch of a sketch. All the points that I shall treat do, I think, play fundamental roles. The same, however could be said of many others that I shall not treat, and I hope the gaps will not result in a picture that is distorted in content or in spirit. But space is limited; and in any case, my sense is that, in a merely philosophical presentation, it is better, and more in keeping with Thomas's own approach, to err on the side of restraint.

Thomas thinks that normal human experience provides a source from which almost anyone can draw a kind of spontaneous inference of there being something divine—something that governs the world and that constitutes a suitable object of worship.[47] The inference has nothing like the force or clarity of a scientific proof, and the conception of the deity that is formed on its basis may be quite crude. It might be a body; it might be nature itself; it might be an especially powerful human being.[48] But Thomas also thinks there are paths of rational reflection that serve both to verify the reality of the divine in a scientific manner and to refine the conception of it.[49] In *Summa theologiae*, I, q. 2, a. 3, he famously traces five such paths or

46. *In Meta.*, VII, lect. 11, §1526.

47. *Scg*, III, cap. 38, §2161; *STh*, II–II, q. 85, a. 1.

48. *Scg*, III, cap. 38, §2163.

49. He also finds Christian doctrine confirming the possibility of philosophical knowledge of God, most conspicuously in St. Paul's Letter to the Romans, 1:20; see *Scg*, I, cap. 12, §77; *STh*, I, q. 13, a. 5. This is what has subsequently come to be called natural

ways. His own words leave no doubt that he considers them scientific (in the Aristotelian sense). He calls them ways by which there being a God "can be proved." Clearly he is seeing them as fitting within his own account, in the immediately preceding article, of the sort of demonstration—the sort of scientific proof—that can be had of there being a God.

Thomas does not present these proofs as necessary prerequisites to faith. He knows that many people take it on faith that there is a God, and he thinks that they may well be doing so quite reasonably. In fact, he seems to hold that nearly everyone must first accept it on faith, assimilating the rational proofs only later, if ever. This is for several reasons: because the proofs are very subtle and abstract; because a good deal of prior knowledge is needed (recall the order of learning); and because many people are just too busy with the cares of life.[50]

Some interpreters have tried to reduce all five ways to one. It seems to me that this does not really fit Thomas's intention. Each way is a different window onto the truth about the deity and presents it under a different guise. The *Summa*'s subsequent treatment of what can and cannot be attributed to God draws now on one, now on another of the conceptions of Him that the various ways provide. Still, it is also true that these conceptions have a good deal in common. Running through all of them is a general notion which, though highly abstract, captures what Thomas regards as the core of the meaning of the word *deus*: "something existing above all things that is principle of all and removed from all."[51] We might say: something more perfect than all the rest, on which all the rest depends, and which is quite distinct from all the rest.

Remarkably, Thomas thinks *deus* means the same for Christians and for pagans.[52] Where they differ is in how they apply it. This should be kept in mind in reading the five ways. Their aim is, in a sense, fairly modest. It is not to prove that there is a being with all the features that we have come

---

theology (with "natural" referring to natural reason). At present the idea of natural theology is not much in fashion, even (especially?) among Christian theologians. Luckily the issue falls outside the scope of this book. But for a spirited defense of the possibility of natural theology, and of Christian faith's own need of that possibility, see Turner, *Faith, Reason and the Existence of God*.

50. *De ver.*, q. 14, a. 10.

51. *STh*, I, q. 13, a. 8 ad 2; cf. *STh*, I, q. 12, a. 12. Here we have, in effect, the famous threefold approach to God of pseudo-Dionysius: causality, negation or removal, and eminence. See Twetten, "Aquinas's Aristotelian and Dionysian Definition of 'God.'"

52. *STh*, I, q. 13, a. 10.

to associate with the name of God: omnipotence, omniscience, eternity, incorporeity, etc. He takes these up in later discussions. He even takes up God's unity later. (He does think it possible to prove that there is only one God.[53]) But he denies that *deus* is a proper name (which is how we tend to treat it). It is not like *Socrates*, but like *man*. It means whatever has a certain nature, the divine nature, whether that be one or many.[54] In Englishing this, *a God* or *the God* would be better than just *God*. At any rate, in the five ways Thomas only wants to show that there must be some being, *at least* one, that merits the name *deus*.

Each of the five ways fixes on some aspect of things in our experience and proceeds to show how it entails the influence of something worthy to be called a God. By "influence" I mean efficient causality.[55] The first three ways, and also the fifth, acknowledge or even insist on other efficient causes standing between the aspect originally invoked and the highest, divine cause. The fourth does not. For various reasons, I shall look at it after the others.

Let me give just a very quick review of the first three ways. The first starts from the observation of some motion. It reasons to a primary source of motion, one whose action of moving things does not depend on its own being moved, by anything—either by others (in that case it would not be primary) or even by itself (nothing moves itself)—and which is therefore entirely unmoved. Between this mover and the motion first observed there can be a whole series of secondary, moved movers, but not an infinite multitude of them, since that would exclude a primary mover. The second way starts directly with the existence of efficient causes and of order among them, such that the causality of one depends on another. Think of an army, or the parts of an animal. Such a series needs a primary, uncaused efficient cause. The third way starts from things that have in themselves the potential both to be and not to be.[56] It argues that not everything can be of this sort; such things depend on something that can only be, something abso-

53. *STh*, I, q. 11, a. 3.

54. *STh*, I, q. 13, aa. 8 & 9.

55. See *STh*, I–II, q. 2, a. 5, obj. 3. I will not even try to give a full treatment of any of the ways here. For a thorough presentation, see Wippel, *The Metaphysical Thought of Thomas Aquinas*, 442–500. For an interesting recent commentary on them, see Weingartner, *God's Existence. Can it be Proven?*

56. Helpful on the third way are Dewan, "The Distinctiveness of St. Thomas' 'Third Way'" and "The Interpretation of St. Thomas's Third Way," and also Grieco, "An Analysis of St. Thomas Aquinas's 'Third Way.'"

lutely necessary. But some necessary things have a cause of their necessity outside themselves. There must be a primary necessary being that has no such cause and that causes the necessity of the others.

The fifth way relies heavily on the notion that was the focus of chapter 2, the notion of nature. This way centers on natural things that do not have cognition. What Thomas gives us in the *Summa* is, in effect, a very synthetic presentation of the discussion offered in Aristotle's *Physics*, Book II, of nature as a cause that acts for an end.[57] And in his own commentary on that discussion, Thomas spells out at considerably greater length the argument given in the fifth way.[58] Here I would like to call attention to just two points about the argument. The first regards the basic phenomenon that it invokes: the fact that natural things lacking cognition usually act in such a way as to attain what is best. In the *Summa* presentation, he does not say what "best" means; he does not specify the good with respect to which the way of acting is deemed best. But in the *Physics* commentary it is clear. It is the good of the thing's own kind, and chiefly the kind's very conservation in being.[59] He is saying that the way things usually act yields results that, on the whole, favor the good of their kinds more than does any of the other results that they may, on rare occasions, bring about.

The other point is what exactly, in the fifth way, God is supposed to explain. "Things without cognition do not tend to an end unless they are directed by a cognizing and intelligent agent, as the arrow is directed by the archer." The thought is not at all that there are events in the physical world which the natures of physical things do not explain and which only a divine intelligence does. Thomas has no hesitation in affirming that the natures of physical things explain physical events; but those very natures themselves need a further explanation. It is not that natural causes are being coordinated, or adjusted, or supplemented, by a divine cause. It is that the very causality of natural causes depends on divine causality.[60] Thomas does not side-step nature to reach God.

---

57. *Physics*, II.8, 198b10–199b33.

58. *In Phys.*, II, lect. 11–14.

59. See *In Phys.*, II, lect. 11, §249[9]; lect. 12, §254[5]; lect. 13, §259[5]. Cf. *STh*, I–II, q. 94, a. 2: all substances tend toward the conservation of their being according to their nature.

60. The point is made explicitly in the reply to the second objection of *STh*, I, q. 2, a. 3. The objector says that everything happening in the world can be traced back either to nature or to the human will. The reply is that this is true, but that both nature (which acts unknowingly for an end) and the human will (which is mobile and contingent) must

Much less does he eliminate it. Heidegger criticizes the doctrine of creation for turning the world into a work of divine craft, thereby suppressing the ancient experience of nature and paving the way for the modern technological attitude toward things. But right there in the *Physics* commentary, Thomas presents a radical difference between divine and human craft. "A nature," he says, "is nothing other than a conception (*ratio*) of a certain craft—namely, the divine—instilled in things, by which the things themselves move toward a determinate end; as if the craftsman who makes a ship could give it to pieces of wood to move of themselves toward taking on the form of a ship."[61] By our craft we can affect the accidental dispositions of things, but we cannot instill the craft itself into the things or make it their inner principle of activity, their nature. God's mind causes natures. Our minds only imitate them. We will return to that point in the final chapter.

As for Thomas's notion of creation, however, the way that brings us closest to it is the fourth.[62] This is the one way that has no room for intermediate causes between God and the effect that is being traced to Him for its full explanation. The reason for this seems clear. The effect in question is the "being (*esse*), goodness, and any other perfection," of absolutely "all beings" (*omnibus entibus*). It is nothing short of all reality, or at least, all the perfection in reality. But nothing is a cause (an efficient cause) except by virtue of some perfection in it; nothing acts except insofar as it is in act, and every act is some sort of perfection. So, if anything other than God, any of the "beings," were an intermediate cause of this effect, it would be acting as its own efficient cause. That was already judged impossible in the second way. It would mean that a thing is prior to itself.[63]

To be sure, this raises a question about God's own status as a being. Is He not part of reality too—is that not the very thing the five ways try to show? I shall discuss this later.

What is it about the perfections in things that shows the need for this universal cause? According to the fourth way, it is the unequal manner in which the perfections are distributed among the things, especially the

---

in turn be traced back further, to a divine cause.

61. *In Phys.*, II, lect. 14, §268[8]. On the relation between nature and creation in Thomas, see Aertsen, *Nature and Creature*.

62. See Dewan, "St. Thomas, the Fourth Way, and Creation."

63. The point is related to the thesis that no creature can be an instrument of creation; see *STh*, I, q. 45, a. 5, ad 1.

perfection of being.[64] They are found in varying grades of strength, *magis et minus*. This indicates that not all things have them on their own. If they did, they would all have them to the maximum. The unequal distribution shows that this is not the case. Rather, things must have these perfections through the influence of a source that does have them to the maximum, as the heat in a house, stronger in some rooms than in others, comes from the fire in the hearth.[65]

Later in the *Summa*, very succinctly, Thomas shows us how this argument is connected with creation. To create is to produce something out of nothing, which is to say, not out of anything. No sort of matter is presupposed to the creator's action. God produces absolutely everything that enters into the creature's constitution; "nothing can be in beings (*in entibus*), unless it is from God." The reason for this is simply that He is the "universal cause of all being (*totius esse*)."[66] And this was just how the fourth way presented Him.

However, the fourth way does not mean to show that God produced the world in a beginning of time. If we take the word *creation* to imply a temporal beginning, then the fourth way does not quite reach God as creator. No merely rational argument does. Thomas does not think the world's having a temporal beginning can be proved. That must be accepted on faith, as something God freely decided.[67] But the interesting thing is that Thomas does think that God's producing the world out of nothing, in the sense of not out of anything, can be proved. This means proving that He causes even matter. And this is the very reason why no temporal beginning is implied. Because creation presupposes no material substrate, it is not really a process or a change (although we cannot help imagining a change and speaking of it as though it involved one).[68] The action of creating does not consist in bringing a subject from one state or condition to another. It is nothing but a causal relation, which takes no time, and need have no beginning.

64. Not many pages later, Thomas indicates why reaching God as cause of the being of all things allows him to go on at once to consider God the cause of absolutely all the perfections of things: "all perfections pertain to the perfection of being, for things are perfect inasmuch as they have being in some way" (*STh*, I, q. 4, a. 2). On this text, see below, 139–41.

65. See Thomas Aquinas, *In Symbolum Apostolorum*, a. 1.

66. *STh*, I, q. 45, a. 2.

67. *STh*, I, q. 46, a. 2.

68. See *STh*, I, q. 45, aa. 2 & 3.

That God, and God Alone, Is His Being Itself

The fourth way is often said to be the most Platonic of the five ways. That may well be so. Of all the ways, however, the fourth is the only one that actually cites any other author; and the author cited (twice) is Aristotle. The references are to the passage mentioned earlier, from *Metaphysics* II, about the correlation between how things are in truth and how they are in being, and about how that which has a feature to the highest degree is cause of that feature in everything else. Thomas almost seems to have anticipated the judgment that the fourth way is Platonic, and to have wanted to insist that it is not, for that reason, less Aristotelian.

In fact, on the subject of God's universal causality, Thomas finds Plato and Aristotle in considerable agreement. Especially insistent upon this agreement is a passage from one of his most mature writings, the little treatise on angels called *De substantiis separatis*.[69] Over and above the mode of becoming (*modum fiendi*) that is by the transformation of matter, he says,

> it is necessary, in the judgment of Plato and Aristotle, to posit another, higher one. For since the first principle must be most simple, it must not be posited to be as participating in *esse*, but as being an *esse* itself. And since there can only be one subsistent *esse*, as has already been shown, all the other things, which are below it, must be thus, as participating in *esse*. Hence in all things of this sort there must come about a certain common resolution, according to which each of them is resolved by the intellect into that which is (*id quod est*) and its *esse*. Therefore, above the mode of becoming by which something comes to be through the arrival of form to matter, another origin of things must be pre-understood, according to which *esse* is conferred upon the whole universe of things by the first being (*a primo ente*), which is its own *esse*.[70]

Now, right here we have Thomas's fundamental way of distinguishing the divine nature from that of everything else, corporeal or spiritual. As mentioned in the first chapter, some of his contemporaries held that all created substances are composed of matter and form, and that God alone is simple, being a pure form. Thomas holds that an angel too is a pure form

69. Thomas also mentions the agreement in two similar earlier passages: *De pot.*, q. 3, a. 5, and *STh*, I, q. 44, a. 1.

70. *De subst. sep.*, cap. 9. The reference is to the previous chapter, where he argued that there cannot be but one subsistent *esse*, "just as any form, if it be considered separate, must be one."

itself, *ipsa forma subsistens*.[71] But the angel is still composite. This is because the essence of his form, which is his essence, is not identical with his
esse; rather, his essence is only that in and through which he receives and
holds on to his *esse*. He only shares in his *esse*, in a manner analogous (not
identical) to the ways in which matter shares in form and a subject shares in
an accident. God's *esse*, by contrast, is not really distinct from His essence,
or from God Himself. And so He alone is absolutely simple.

Thomas's so-called real distinction, in creatures, between essence and
esse, has been debated for centuries. Recently, both it and his character-
ization of God as a subsistent *esse* itself, *ipsum esse subsistens*, have been
criticized for being too much of a concession to Platonism and inconsistent
with his own Aristotelian principles. I have discussed this issue at some
length in other places.[72] In what follows I am not going to try to resolve any
of the debates, or to give a full presentation of Thomas's thought in these
areas.[73] In the subsequent sections of this chapter I will say a few things
about the Platonism issue in relation to Thomas's conception of God. As
for the real distinction, there is just one point about it that I would like to
make. This is how very fine the distinction is, as Thomas conceives it. This
does have some bearing on the question of the Aristotelian credentials for
the distinction, because it can seem that Aristotle's doctrine of substance
has no room for a substantial act that is really distinct from substantial
form. As we have seen repeatedly, Aristotelian form itself is act and makes
what has it be in act. I would like to suggest that this is a problem only if
we exaggerate the distinction in a way that Thomas does not mean to do.

The point then is this. The distinction that Thomas means to draw is
primarily between a substance, or the essence of a substance, and what we
have called the substance's unqualified *esse*, which is its substantial *esse*.
This is the *esse* that it has through its substantial form. It is quite close to

71. *STh*, I, q. 50, a. 2, ad 3; q. 50, a. 5.

72. The most forceful and philosophically interesting formulations of the criticisms that I have seen are those offered, in a number of writings, by the eminent Italian
philosopher and Aristotelian scholar, Enrico Berti. Two of the earliest are "Il problema
della sostanzialità dell'essere e dell'uno nella *Metafisica* di Aristotele" and "Aristotelismo
e neoplatonismo nella dottrina tomistica di Dio come «*ipsum esse*»," both of which are
included in Berti, *Studi Aristotelici*, 221–52 and 423–29. For more bibliography, and an
attempt to address the issues, see my "On Whether Aquinas's *Ipsum Esse* is 'Platonism.'"
Also pertinent is my "Harmonizing Plato and Aristotle on *Esse*: Thomas Aquinas and the
De hebdomadibus."

73. On the real distinction, a thorough overview of Thomas is offered in Wippel, *The
Metaphysical Thought of Thomas Aquinas*, 132–76.

the form. Indeed, the word *unqualified* may be somewhat misleading. It is not at all meant to suggest that this *esse* does not admit any complement or specification. Quite the contrary. The substantial *esse* of man, which is distinct from man and from the essence of man, is *esse hominem*; that is, it is the act of *being a man*.[74] The *esse* of a horse is its act of *being a horse*. Generally, that of a living thing is its *life*. Calling it unqualified means merely that it is the *esse* according to which the substance simply is or exists, period. It is the substance's first *esse*. Without it, the substance simply is not. It is opposed to any *esse* or any act according to which the substance is in act in some additional, non-substantial way: an act of being hot, of being virtuous, etc. Without these, the substance can still be. But even in the case of these acts, there is a distinction between the form and the *esse* that the form gives. An example of Thomas's is the distinction between *knowledge* and *being knowledgeable*.[75]

So clearly the distinction is rather fine. It is not between a thing's essence or form and some extraneous, unspecified, and (as it were) amorphous nature that is called simply *esse* and nothing else. Rather, the *esse* of diverse things is itself diverse in each of them. That is, diverse thing are diverse *according to* their *esse*. This means that *what* their *esse* itself *is* is diverse.[76] Why? Because in each case it is a direct function of a diverse form or essence. But it is not the form or the essence. It is the act of an essence.[77]

This, however, does not mean that it is another act, *added* to that act which is the thing's form. There are two distinct items that are called act here, but there are not two acts. Rather, *esse* is called act just by reason of itself. Form is called act by reason of its immediate connection with *esse*—its functioning, in virtue of itself, as that through which a thing has *esse*.[78] Form is essentially act, but *esse* is, as it were, the very actness—*actualitas*, as Thomas often calls it—of any act.

If a form cannot quite be identified with the *esse* that it brings, the reason is that it also carries a dimension of potency. The *esse* is act and

74. See *De ver.*, q. 2, a. 11.

75. Ibid.

76. Ibid.; also *De ente*, cap. 4; *STh*, I, q. 3, a. 5.

77. *De pot.*, q. 5, a. 4, ad 3. Cf. *In Sent.*, 1, d. 4, q. 1, a. 1, ad 2; d. 19, q. 5, a. 1, obj. 1; d. 33, q. 1, a. 1, ad 1; d. 37, q. 1, a. 2; *De ver.*, q. 10, a. 1, obj. 3; *De pot.*, q. 9, a. 5, ad 19; *De spir. creat.*, q. un., a. 11; *STh*, I, q. 54, a. 1; *In Meta.*, IV, lect. 2, §558; *In Peryerm.*, 1, lect. 5, §73.

78. "Each thing is a being in act through a form, either according to substantial being or according to accidental being, *whence* every form is act": *De spir. creat.*, q. un., a. 3, c. (emphasis added).

nothing but act. One way of seeing the potency of the substantial form, I think, is to consider how it disposes the substance for *further* acts, beyond the substantial *esse*—the acts that the substance needs in order to be fully perfect or complete.[79] I am not now talking about the form's role as an active principle of those further acts, but about its role as a sort of receptive principle of them. The soul is such a principle, and even angelic forms are: their powers of intellect and will, and the activities of these powers, are received in the angel's substance, which is pure form.[80] But this means that the form cannot be the substantial *esse* itself. For a receptive principle, as such, relates to what it can receive as potency to act. What is nothing but act, *esse*, cannot be receptive of act. And so the substantial form, having a dimension of potentiality, cannot be identical even with the substantial *esse*; it must be a receptive principle with respect to substantial *esse* itself.

In this respect, as having potentiality, substantial form is somewhat comparable to matter.[81] And indeed, just as matter contracts form to a determinate individual, a substantial form that is not its *esse* contracts the *esse* to a determinate nature, a finite grade.[82] However, a form's relation to *esse* also differs from matter's relation to form. The form is totally determined to the *esse* that is received through it, and this *esse* is inseparable from it, following on it immediately and in virtue of itself. Matter's potency for form, and form's potency for *esse*, are very different senses of the term *potency*.

In the case of God, the form does not contains any potency at all, nor is it a receptive principle, nor does it contract the act of being in any way. A sign of this is that God can have no accidents or additional perfections or acts of any sort.[83] The deity is the only subsistent entity that is identical with its own *esse*. But I have stressed the fineness of the distinction between form and *esse* in creatures, partly because I think it is sometimes not fully appreciated, and partly because I think it sheds light on what the identity, or the absence of the distinction, in the case of God, amounts to. To repeat, the distinction in the creature is not merely between, e.g., man, or man's form, and *esse* taken without specification; it is between man, or man's form, and

79. I develop this line of thought in "How Many Acts of Being Can a Substance Have?"

80. See *STh*, I, q. 54, a. 3, ad 2; q. 77, a. 1, ad 6.

81. See *STh*, I, q. 90, a. 2, ad 1.

82. *STh*, I, q. 7, a. 2; q. 50, a. 2, ad 1 & ad 4; q. 54, a. 2.

83. *STh*, I, q. 3, a. 6.

esse hominem, being man. And in the case of God, the identity is between God, or God's form, and *esse deum*, the act of being God. It is between God and *His* own *esse*.[84] In God's case, too, the word *esse* admits a complement or a specification, in accordance with God's form. And I shall want to argue we are not to understand God, or God's form, to be identical with the nature of *esse* itself, taken universally or without specification.

This way of stating Thomas's view, however, takes it for granted that he thinks there is such a thing as God's form. There are reasons for doubting this assumption. In my opinion, the question goes to the heart of Thomas's metaphysical teaching about God.

That Godhead Exists

One reason for doubting whether Thomas thinks that God has a form is that, if he does, then this form, and God Himself, would seem to be nothing other than the Platonic Idea of *esse*, Being Itself. This is inconsistent with very fundamental positions of Aristotle, who insists that being cannot be the essence of anything at all, and who in any case considers it far too varied and diverse in things to be the essence of a single entity. Thomas expresses agreement with these views. Seeing God's essence as nothing other than *esse* itself also seems hard to square with the divine transcendence. If everything participates in *esse* and has *esse* in it, then must not everything have the divine nature in it, albeit in reduced mode? The divine nature will not be strictly proper to God. And we will have grasped or conceived it, inasmuch as we do have a concept of *esse*.

Or do we? Some interpreters have held that, for Thomas, there is no such concept, no such thing as *what being is*, and that in denying the distinction between essence or form and *esse* in God, Thomas is not so much saying that *esse* is God's essence or form as he is denying that there is any such thing as God's essence or form. We do not know what *esse* is because there is no such thing as what *esse* is, and likewise we do not know what God is because there is no such thing. And the fact that all things participate in *esse* does not mean that everything has the divine nature in it, again because there is no such thing as the divine nature, and because *esse* cannot be identified with God except when it is found separately, subsisting by itself, positively detached from any essence or nature or form.

84. See *De ver.*, q. 2, a. 11.

Luckily I do not need to go into the question whether, for Thomas, there is any such thing as a concept of *esse* or what *esse* is. The question has been handled thoroughly in a recent doctoral thesis.[85] The thesis, which is excellent, leaves no doubt: yes, there is such a thing. And there is also such a thing as what *esse* is. Although not very often, Thomas does occasionally speak of the nature or even the essence of *esse*, both in early and in very mature works.[86]

It is probably significant, though, that he does not do so very often.[87] I suppose that this has to do with the fact that, as we saw, *esse* is something diverse in diverse things. Taken universally or without specification, it is *one* essence only in a very weak and qualified way. It is not one in species or even in genus, but only as a common proportion.[88] It is common to all things in the way that act and potency are. That common proportion would be what the general concept expresses. So it is more the actuality of this or that essence than an essence in its own right. This weak unity of *esse*, however, would pose a problem for Thomas only if he did identify *esse*, taken without specification, with the essence of God. For if there is such a thing as the essence of God, it must surely have a stronger unity, indeed immeasurably stronger, than that of a mere proportion.

But is there after all such a thing as God's essence, for Thomas, or not? Now, he does on several occasions say that God is *esse tantum*, "only *esse*." In one of them, the youthful *De ente et essentia*, he also remarks that "some philosophers are found saying that God does not have a quiddity or an essence, because His essence is not other than His *esse*."[89] As Étienne Gilson perceived, Thomas evidently hesitated to embrace such "uncompromising language." After all, to say that God has no essence sounds like saying that there is no such thing as what God is; and this sounds like saying that what God is is nothing—i.e., that there is no God. But Gilson did think that

---

85. Vargas Della Casa, "Thomas Aquinas on the Apprehension of Being."

86. In the (probably) early *Expositio libri Boetii De ebdomadibus*, lect. 2, §25, Thomas quotes Boethius: "*esse* itself has nothing else mixed in," and to this Thomas adds, "outside its essence." A similar thought is found in *Scg*, I, cap. 23, §214. In *Quodl.*, III, q. 1, a. 1, he says "the nature of *esse* belongs to God infinitely." He also says that God knows the "nature of *esse*": *De ver.*, q. 2, a. 15, ad 3; *Scg*, I, cap. 50, §1; *STh*, I, q. 14, a. 6.

87. And in one place he shows some reservation about it, saying ". . . so to speak, the nature of *esse*" (. . . *ut ita dixerim, naturam essendi*): *STh*, I, q. 45, a. 5, ad 1.

88. See I, q. 4, a. 3.

89. *De ente*, cap. 4 (very near the beginning). On the meaning of the term *quiddity*, see above, 60n29.

Thomas saw a point to such language. "To say that God has no essence really means that God is as a beyond-essence. This is best expressed by saying that God is the being whose essence is to be beyond essence or, in other words, God is the being whose essence it is to be."[90] Similar readings have been proposed quite recently. These mesh with a broader recent tendency to read Thomas's theology as highly apophatic, that is, as holding that there is little or nothing that can be affirmed about God, and that ultimately even such judgments as that God is a subsistent *esse* are rather negative than affirmative.[91]

Now, as a matter of fact, in his commentary on the *Sentences*—nearly contemporaneous with the *De ente et essentia*—Thomas attributes the view that God has no essence to two thinkers, Avicenna and Maimonides.[92] He then explains that their theology was quite apophatic, denying that any term taken from creatures could be attributed to God in a proper (non-metaphorical), absolute (not merely relative), and positive sense.[93] As said of God, terms such as wisdom, goodness, essence, etc., either mean merely that He causes these features in creatures, or else serve merely to negate their opposites (foolishness, badness, privation) in Him. Further on in this passage, however, Thomas says that their reason for this view was simply that they wanted to deny that what such terms apply to, when they are said of creatures, could be attributed to God. Thus, regarding essence, they wanted to deny that it could be said of God in the sense in which it applies to "a certain thing that does not subsist." But they do not mean to say that God lacks any "mode of perfection."[94] And still in this same passage, Thomas describes with approval the theology that does attribute such terms positively to God. He says that what these terms signify truly is in God, although it is so in a way that exceeds our conception.[95]

90. Gilson, *The Elements of Christian Philosophy*, 145–46.

91. For example, Porro, *Tommaso d'Aquino*, 245 ff., 258, 408; Marion, *God Without Being*, 229–236. There are many eminent readers of Thomas, however, who do not make him out to be so apophatic: e.g., Davies, Dewan, Elders, Kretzmann, Stump, te Velde, and Wippel.

92. On the Neoplatonic background to the Avicennian doctrine of God as being alone, beyond essence and form, and also on this doctrine in the *Liber de causis*, see Taylor, "Aquinas, The *Plotiniana Arabica*, and the Metaphysics of Being and Actuality."

93. Relative terms include those that indicate causality. A relative term does not immediately express much, if anything, about the intrinsic constitution of that to which it is attributed.

94. *In Sent.*, I, d. 2, q. 1, a. 3.

95. In fact, since everything in God is God, and God is His own essence, the

Moreover, in the *De ente et essentia* itself, Thomas says generally of simple or immaterial substances—angels and God—that essence is in them "in a truer and nobler way, inasmuch as they also have *esse* in a nobler way."[96] This is hardly going in the direction of denying essence of such substances. Nor is it easy to square with the notion that God's essence is to be beyond essence because His essence is to be.[97]

Later in the *De ente*, Thomas says that "although God is only *esse*, He need not lack the other perfections and excellences (*nobilitates*), indeed he has all the perfections in all genera."[98] It seems to me that Thomas is definitely seeing *essence* itself as signifying a perfection. It is one that extends to all things, and one that approaches closer and closer to the perfection of *esse* itself as we ascend on the scale of the perfection of *esse* itself. The young Thomas did nod to the view that God has no essence, but that was hardly even a flirtation with it. And the very fact of his being aware of it only strengthens the significance of his repeatedly asserting the contrary.

Now, among creatures, more perfect are those essences that are without matter, subsisting forms. Indeed, there is a definite kinship between the notions of perfection and form, so much so that in the *Summa theologiae*, Thomas treats the likeness of creatures to God within the *quaestio* on God's perfection, and he says there that likeness is a function of agreement or communion in form.[99] And this is what I would especially like to stress: that Thomas ascribes form to God.[100]

The texts are far too many and too strongly worded to be swept under the rug. Here are a few from the *Prima pars*. God is "by His essence

---

knowledge that these terms express must be some sort of knowledge of God's essence. Thomas certainly denies that any of our knowledge of God is "quidditative." That is, none of it provides even a partial answer to the question, "What is God?" But this is not to say that we have no knowledge *about* what God is. Indeed, Thomas insists that it is impossible to know that a thing exists without knowing something about what it is, at least in some imperfect and confused way. In the case of God, he explains, this consists precisely in the threefold way of negation, causality, and eminence; see *In De Trin.*, q. 6, a. 3.

96. *De ente*, cap. 1.

97. On a valid sense in which God or God's essence could be said to be beyond essence, see below, 141n123.

98. *De ente*, cap. 4.

99. *STh*, I, q. 4, a. 3.

100. Gilson does not deny this, but he certainly downplays it, often couching it in hypothetical terms ("Let us suppose God is pure form . . ."), and presenting it as a mere phase in Thomas's account of God, from which we "jump" into the true Thomistic world of God as *esse*; see Gilson, *The Elements of Christian Philosophy*, 126–28.

form" (q. 3, a. 2). "That sort of form which is not receivable in matter, but is self-subsistent, is individuated by the very fact that it cannot be received in anything else; and God is such a form" (q. 3, a. 2, ad 3). God is most appropriately called "He who is" because His *esse* is His essence and "each thing is denominated by its form" (q. 13, a. 11). God "is a simple form to the highest degree" (q. 13, a. 12, obj. 2). "God is called infinite as a form that is not terminated by any matter" (q. 86, a. 2, ad 1). And the *Prima pars* alone has over a hundred instances of the word *deitas*, Godhead. This signifies a form.

The higher substances lack the composition of form and matter. They are only forms, without matter. But although the very highest being lacks the *composition* (which implies the *distinction*) of *esse* and essence or of *esse* and form, and indeed is only *esse*, this does not at all mean that He is without essence or form. (Nor, as I shall argue in the next section, does it mean that when we think of His essence or His form we should think of nothing but *esse*.) There is no such thing as a form that is identical with its own matter, but there can be *esse* that is identical with its own form. This is because *esse* itself is "most formal."[101] Matter cannot be form because matter is potency and form is act. The very notions are opposed. But a form *can* be an *esse*, for that very same reason: form is act. What would be the difference between thinking of God as existing without form, and thinking of matter in that way—which, Thomas said, involves a contradiction?[102] To be sure, *some* form has an aspect of potency, and *that* form cannot be an *esse*. But the mere notions are not opposed. And if a form that is an *esse* is more perfect than a form that is not, an *esse* that is a form is also more perfect than one that is not. It is more *self-sufficient*. Form is a thing's power, or energy, to be. In God's case, it is identical with the to be.

So we need to see God's *esse* as containing in itself the perfection of form: the energy, the *virtus*, of being and of acting, that this word conveys. We already saw Thomas defending the idea of something that is its own form. He was speaking of the Persons of the Trinity and their being "of one essence," an expression that signifies essence in the function of form. Connected with this notion is the equality of the Persons. Equality, Thomas says, pertains to quantity. Of course, in this context, it cannot be quantity of extension. It is rather quantity of *virtus*, according to the perfection of some form or nature. Its *root*, he says, is the perfection of the form or nature itself;

101. *STh*, I, q. 7, a. 1; *Scg*, I, cap. 23, §214.
102. See above, 42–43, 49n74.

then it can be considered in the *effects* of form, the first of which is *esse*, and the second, activity. Things with more perfect forms are more enduring in being and more potent in action. What is striking is that he says all this, and quite matter-of-factly, in a discussion of the Trinity.[103]

Clearly we also need the notion of form in the doctrine of God's knowability and God's knowledge. Thomas's whole account of knowledge is in terms of form. In fact, Thomas associates God's knowledge in a special way with the very word *deus*. That word signifies what has the divine nature, not as it is in itself—we cannot know or name it in that way—but as that which underlies His universal providence over things.[104] Providence is an exercise of intellect (and of will).[105] Here of course the fifth way is particularly relevant.

But it is perhaps with respect to God's own knowability that the extreme versions of apophatic theology are hardest to square with Thomas's teaching. If they do not leave us thinking that there is no such thing as what God is, and therefore no such thing as God, they at least make us wonder whether His unknowability is only in relation to us, or whether He is unknowable, period—even to Himself. On the previous page I quote a text from the *Prima pars* saying that God is infinite as a form that is not terminated by any matter. Thomas's point there is that, in Himself, God is quite knowable. And He is quite knowing, for the same reason. As we saw, this same notion of form not contracted by matter is what Thomas uses to establish God's being at the summit of cognition.[106]

In reality His knowledge and His knowability are the some thing. What He primarily knows, and that through which He knows everything else, is Himself. His intellect is identical with His intelligible likeness or *species*.[107] This is the form that specifies His intellectual operation, and it is nothing other than His essence, which is that by which the divine understanding, "or rather, God Himself," is specified.[108]

---

103. *STh*, I, q. 42, a. 1, ad 1.

104. *STh*, I, q. 13, a. 8. Notice that, as to *what* the word signifies, "God" is a more suitable name for God than "He who is" (*STh*, I, q. 13, a. 11, ad 1).

105. *STh*, I, q, 22, Proem.

106. *STh*, I, q. 14, a. 1; as we also saw, the article sends us back to I, q. 7, a. 1, on God's infinity.

107. *STh*, I, q. 14, a. 2.

108. *STh*, I, q. 14, a. 5, ad 3. When He is seen by a creature, His essence itself (not a likeness of it) becomes the created intellect's intelligible form: *STh*, I, q. 12, a. 5.

So there is even such a thing as God's species, the kind of thing that God is. Obviously He is one of a kind. And obviously His is not a species *of* some genus. He cannot be defined in genus and difference. Even that would be a sort of composition in Him, and it would mean that He is limited, confined to that genus, so that He would not be principle of all *esse*.[109] But knowability is not the same as definability; to define a thing is to express it in terms of other things, but it is possible to know a thing through itself. And having a form does not entail being limited, though it does entail being *this* and not *that*.[110] The forms that limit *esse* and contract it to a species of a genus are forms that are distinct from *esse* and contain potency—imperfect forms, forms that are not act *alone*.

There are such things as what *esse* is, and what God is, and God's species and form; and God's form is God's *esse*, which is subsistent *esse*, and is cause of everything that in any way shares in *esse*. One can see why some have found it hard to avoid concluding that Thomas's God is the Platonic Idea of being or of *esse*. That is, God's essence and the essence of *esse* or of being would be the very same. In the next section I shall try to show why this is not the case. To conclude this one, let me simply say something about Thomas's language.

He does indeed say, in many places, that God, or God's essence, is *ipsum esse subsistens*. In quite a few of these, he adds the word *suum*: God is "His *esse* itself, subsisting." Now, this expression, by itself, in no way warrants identifying God's *esse* with *esse* taken universally or without specification, or identifying His essence with the sheer essence of *esse*. But what about the cases in which Thomas does not add *suum*? Then it does sound as though he is saying that God is *esse* itself, subsisting. And that is how it is often rendered. But it does not have to be rendered that way. Notice, for instance, that Thomas speaks in several places of God or angel as *ipsa forma subsistens*. No one takes this to mean that God or angel is simply form itself, subsisting—that is, the universal nature of form existing by itself. Rather, in this case, the expression is translated with the indefinite article. An angel is *a* form itself, subsisting. Why should we not render *ipsum esse subsistens* in the same way? God is *an* act of being itself, subsisting. As it turns out, He is the only one. There cannot be many. But that does not amount to an identification of His *esse*, or of Him or His nature, with the common nature of *esse*. What I now wish to show is that, for Thomas, they cannot be

109. See *STh*, I, q. 3, a. 5.
110. See *STh*, I, q. 7, a. 1, obj. 3 & ad 3.

identified, because His nature stands above the common nature of *esse*, as its very cause.

That God, and Godhead, and God's Being are Beyond Being Itself

First let me present just a couple of texts in which Thomas sets God above common being, as its cause. One of the texts relates being to God's will; the other relates it to his intellect. Afterwards I shall try to lay out how he reaches a conception of God's nature, and even of God's very being, as beyond the nature of being itself, not to be identified with it.[111]

The text regarding God's will is from the *De interpretatione* commentary, within a discussion of determinism. Thomas is arguing that the infallible efficacy of God's will, which extends to everything, does not make everything necessary. "For the divine will must be understood as standing outside the whole order of beings, in the manner of a cause pouring forth the whole of being (*totum ens*) and all its differences."[112]

The other text, regarding God's intellect, is from the commentary on the *De divinis nominibus*. Thomas is explaining how God is prior to every limit and boundary.

> And He is the cause of the limiting of all, and not only of the things that are, but of *esse* itself. For created *esse* itself is not limited, if it is compared to creatures, because it extends to all; yet if it is compared to uncreated *esse*, it is found deficient and out of the forethought of the divine mind, having the boundary of its own conception (*ratio*).[113]

This is quite striking. Clearly *esse* does have a concept, a *ratio*. And this sets a sort of boundary, one that God has, so to speak, excogitated. Every creature, of course, shares in *esse* only in a limited fashion. But even if we prescind from anything that puts a limit on created *esse*, anything extraneous to *esse* itself, so that what remains is unlimited or infinite with respect

---

111. On this see Dewan, "St. Thomas and Creation: Does God Create 'Reality'?"

112. *In Peryerm.*, I, lect. 14, §197[22]. He goes on to explain that necessity and contingency are differences of being. God's will infallibly makes necessary things happen necessarily, and contingent things happen contingently. His will itself, unlike any other will or cause, "transcends the order of necessity and contingency." See Goris, *Free Creatures of an Eternal God*.

113. *Super Librum Dionysii De divinis nominibus*, cap. XIII, lect. 3, §989.

to *esse*, nevertheless it is still something limited: it still falls within the boundary of the concept of *esse*. Thomas says that this is deficient in comparison with uncreated *esse*. Evidently uncreated *esse* does not fall within the boundary of the concept of *esse*. It is certainly an infinite *esse*, but it also goes beyond that.

We can speak, truly and properly, of God's *esse*, but we must not think of it as falling under the common notion of *esse*. Or to put it another way, we may speak of God as something real, but we must not think of Him as part of reality. He does not stand within the hierarchy of lesser and greater strength of being, even as the greatest within it. We must think of Him as the source of the whole hierarchy and beyond the greatest within it. How can we form any notion of this?

Let me go back to the *Summa* for a moment. After presenting the five ways, Thomas takes up the question of God's mode of being. He says that since we cannot know what God is (*quid sit*), neither can we know how He is (*quomodo sit*). This, however, does not mean that we cannot know anything positive about Him, but that we cannot know His proper mode of being, which is (so to speak) a function of what He properly is. But we can know how He is not, removing or negating features that do not suit Him. Indeed we can know that certain negations are proper to Him, true of nothing else.

The first such thing that Thomas seeks to remove is composition.[114] God, and only God, is absolutely simple, free of composition, in every way. There is no composition of bodily parts, of matter and form, of individuating principle and essence, of essence and *esse*, of genus and difference, or of subject and accident; nor is He composed with anything else.

Then, immediately after considering God's simplicity, Thomas treats His perfection.[115] This is certainly a positive item. However, we cannot know the perfection that is proper to God, His distinctive mode of being perfect. Nevertheless, we can know that there is no perfection which He lacks. Again, this is proper to God.

Now, the reason given by Thomas for treating God's perfection after His simplicity is that "in bodily things, the simple ones are imperfect and parts."[116] He is considering that we are apt to judge everything on the model of bodily things, which are our mind's starting-points. Your computer is

114. *STh*, I, q. 3.
115. *STh*, I, q. 4.
116. *STh*, I, q. 3, Proem.

more complex than its screen. And you are more complex than your computer. From our point of view, simplicity and perfection are rather in tension with one another. Thomas is pressing and exploiting this tension. Having taken us to the extreme of simplicity, he now takes us to the extreme of perfection. And he wants us to understand that these extremes are one and the same thing. He thinks we can come to see that they must be. But the very tension makes it abundantly clear that we cannot see how. That is, we cannot see the *form* according to which they are one. Right here, it seems to me, Thomas is giving his fundamental account of God's transcendence, showing by rigorous reasoning that He lies beyond anything reason can conceive. It is not the extreme simplicity alone, nor the extreme perfection alone, that establishes this, but the two together.

Let me spell this out briefly, using mainly the second article from the question on God's perfection. In the first article, it is determined that God is indeed perfect. He is the first active principle, and so He must be in act to the highest degree; and something is perfect insofar as it is in act. This is confirmed by the fact that His essence is (an) *esse* itself; for *esse* is the actuality of all things, and even of the forms themselves. If anything can be added to an *esse*, it is only in the manner of what receives it, in material fashion; *esse* itself is formal and received. Of course, nothing can be added to God, even as a recipient.

Then in the second article, Thomas determines that the perfections of all things are in God. He gives two arguments. One is that God is the first efficient cause of all things, and that the perfection of an effect must pre-exist in its efficient cause, either in an equal way, if cause and effect are of the same kind, or in a more eminent way, if they differ in kind; and hence all the excellences of things pre-exist in God in a more eminent way. The other argument, which is what chiefly interests us, rests precisely on the fact that God is (a) self-subsistent *esse* itself.[117] The first thing that follows from this is that He contains in himself "the whole perfection of *esse*." To illustrate this, Thomas imagines a subsistent heat, a heat not received in and conditioned by any subject. Such a heat could not be lacking in any of the perfection—the *virtus*—of heat. In the same way, the subsistent *esse* of God cannot lack any of the perfection of *esse*. But this means that He must contain absolutely all the perfections in things. For all perfections "pertain

---

117. I think the insertion of "a" here is quite justified, given that an earlier version of the same argument rests on God's being *His* own *esse*: *Scg,* I, cap. 28, §259–61.

to the perfection of *esse*." Things are perfect just insofar as they have *esse* in some way.

Now, this last assertion may sound as though *esse* itself is the only real perfection. But this is not what Thomas means. He also recognizes other perfections, distinct from *esse*. This is clear in similar passages from other works.[118] In the *Summa contra gentiles*, he gives the example of wisdom. The wisdom of Socrates is certainly not his substantial, unqualified *esse*. It is not even his act of *being wise*. But the wisdom of Socrates is still a perfection, precisely because *through* it, Socrates *is* wise. His wisdom is a form, according to which his act of being wise is constituted. It pertains to his being wise; it is a *principle* thereof. If the entire perfection of *esse* is in God, then all the various forms of things must also be in Him. Every perfection of *esse* is tied to the *virtus*—as it were, the energy—of some form.

Along this line, the article's first two objections are particularly significant. The first is that the perfections of things are many and diverse, whereas God is simple. The second is that the species of things are perfected by their differences, and these are opposites; but opposites cannot exist in the same subject. Thomas answers the two objections together, very briefly. He does not at all deny that the perfections and differences in things are diverse and even opposed. He simply asserts that things diverse and opposed in themselves pre-exist in God as one, without detriment to His simplicity; and he cites pseudo-Dionysius, who likens God to the sun, which, being one, pre-contains all the substances and qualities of sensible things "uniformly."[119] *Uniformly*, of course, means *in a single form*.

The early, *De ente* version of the argument even speaks in terms of qualities: "just as, if someone, through one quality, could effect the actions of all qualities, then he would have all qualities in that one quality; so God has in His *esse* itself all perfections."[120]

Now what, on this account, is the difference between the way in which the perfections of things are in the things themselves, and the way in which they are in God? It is not just a difference of strength or intensity—not even an infinite one. It is a difference in *what* the perfection is, a difference in its very nature. This is clear because, in the things themselves, the perfections

---

118. E.g., *De ente*, cap. 5 (Leonine edition vol. 43, 378, ll. 30–43); *De pot.*, q. 6, a. 6; *Scg*, I, cap. 28, §260.

119. Cf. *STh*, I, q. 14, a. 6, explaining how God knows the proper natures of all things, just by knowing His own essence perfectly.

120. *De ente*, cap. 4.

differ in nature from each other; whereas in God, their nature is nothing other than the nature of God, which is absolutely simple.

In some cases this is extremely obvious. What the perfection of *lion* is, in a lion itself, is something that makes the lion be a lion. But as it is in God, the perfection of lion does not make Him be a lion. He is a lion only metaphorically. This is because in the proper sense, the name *lion* also implies imperfection or limitation and excludes many other perfections.[121]

But even in the case of perfections whose names do not of themselves imply imperfection or limitation or exclude some other perfection, what the perfection is, considered in itself, differs from what it is in God. For in itself, what it is differs from what other perfections are. But in God, what each perfection is does not differ from what any of the others is. What each one is, is God. It is not a component of God, distinct from the others; God does not have components. He is not the synthesis of all perfections. For he is not a synthesis at all. He is a maximally simple form.

In short: absolutely speaking, what wisdom is and what love is are not the same. But in God, what wisdom is and what love is are absolutely the same; they are what God is. Wisdom is not God. But God's wisdom is God. And so, what wisdom is, and what God's wisdom is, are not the same.

This is the core of Thomas's doctrine of the non-univocity of all names said commonly of God and creatures.[122] Each name signifies some perfection. It does so according to a concept that "circumscribes and comprehends" the perfection, i.e. that expresses just what it is, and that distinguishes it from the others that its subject has. And this is how each perfection really is in any creature: circumscribed and distinct from the others, according to what it is. But with God, while preserving the perfection that is circumscribed by the concept that the name signifies, we must remove the circumscription. The concept must include its own failure to express what the perfection is and include its not distinguishing what that perfection is from what those signified by other names are. This is not to make the various names that apply to God synonymous. The concepts that they signify still differ. But the nature of the thing conceived is the same, and each concept reflects this fact by its lacking circumscription and by its thereby leaving that nature unexpressed and transcending the concept's own positive content.[123]

121. *STh*, I, q, 13, a. 3.

122. *STh*, I, q. 13, a. 5.

123. This doctrine is extremely important with regard to the Trinity. See, e.g., *STh*, I, q. 28, a. 2, ad 2: in a divine person, the divine essence that is common to the persons

A name said commonly of God and creature is not univocal. It does not have the same meaning in the two cases. But neither is it wholly equivocal. The meanings are connected, according to a definite relation; we have just seen how. That is why we can draw conclusions about God's perfections using our knowledge of those perfections as they are in creatures. In Thomas's terminology, a name that is said of many things neither univocally nor wholly equivocally is said *analogically*. Analogy means proportion. A name said analogically primarily signifies one thing, and in a subordinate way it signifies one or more relations or proportions to that one thing. So we can ask: of the names said commonly of God and creatures, which is primary, what it signifies as said of God, or what it signifies as said of some creature?[124]

Here again we must distinguish what is primary for us and what is primary simply. What is primary for us—that to which we first apply such a name, being what we first know—is in a creature. And thus, in the definition of what the name means as said of God, we put what it means as said of the creature. *Good*, as said of God, means *that in which what we call goodness in creatures pre-exists in a higher way* (the way described above).[125] But this very formulation also indicates that what is primary simply is what the name means as said of God. He is good most *truly*. What goodness is in creatures is an effect, and a more or less imperfect likeness, of what it is in God. It is relative, proportioned, to the goodness of God.

Now let us go back to the question of *esse*. What we said above about wisdom applies equally well to *esse*. Absolutely speaking, what *esse* is, and what essence or form or power or wisdom or love is, are not the same. But in God they are identical; each is just what God is. And so, what *esse* is, and what God's *esse* is, are not the same. *Esse* is just *esse*. God himself, Thomas says, is *esse tantum*, just an *esse*; but Thomas is also saying that God's *esse* is not just *esse*! In raising our thought to God, we must certainly strip matter

---

is not really distinct from the relation that constitutes and distinguishes that person. It is in this sense that we might speak of God's essence as "beyond essence." The simple reality of the divine essence contains more (not less!) than what is signified by the word *essence*. The signification of *essence*, as ascribed to a complete subsistent thing, extends only to what belongs to the thing considered absolutely or just in itself; what is relative to something else is signified in some other way. In creatures the absolute and the relative are really distinct; in God they are one simple reality that goes beyond either signification. And thus the divine relations are also "beyond relation."

124. *STh*, I, q. 13, a. 6.
125. *STh*, I, q. 13, a. 2.

from form, leaving form uncontracted. But we must not then strip all forms or other perfections away from *esse*, leaving *esse* unspecified. Nor do we strip common *esse* from His *esse*, making the word purely equivocal, or rather meaningless. Rather we consider the intrinsic kinship that all forms and perfections have with common *esse*, and we fold them all into it; and then we smooth out the folds, leaving something that is absolutely simple, and that is therefore outside the whole panorama of created perfections and outside common *esse* itself.[126]

Now although this is supremely knowable in itself, it does leave *us* in the dark.[127] "The divine essence is something uncircumscribed, containing supereminently in itself whatever can be signified or understood by a created intellect; and this can in no way be represented by any created intelligible likeness, because every created form is determined according to some concept, whether of wisdom, or of power, *or of* esse *itself*, or such like."[128] This is not an *esse* without essence or without form. It is a form that is an *esse*, and a wisdom, and a power, and the perfection of a lion. But none of these terms expresses its essence. Its essence cannot be expressed in terms of anything but itself.

We name God with many names because none of them perfectly expresses Him as He is in Himself. This does not yield falsehood, so long as we include the failure in what the names mean. And we had better learn to do so, because as regards the names that signify our own conceptions of Him, the failure cannot be fully overcome. Ever.

> But if our intellect saw God through Himself, it could impose one name on that conception, which will be in the Fatherland; and so it is said in Zechariah (14:9), *On that day the Lord will be one, and His name one*. But that one name would not signify goodness alone, or wisdom alone, or something of that sort, but it would include the significations of all these [names]. But nevertheless, if an intellect seeing God through His essence were to impose a name on the reality that it saw, and to name by way of a conception thereof that it has, it would still have to impose many names; for

126. Analogous to this mystery of a being that is at once absolutely simple and in possession of all perfections is the mystery of God's duration in being, which also is simple—without any real succession of temporal parts—and at the same time "includes" all the parts of time; its measure is not time but something beyond that called *eternity*. See *STh*, I, q. 10, aa. 1 & 2; q. 13, a. 1, ad 3; q. 14, a. 9.

127. Cf. *In Sent.*, I, d. 8, q. 1, a. 1, ad 4.

128. *STh*, I, q. 12, a. 2; emphasis added.

it is impossible that a conception of a created intellect represent the whole perfection of the divine essence. Whence, seeing one thing, it would form diverse conceptions, in the way that Chrysostom also says that the angels praise God, some as majesty, some as goodness, and so forth. But the conception that perfectly represents Him is the uncreated Word. And therefore it is just one.[129]

129. *In Sent.*, I, d. 2, q. 1, a. 3. I have not been able to trace the Chrysostom reference. The fundamental thought here, I believe, is the same as that of the passage that I have quoted in the previous paragraph, from *STh*, I, q. 12, a. 2: no created form can represent the divine essence as it is in itself. If a created intellect does know the divine essence as it is in itself, this is not through a created form representing the essence, but through the essence itself, united in its own being to the created intellect (*STh*, I, q. 12, a. 2, ad 3). But if the created intellect that thus knows the divine essence forms a conception expressing its knowledge, and names God according to that conception, even this name will fall short of His essence, because that conception too will be a mere created form.

6

Ends

Metaphysics in Moral Philosophy, the Question of the Last End, and Natural Law

Thomas's Metaphysics of Morals

A T THE BEGINNING OF the proem to his Commentary on Aristotle's *Metaphysics*, Thomas offers a rather striking explanation of the dominant role of metaphysics in human knowledge, and indeed in human life. "As the Philosopher teaches in his *Politics*," he says, "whenever many things are ordered to one end, one of them must be regulating or ruling (*regulans sive regens*), and the others regulated or ruled (*regulata sive recta*). . . . But all the sciences and arts"—all the human disciplines—"are ordered to one thing, namely the perfection of man, which is his bliss. And so it is necessary that one of them be to all the others as the ruler (*rectrix*), which rightly merits the name of wisdom. For it belongs to the wise man to order things."[1] Of course, Thomas goes on to identify this wisdom with metaphysics. What does its ruling function consist in? It is just what we saw in chapter 4. Metaphysics is the architectonic science. A passage from Thomas's *Ethics* commentary sums it up: "wisdom directs all other sciences, inasmuch as

---

1. *In Meta.*, Proem. The *Politics* reference is I.2, 1254a27–31. The last remark, that ordering belongs to the wise man, is an allusion to *Metaph.*, I.2, 982a17–19.

all others assume their principles from it."[2] To repeat, metaphysics is the science of truth. All sciences are ordered toward truth, and that is how, as sciences, they contribute to man's end. Each science confers mastery over a certain field, disposing the mind to reason rightly to true conclusions about the field. The reasoning starts from certain first principles. Each science, then, is ordered toward truth by virtue of its principles. But metaphysics judges and confirms the principles themselves. In doing this, it orders or directs all the sciences toward truth.

We may tend to think that Thomas is talking only about the specula-tive sciences. But that remark about directing all the sciences is in the *Ethics* commentary, after all; and the *Metaphysics* proem speaks not only of the sciences, but also the arts, which for Thomas are mostly practical disci-plines. What I shall wish especially to focus on in this chapter is the role, or set of roles, that Thomas gives to metaphysics in ethical science and in practical thinking generally. First let me give just a little information about his work in this area.

Thomas's writings on moral matters span his entire career. The major ones include large portions of both the *Sentences* commentary and the *De veritate*; the (unfinished) *De regno ad regem Cypri*; the last third of Book III of the *Summa contra gentiles*; the *Disputed Questions on Evil*; the commen-taries on Aristotle's *Nicomachean Ethics* and *Politics* (the latter breaking off at Book III, chapter 6); the *Disputed Questions on the Virtues*; and the *Secunda pars* of the *Summa theologiae*, which is Thomas's most complete treatment of the moral life. Much of this material is theological, but as usual, it also contains a great deal of philosophy.

On the whole, Thomas's chief philosophical source in morals is surely Aristotle. In fact, the commentaries on the *Ethics* and the *Politics*, as well as the *Tabula Libri Ethicorum*, seem to have served as direct preparation for the *Secunda pars*.[3] Aristotle figures noticeably even in Thomas's treatment of the theological virtues, especially charity. Thomas understands charity as a kind of friendship—friendship with God—and his conception of friend-ship in general owes much to the account of human friendship offered in *Nicomachean Ethics* VIII and IX.[4] On the other hand, Thomas organizes

2. *In Eth.*, VI, lect. 6, §1184.

3. See Torrell, *Initiation*, 331–37, 341. On Thomas's Aristotelian approach to moral thinking, see Flannery, *Acts Amid Precepts*. For an illuminating reflection on how con-temporary, analytical virtue ethics stands in relation to Aristotle and Aquinas, see Vogler, "Aristotle, Aquinas, Anscombe and the New Virtue Ethics."

4. See Torrell, *Saint Thomas d'Aquin, maître spirituel*, ch. 12, 367–409; Torrell, *Christ*

the moral virtues around the four so-called cardinal virtues of prudence, justice, courage, and temperance; and in this he knows that he is not following Aristotle.[5] He is following Christian authors such as Ambrose, Augustine, and Gregory the Great. On particular moral topics, other important sources include Cicero, Seneca, the Roman jurists, Macrobius, Nemesius' *De natura hominis* (which Thomas attributes to Gregory of Nyssa), and Maimonides.

Thomas makes significant contributions on many specific issues in moral philosophy. If there is anything that especially characterizes his overall handling of the field, however, I think it would be the tendency to adopt an overtly metaphysical viewpoint.[6] This is especially visible in the *Secunda pars*, but it is also present in his other moral writings, including the commentaries on Aristotle. Of course, important connections between ethics and metaphysics can be found in Aristotle himself. For instance, in the *Nicomachean Ethics*, Aristotle relegates the most accurate treatment of the good to "another part of philosophy," which is surely metaphysics.[7] And in the *Metaphysics* itself he treats two very fundamental elements of his moral thought: the fact that rational powers are open to opposite ways of operating and are determined to one or another by choice, and the distinction between transitive action or production (*poiēsis*), and immanent action or conduct (*praxis*).[8] Nevertheless, metaphysical treatments of ethical matters are far more abundant in Thomas. This is not very surprising, since he has so much more to say about man's relation to God.

Man's relation to God is in fact so fundamental for Thomas's understanding of the moral life, and revelation is so crucial for his understanding of that relation, that some interpreters have wondered whether his thought really even allows for a purely philosophical science of morals. Later we will take a look at this question. But as a matter of mere fact, it seems undeniable that he considers moral philosophy a valid discipline. Indeed we find him giving it a quite explicit role of "leading by the hand" in theological matters. He applies its order to the account of what we might even call the morality of God Himself. "Having considered the things that pertain absolutely to

---

and Spirituality, 45–64.

5. See *In Eth.*, I, lect. 16, §193.

6. See Dewan, *Wisdom, Law and Virtue*, passim.

7. I.4, 1096b30–35.

8. On rational powers, IX.5, 1047b31–1048a24; on action and production, IX.6, 1048b18–36; IX.8, 1050a23–b6; and see above, 71.

the will"—he means God's will and its possession of such perfections as love and mercy and justice[9]—"we must go on to those that regard intellect and will together. But providence is of this sort . . . . For in moral science too, after the moral virtues, prudence is treated, to which providence seems to pertain."[10] By moral science here he can only mean moral philosophy. For the order that he invokes is that which is observed in the *Nicomachean Ethics*, and it is the very opposite of that which he himself observes in the *Secunda secundae* of the *Summa*, i.e., in moral theology. There he treats prudence prior to justice and the other moral virtues.

But not all of the metaphysics in Thomas's morals directly regards God. For example, he applies the metaphysics of being and goodness in created substances, which he lays out in the *Prima pars*, extensively to the analysis of the morality of human actions.[11] Likewise, he applies his metaphysics of evil to the treatment of sin.[12] This is all the more striking because, in the order of philosophical learning, he puts morals before metaphysics, not after.[13] He almost seems to think that, in moral matters, theology gives the deliverances of reason more weight than philosophy itself does; or at least, more than Aristotle does. He says that whereas Aristotle only calls bad someone who harms other—and not, e.g., one who is prodigal with his wealth—"we call bad, in a general way, everything that is repugnant to right reason."[14]

The following presentation of Thomas's thought in the area of moral philosophy must of course be very partial and sketchy. Thomas says that sketchy or general discussions are not of much use in moral matters, because actions are in particulars.[15] So I shall not even attempt to give a complete overview of his thought in this field. Rather, for the reasons just indicated, I shall focus mainly on what can be called, for lack of a better expression, his metaphysics of morals. Along the way I shall hazard some inferences about his relation to Aristotle in this area. I do think that this discussion can be of some use. It may not provide much guidance for concrete moral thinking, but it addresses the question of the very possibility of

9. *STh*, I, qq. 19–21.

10. *STh*, I, q. 22, Proem.

11. *STh*, I, qq. 5–6, & I–II, qq. 18–21.

12. *STh*, I, qq. 48–49, & I–II, qq. 71–89.

13. *In Eth.*, VI, 1ect. 7, §1211, quoted above, 83.

14. *STh*, I, q. 18, a. 9, ad 2.

15. *STh*, II–II, Proem.

intelligibility and truth in moral matters. Today that is certainly a question, and not just a theoretical one.

Moral Philosophy among the Sciences

At the very beginning of his commentary on the *Nicomachean Ethics*, Thomas lays out a broad division of the human sciences. Governing the division is the notion of order. Grasping order, he says, is proper to reason, and setting things in order belongs above all to reason's foremost perfection, which is wisdom. This is the idea that he invoked in the proem to the *Metaphysics* commentary. But here he develops the point in a different way. Order, he says, is related to reason in four different ways. First, there is order that reason only considers and does not make. Considering this sort of order belongs to what he here calls natural philosophy. He is taking this expression broadly, as the Stoics did, to cover not only the science of mobile things but also mathematics and metaphysics. These are the sciences that Aristotle calls theoretical or speculative, regarding things that we can look at and think about but cannot make or do. Then Thomas cites three fields in which reason both considers and makes order: (a) its own operations, which pertain to logic; (b) the operations of the will; that is, voluntary actions—also called human actions—which pertain to moral philosophy; and (c) the external things that reason causes, which pertain to the mechanical arts. Moral philosophy, then, is not speculative or theoretical, but rather active or practical.

Thomas also observes that order is twofold. There is the order among the parts of a whole or a multitude, and there is the order of the whole or the multitude to its end. The order to the end has priority, because the other is for its sake, as the order among the parts of an army is for the sake of the whole army's order to its commander. Further on, Thomas reasons that just as the subject of natural philosophy—now taken in the narrower sense— is motion or (to put it concretely) mobile reality, so the subject of moral philosophy is human operation ordered to an end or (to put it concretely) man insofar as he acts voluntarily for an end. In making this comparison, perhaps Thomas has in mind that motion too involves order to an endpoint.

Thomas then divides moral philosophy itself into three parts. The first concerns the actions of individuals. He calls this *monastica* (from Greek *monos*, single). This is not a reference to monasticism; he says that it is what the *Nicomachean Ethics* is about, and ethics is just what we would call it. The other two parts of moral philosophy concern the multitudes to which human beings naturally need to belong, on account of their lack of individual self-sufficiency: the family or domestic community, which is the concern of *oeconomica* (from *oikos*, household), and civil society, the concern of *politica* (from *polis*, city). These multitudes, Thomas says, have only a qualified sort of unity, unity of order. In a multitude with this sort of unity, not all the operations of the parts are operations of the whole. This is why *oeconomica* and *politica* are distinct from each other and from *monastica*.

The bulk of Thomas's writings on moral matters pertains to ethics. Most of what he has to say about domestic life is in his treatments of the sacrament of matrimony, the longest being that of the commentary on the *Sentences*.[16] His two overtly political works, the commentary on the *Politics* and the *De regno*, are unfinished and do not offer anything close to a complete political theory.[17] However, the *Secunda pars* of the *Summa theologiae* devotes much attention to topics with obvious political bearing: law, the virtue of justice, the common good, commerce, etc.[18] And the treatment of the Old Law contains lengthy discussions of the political conditions in ancient Israel.[19]

Returning to the fourfold division of the sciences, clearly this is itself an ordering. Each science considers order in some field, but there is also order among the sciences. Here they are distinguished by the relations between their subjects and reason. And the order in which Thomas lists them also seems to be the order in which he thinks that, on the whole, their subjects fall under reason's apprehension. In other places, Thomas indicates that reason first considers the things whose order it only knows and does not make; among these, the very first are mobile, sensible things. Then reason considers its own operations; then voluntary or moral actions; and finally, external things to be produced through and for the sake of moral actions. At least in this respect, then, natural or speculative philosophy has priority over moral philosophy.

Which science is it that considers this fourfold division and order? It is surely not moral philosophy. In that case, it would be an order pertaining to

16. IV, dd. 26–42. Much of this material, somewhat rearranged, makes up *STh*, *Supplementum*, qq. 41–68.

17. On the need for caution in reading the *De regno*, see Torrell, *Initiation*, 247–49.

18. On Thomas's legal and political thought, see Finnis, *Aquinas: Moral, Political, and Legal Theory*.

19. *STh*, I–II, qq. 98–105.

voluntary activity, one that reason not only knows but also makes. This cannot be right. Reason itself is not the cause of the fact that what it considers relates to it in this fourfold way. It can only consider this fact. The fourfold division pertains to reason's very nature, which reason does not make. The division is something natural, in the sense of something speculative. Moreover, as a whole, the division covers absolutely everything that reason can consider, which is to say, all beings. Its consideration pertains to metaphysics. The things that reason causes—its own operations, voluntary actions, artifacts—are beings too, and they fall within the metaphysical domain. Evidently, then, it is no accident that Thomas begins the discussion with a reference to wisdom, this being—within philosophy—just another name for metaphysics. In the *Ethics* commentary, it is Thomas the metaphysician who is introducing us to moral philosophy.

Wisdom and Morals

What has just been said should not be taken too far. Thomas does recognize a way of considering all the sciences, including metaphysics, that belongs to moral philosophy itself. Both the *Nicomachean Ethics* (in Book VI) and the *Secunda pars* of the *Summa theologiae* (in scattered places) offer extensive discussions of the intellectual virtues. These are qualities of mind that enable us to hit upon truth in a reliable way, and among them are the sciences. What ethics teaches about the sciences is not what their subjects are or how these relate to human reason, but how the sciences themselves relate to the human will. All intellectual virtues are human perfections or human goods, which is to say, suitable objects of the human will; and their acquisition and exercise, being voluntary activities, are subject to the direction of practical reason.[20] Reason both considers and causes an order in the pursuit and use of truth, and this is a topic for moral philosophy. The question of how to give metaphysics itself its due place in human life as a whole is a moral question.

On the other hand, addressing this question presupposes a judgment as to what that due place is. The beginning of the *Ethics* commentary gave us Thomas's judgment: wisdom is reason's, and hence man's, foremost perfection. He likewise regards wisdom's exercise, sapiential contemplation, as the very best human activity. The life that is most humanly satisfactory, or that achieves the happiness most fully proportioned to human nature, is

20. See *STh*, II–II, q. 47, a. 2, ad 2.

the philosophical life. The active life, dedicated chiefly to external affairs, does lead to a sort of happiness, but it is only a secondary sort. Thomas's main reason for this view, gotten from Aristotle, is that wisdom considers beings that are better than man, divine beings.[21] This is as much as to say that if there were nothing divine, the value of purely speculative thought in human life would be much reduced. Along this line, Thomas says that if man were his own ultimate end, his happiness would lie in the activity of practical intellect considering and ordering his actions and passions.[22] The reason why man is not his own ultimate end is that there is something higher, the divine, and he is ordered to it.

Notice, moreover, that the task of judging wisdom in this way—as to how its object compares with that of the other virtues—belongs to wisdom itself. It is not moral thought that determines wisdom's object or that ranks its object in relation to those of other habits of mind. Moral thought only receives this ranking and uses it to formulate rules of action.

Moral philosophy, then, is not the most excellent science. In fact, it is not even the most excellent intellectual virtue concerning human action. That virtue, which we can call a sort of wisdom, but only qualified and practical, is prudence. For moral science, in itself, is confined to universal considerations, whereas action is realized in particulars. Prudence is the quality that perfects reason's ability to put order into action. However, prudence too is outranked by metaphysics. Prudence does not rule over wisdom, Thomas says (again following Aristotle), but only "leads into it, preparing the way to it, as the doorkeeper to the king."[23]

If anything, then, it is wisdom or metaphysics that rules over prudence, and hence over moral philosophy. In part, this is simply because it rules over all human disciplines, as we saw. To be sure, that is not a practical sort of direction. It only regards the content of the sciences, not their pursuit or exercise. Unlike theology, metaphysics is a purely speculative science.[24] Speculative thought aims at nothing but the consideration of truth. Evidently, however, this does not mean that the ruling or directing function of metaphysics extends only to other speculative disciplines. Practical disciplines also seek truth. What distinguishes them is that they seek truth,

---

21. *In Eth.*, VI, lect. 6, §1189.

22. *STh*, I–II, q. 3, a. 5, ad 3.

23. *STh*, I–II, q. 66, a. 5; *In Eth.*, VI, lect. 11, §1290–91. See also the more general considerations in *In Eth.*, I, lect. 2, §25–31.

24. See *STh* I, q. 1, a. 4; II–II, q. 45, a. 3, obj. 1.

not for its own sake, but in order to guide action by it. But with respect to the nature of truth, this difference is accidental. The intellect may work speculatively or practically, but its nature is the same, and so is the nature of truth, which is its proper object and perfection.[25] Metaphysics can very well have a role in directing practical disciplines toward truth, insofar as they too have principles whose truth it can judge and confirm.

In the case of moral philosophy, such principles are manifold. One is the very existence and nature of its subject, voluntary or free action. Thomas offers extensive analyses of the nature of the human will and of its freedom—quite metaphysical analyses, leading all the way back to the causality of God. Another principle of moral philosophy is the will's object, the good, along with its opposite, evil. Moral philosophy takes the notions of good and evil for granted. Taken absolutely, these are metaphysical notions, and determining their nature—determining whether there even is such a thing as their nature, whether they are anything objective—is a metaphysical task to which Thomas devotes considerable effort; and, as mentioned earlier, he also treats the good and evil proper to human actions, moral good and evil, from a highly metaphysical viewpoint. He does the same with principles of human action other than the will, such as the passions, the habits (virtues and vices), and law. More will be said in the following sub-sections about Thomas's handling of moral principles.

Moral Philosophy and Moral Theology

Moral philosophy is a practical science. As we saw, this means that it is not only about order in action, but also a source of such order. It consists in knowledge by which to guide or direct the actions that are in our power, those subject to our will or choice. As with any science, this knowledge is reached by reasoning, and the reasoning has starting-points.

Now, the starting point of any practical reasoning, Thomas holds, is an end or a goal. Having a goal in mind, one reasons about what is involved in attaining it, so as to order one's actions accordingly. In particular fields of action there are particular goals. But moral philosophy treats the entire field of voluntary action, insofar as reason can shed light on it. But if this whole field can be approached as a unity and in a practical way, it is because there is an end to which all human actions are ordered, an end that we are seeking by the sheer fact of acting voluntarily at all. This overarching

25. *STh*, I, q. 79, a. 11; see I–II, q. 64, a. 3, and above, 85.

goal constitutes the most fundamental practical principle. Thomas calls it the last or ultimate end—as it were the endliest end. Its attainment is what he calls happiness (*felicitas*) or bliss (*beatitudo*). We all want it. We differ, however, as to what it consists in. Moral science depends above all on the truth about the last end.

Any moral theory that does not give absolute primacy to the last end, then, can hardly be considered Thomistic. The *Secunda pars* could hardly be clearer about this, beginning as it does with no less than five Questions on man's last end. At the same time, however, Thomas's actual teaching about the last end raises a problem for the very possibility of a Thomistic moral philosophy. In fact, the problem is already implicit in the very first article of the *Prima pars*. There Thomas says,

> it was necessary for human salvation that, besides the philosophi-
> cal disciplines, which are built up by human reason, there be a
> teaching according to divine revelation. This is chiefly because
> man is ordered to God as to an end that surpasses the grasp of his
> reason, as it says in Isaiah (64:4): "The eye hath not seen, O God,
> apart from Thee, what things Thou hast prepared for them that
> wait for Thee." But the end must be pre-known by men, who have
> to order their intentions and actions to an end.[26]

Being voluntary agents, we cannot but order our actions to some end or other; there is no such thing as acting voluntarily with no end at all in view. But if we do not know what the true end is, we will likely adopt a false one, thereby obstructing the attainment of the true one.

As a way of bringing out the problem that this passage raises for moral philosophy, let me try to forestall two objections that it might raise. One is what we saw in the previous chapter: Thomas thinks that reason can know God. How then can he say that God is an end that surpasses reason? The other is that God obviously exists quite independently of anything we can do. How then can He be an end of our action?

The second question can be answered easily with a distinction. God can be an end of our action, not as a product or result, but as a target to which we can move and cling. Thomas is seeing God as a target whose attainment brings human life to perfect fulfillment, and life is inseparable from activity. Its perfect fulfillment cannot consist in a transitive action or production, since this is itself fulfilled in a product or result; nor can it con-sist in a motion, since this is fulfilled in a completion that coincides with its

26. *STh*, I, q. 1, a. 1.

cessation. The fulfillment must be in immanent and complete activity. But this can still have an object distinct from it, and God can be our end as an object of immanent and complete activity.[27] This, we said, is cognitive and appetitive activity. Bliss lies here, in a union with God by knowledge and love.

This brings us back to the first question. How is God an end unknown to reason? He is so as the object of a knowledge and a love that are themselves unknown to reason. Thomas, we saw, holds that God as He is in Himself, in His very essence, surpasses reason's grasp. But since the actuality of knower and known are the same, this means that the knowledge of His essence, and the love that such knowledge elicits, likewise surpass it. What Thomas argues in the first five questions of the *Prima secundae* is that the perfect bliss promised by God, that which goes by the name of eternal life, must consist in this knowledge and love. The point that Thomas is making in the *Summa*'s very first article is that natural reason lacks not only the experience of this end, but also the power to envision or preconceive it, at least with enough determinacy or concreteness to guide action. An end that is not grasped in itself can be concretely envisioned only in the causes by way of which it can be realized, and nothing within reason's grasp is sufficient to cause this end.[28] Without revelation we do not even know that an order or way to this end exists. The article's argument for revelation rests on revelation.

This, however, means that moral philosophy, which is a work of natural reason, proceeds in ignorance of our true last end. Here lies the problem. As practical, moral philosophy must assume an end. As bearing on human action as a whole, it must assume an end that is quite global or universal, and in that sense quite ultimate. If it is ignorant of our true last end, will it not assume a false one? Readers of Thomas do not seem to have worried much about this question until the last century, when it received a good deal of attention, as well as a rather wide variety of answers. Without tracing all of the ins and outs, here is a sketch of the debate.

27. This is why wisdom is higher than prudence. It does not determine the means to happiness, but it considers the very object that defines happiness itself, that object being the highest intelligible: *STh*, I-II, q. 66, a. 5, ad 2.

28. We might put it thus: John 1:18—"No one has ever seen God; the only-begotten Son, who is in the bosom of the Father, he has revealed him"—goes with John 14:6—"No one comes to the Father except through me."

The first to raise the issue, as far as I know, was Jacques Maritain.[29] On his view, for the reason just indicated, a "moral philosophy adequately considered" must be one that is "subalternated" to moral theology. That is, it must suppose a principle taken from moral theology: the truth about man's last end. Otherwise it will assume a false end and be vitiated at the root. It will nevertheless be distinct from moral theology, because it will be confined to the partial or imperfect direction, toward the last end, that natural reason can furnish.

In sharp disagreement with Maritain was the great Dominican master, Santiago Ramírez.[30] As Ramírez saw it, Maritain's moral philosophy would be nothing other than those portions of Thomas's moral theology that fall under reason's competence. In favor of an independent moral philosophy, Ramírez invoked Thomas's repeated assertion of a twofold last end. There is the unqualifiedly last end, which is the perfect bliss of the supernatural vision of God in Himself, and which is attainable only in the afterlife. But there is also an end that can be called last in a qualified sense: the full perfection that man's own nature enables him to attain. Thomas seems to regard this qualified, natural end as more or less identical with the this-worldly bliss that Aristotle's ethics has in view. As Aristotle himself indicates, it is an imperfect bliss. Its possessors are blissful, not simply or unqualifiedly, but "as men."[31]

With this distinction, Ramírez held, moral philosophy can assume a last end that is other than the revealed, supernatural end, but nevertheless is not false, because it is only qualified. Rather than directly opposing the true unqualified end, it merely abstracts from that. In practical as in speculative science, abstracting does not yield falsehood.[32] Besides, Thomas sees the natural end as essentially a likeness of true bliss and as quite fit to be ordered to it. For it too has God for its principal object; not, of course, according to His own form or essence, but through and in terms of His naturally knowable effects. The natural last end, in fact, consists chiefly in philosophical contemplation. Secondarily, it consists in morally virtuous action; this is a share in bliss insofar as it too is according to reason and

---

29. Maritain, *De la philosophie chrétienne*, esp. par. 3 & Note II, and *Science et sagesse*, Deuxième partie.

30. Ramírez, "Sur l'organisation du savoir moral" and "De philosophia morali christiana."

31. *NE*, I.10, 1101a14–21. See *STh*, I–II, q. 3, a. 2, ad 4; a. 6, ad 1.

32. *Physics*, II.3, 193b35.

driven by truth. Thomas even calls the exercise of the speculative virtues an *inchoatio*, a germ or rudiment, of perfect bliss.[33] On this account, Thomas's moral philosophy would on the whole coincide with Aristotle's, with additions on specific topics from the other authors mentioned at the beginning of the chapter.

More recently, however, there has been a great deal of discussion about the correct way to understand the very distinction between the natural and the supernatural in Thomas. To many, it has seemed that views like Ramirez's make nature and grace too accidental or too extrinsic to each other and overlook the passages where Thomas refers to an openness in human nature itself toward grace and the supernatural.[34] And this has led to doubts about whether the mere presence in Thomas of the concept of a natural last end, or the mere validity of the concept in itself, suffices to justify the idea of a whole practical order or practical science that is distinct from that of moral theology. Thus, Denis Bradley holds that Thomas's view allows for no distinct moral philosophy at all.[35] Against Maritain, he argues that a science subalternated to theology is theological, and that it is arbitrary and artificial to isolate the direction toward bliss that natural reason can furnish and make it a distinct science. Against Ramírez, he argues that Thomas's imperfect bliss is not formally distinct from perfect bliss. It is only the closest approach or approximation to perfect bliss that is possible in this life. It is not really an ultimate of any sort, even qualified. So it does not generate a distinct science.

Now it seems to me that, as a reading of Thomas on moral philosophy, Bradley's view is not tenable. Nowhere does Thomas suggest that revelation or moral theology simply supplants moral philosophy. As we saw, he draws upon moral philosophy in his very discussion of God in the *Prima pars*. He also acknowledges its distinction from moral theology in the *Secunda pars* itself.[36] Most importantly, he comments on Aristotle's *Nicomachean Ethics*,

---

33. *STh*, I–II, q. 57, a. 1, ad 2; q. 66, a. 3, ad 1; q. 66, a. 5, ad 2; q. 69, a. 3.

34. Man is naturally *capax Dei*: *STh*, III, q. 4, a. 1, ad 2.

35. Bradley, *Aquinas on the Twofold Human Good*. Bradley relies heavily on Henri de Lubac's *Surnaturel* and its famous interpretation of Thomas's notion of a natural desire for the vision of God (cf., e.g., *STh*, I, q. 3, a. 8). This interpretation has been contested in an exhaustive study by Lawrence Feingold, *The Natural Desire to See God*. For a summary of the general issue, see McInerny, *Praeambula Fidei*, 69–90. Personally I find Feingold's arguments persuasive, but I shall not address the question here (except regarding a small point: see below, 158n37).

36. *STh*, I–II, q. 71, a. 6, ad 5.

separately and as a whole, without ever expressing theological doubts about its legitimacy. Moreover, there are places where he indicates that there is a sense—even if merely qualified—in which what is naturally attainable is indeed a formally distinct perfection from the supernatural end and not just an imperfect share therein.[37] This suggest that it can function as a genuine principle of practical ordering.

At the same time, I think it would be wrong to say that Thomas's own moral philosophy, if he had written one, would differ from Aristotle's only by the addition of certain details taken from other authors. I think we can identify at least two points of difference that are quite fundamental: what the rational (and so philosophically sound) outlook is on natural or this-worldly bliss, and what the rational way is for God to function as a moti-vating factor in human action. These points will be the focus of the next section. I hope the discussion will serve to allay the fear that positing a distinct moral philosophy must be tantamount to making the natural order closed or to making the supernatural order merely accidental to it.

The Time of Bliss, the Love of God, and Moral Philosophy

There is at least one place where Thomas explicitly pronounces Aristotle's conception of bliss erroneous. It appears in his commentary on the dis-course on the Beatitudes in the fifth chapter of the Gospel of Matthew.[38] In this discourse, Thomas says, the Lord repudiates several false opinions about bliss. Among these is the view held by some, "such as Aristotle," that it consists in the virtues of the contemplative life. Against this is the eighth verse, *Blissful are the clean of heart, for they shall see God.* Thomas argues that the future tense ("they shall see," not "they see") shows that Aristotle's

---

37. See *In Sent.*, 3, d. 14, q. 1, a. 3, qc. 1, ad 1; *De ver.*, q. 8, a. 4, ad 13. Notice that what is in man's natural power differs from the supernatural end, not only as imperfect from perfect, but also in kind; see *STh*, I–II, q. 5, a. 5, ad 3 (and cf. I–II, q. 63, a. 4). I think it is clear that Thomas would not call man's capacity for the vision of God a natural potency; it is a specific "obediential" potency (the obedience being to God); see *De virtutibus*, q. 1, a. 10, ad 13. This reading is sometimes rejected on the grounds that it would make grace miraculous and so in some way accidental to human nature. But obediential potency is not only for miracles. Miracles are effects of natural causes operating outside their natural order (*STh* I, q. 105, a. 7, ad 1; q. 110, a. 4, obj. 3). Grace is the work of no natural cause at all. And it pertains to God's role as man's *naturally* immediate superior: see *STh*, II–II, q. 2, a. 3.

38. *Lectura super Matthaeum*, cap. 5, lect. 2. This work probably dates from around 1269–70; see Torrell, *Initiation*, 81–82.

view errs "with respect to the time." Aristotle rightly located man's bliss in the contemplation of divine things, but he erred by identifying this with the exercise of the speculative virtues, which pertain to this life.

Now, Thomas cannot mean that Aristotle thought that a vision of the divine essence could be reached in this life through the speculative virtues. Thomas often ascribes to Aristotle the view that knowledge in this life, starting as it does from sensible things, cannot reach the essence of any immaterial substance, let alone God's. The bliss that is attainable through the speculative virtues is imperfect, consisting in a true but deficient knowledge of the divine in light of its effects, rather than a vision of it in its own essence.[39] Yet, even though Matthew 5:8 speaks of seeing God, the error in Aristotle's conception of bliss that Thomas finds signaled there is not its falling short of the beatific vision, but simply its time. Why is this? My suspicion is that Thomas is thinking that whereas Aristotle's ignorance of the promise of the vision of God was invincible, his placing man's final bliss—whatever it consists in—in this life rather than in the afterlife was an error that could and should have been avoided.

This suspicion is supported by a remark in Thomas's *Ethics* commentary, regarding the passage where Aristotle calls those who are blissful in this life blissful "as men."[40] Again, Thomas calls it an imperfect bliss. However, he does not compare it with supernatural bliss or the vision of God, but with the general conditions of happiness that Aristotle himself had previously laid down, particularly the condition of stability. In this life, Thomas says, men are subject to mutability, and so they cannot have perfect happiness. But since we naturally desire perfect bliss, and "since natural desire is not idle, it can be rightly supposed (*recte aestimari potest*) that perfect bliss is reserved for man after this life." This last remark reflects nothing in Aristotle's text. Indeed, it is hard not to see the remark as a muted criticism of the Philosopher. It is Aristotle, after all, who teaches that nature does nothing idle.[41] And Thomas thinks Aristotle proved the immortality of the human soul.[42]

---

39. See *Scg*, III, cap. 48, §2254–61. Here he says Aristotle "seems" to have judged that man can have only the imperfect bliss of this life.

40. *In Eth.*, I, lect. 16, §202.

41. Aristotle, *De caelo*, I.4, 271a33.

42. *In De an.*, III, lect. 10, §743. In one place Thomas imagines a philosopher taking the consideration of the soul's immortality as the occasion for adopting some course of action: *De ver.*, q. 14, a. 4.

Elsewhere Thomas leaves no doubt that, on his view, it is not only contrary to the Christian faith but also unreasonable to suppose that the ultimate perfection possible for man is in this life.

> The last end of man, which all naturally desire, is bliss. Some have held that man is able to attain it in this life, and so they had no need to admit another life after this, wherein man would attain to his final perfection . . . . But this opinion is confuted with sufficient probability by the changeableness of fortune, the weakness of the human body, and the imperfection and instability of knowledge and virtue, all of which hinder the perfection of bliss, as Augustine argues at the end of *The City of God* [XXII, 22].[43]

Even within the limits of natural reason and philosophy, then, to identify the perfection attainable in this life, or man's natural last end, with his unqualified last end, is unwarranted. Although the possibility of a more perfect happiness in an afterlife cannot be strictly proved, it is the most reasonable thing to suppose. At least in this respect, Thomas would evidently have found Plato more satisfactory than Aristotle.[44]

There also seems to be another way in which, from Thomas's perspective, Aristotle's conception of human happiness looks defective, even philosophically. As we saw, Thomas agrees with Aristotle that sapiential contemplation is the best human activity because its object is the best reality. This agreement, however, should be seen alongside a rather radical distinction that Thomas draws between two possible motives for this contemplation.[45] In the contemplative life of the "philosophers," he says—meaning by this term the pagan lovers of wisdom—knowledge was attractive as a perfection of the knower, and the attraction to it proceeded from self-love (*ex amore sui*). By contrast, in the contemplative life of the "saints," knowledge is attractive because of the object in which it terminates, and the desire to contemplate proceeds from the love of the object—that is, the love of God.

Thomas is not saying that the philosophers only wanted to contemplate and did not care what the object contemplated was. They wanted to contemplate the best object. But they did so only because that is the best

---

43. *STh, Supplementum*, q. 75, a. 1 (= *In Sent.*, IV, d. 43, a. 1, qc. 1).

44. However, he finds Aristotle's view of the hylomorphic relation between soul and body both more rational and more in support of the doctrine of the resurrection of the body (ibid.).

45. *In Sent.*, III, d. 35, q. 1, a. 2, qc. 1.

contemplation and best activity of the one contemplating—because it is, so to speak, the best way to "enjoy oneself." Of course, the saints enjoy it too, and even more. But their chief motive is rather to unite themselves to the one contemplated and, so to speak, to render themselves enjoyable to Him.

The issue here is even more fundamental than that of the time of bliss's attainment (now or in an afterlife), or even that of its object (God as represented by His effects or God in His own essence). It regards the very end of human bliss—the end in the sense of the person *out of love for whom* it is desired. To use the example cited at the start of the *Ethics* commentary, it is in this sense that an army's end is its commander. Obviously the commander is not the goal to be effected by military action. That is victory. Nor is he even the action's target, which is the enemy. But he can be the army's end in the sense that the army fights for victory over the enemy out of love for him.

Thomas did not invent this example. He got it from Aristotle. It appears in Book XII of the *Metaphysics*, in the account of how the first unmoved mover is the highest good—the primary end—of the universe. Thomas identifies the unmoved mover with God.[46] He finds Aristotle conceiving God as the provident commander and lord of all things.[47] He even finds Aristotle holding that it is out of love for God that the lower separate substances execute His command to move the celestial spheres.[48] Such readings of Aristotle are, to say the least, controversial.[49] But the point is that, despite them, Thomas never ascribes to Aristotle, or to any pagan, the idea that one should act more from love of God than from love of oneself. On the theme of God's due role as a motive of human action, Thomas's debt to Aristotle is slight.

But is the requirement of loving God above oneself—of acting as saints do—a matter for moral philosophy at all? Is it not revealed, theological? Thomas's answer does not seem to be simple. On the one hand, he holds that loving God above oneself is a demand of nature and natural reason. It is a primary precept of the natural law.[50] It flows from the truth, naturally knowable, that one's whole being is from Him and that one's whole

46. *In Meta.*, XII, lect. 12, §2663.
47. *De subst. sep.*, cap. 3.
48. *In Meta.*, XII, lect. 7, §2529; lect. 8, §2536.
49. See my "The Causality of the Unmoved Mover."
50. *STh*, I–II, q. 100, a. 3, ad 1.

good, including one's very self, is more His than one's own.[51] But on the other hand, Thomas holds that in man's fallen state, fulfilling this precept is impossible without grace.[52] He also judges that sin has so obscured the natural understanding of it that a revealed expression of it was needed.[53] Perhaps he would say it is a topic on which revelation can guide and stimulate philosophical thought; he does not seem to hold that philosophy, to be genuine, must shun such influences. However, as far as I know, he nowhere indicates how the love of God, or for that matter the practical implications of the immortality of the soul, should figure into moral philosophy.

But in any case, since he thinks that even philosophy, if it is fully rational, looks to a bliss beyond this life, his view allows for a distinct philosophy of morals that is ordered to the natural, this-worldly end but that does not treat it as though it were man's unqualified last end. Neither does it make grace look merely extrinsic or accidental to the natural end. However, this moral philosophy would no doubt look somewhat more metaphysical than Aristotle's.

We might still ask what need a theologian would have for moral philosophy, even a highly metaphysical one. I think Thomas's answer would be the same as for philosophy generally: strictly speaking it is not necessary, but it can be very useful. It can help to lead us by the hand toward the things lying beyond natural reason. Thomas is convinced, and astonishingly consistent with his conviction, that being more rational, as such, means being better disposed, not worse, for adhering in thought and action to the mysteries of the faith. As we have seen, the root of the soul's immortality is its rational nature; and the root of our capacity for faith and grace is reason's natural understanding of universal being and good.[54] And what favors living according to reason in this life favors life in the hereafter too. Of course, it is not that moral philosophy can order us directly to the supernatural end. Even with grace, reason never really masters that order.

This point emerges briefly but strikingly in a passage within Thomas's treatment of suicide. Here we also see those two crucial truths—that of the afterlife and that of our being more God's than our own—working together.

---

51. See *STh*, I, q. 60, a. 5; II–II, q. 26, a. 3.

52. *STh*, I–II, q. 109, a. 3.

53. *STh*, I–II, q. 100, a. 5, ad 1.

54. *STh*, II–II, q. 2, a. 3, quoted above, 97.

Unlike the affairs of this life, he says, the passage out of this life to a happier one is not subject to man's free choice, but only to divine power.[55]

Similarly, the virtues that natural reason can generate, the so-called acquired virtues, are not fully proportioned to the absolutely last, supernatural end, but only to an end that is ultimate in some particular field or other. All the virtues proportionate to the absolutely last end, whether regarding the end itself (theological virtues) or regarding the means to it (moral virtues), must be infused by God.[56] But among the demands of the order to the supernatural end are many things that reason does master, things that it sees for itself. These are the dictates of natural law, which for Thomas are in no way abrogated by revealed law, but rather confirmed and revitalized.[57] Moreover, the acquired virtues have one feature that the infused lack. The process of acquiring them involves the suppression of contrary dispositions, such as unruly passion.[58] They do not move directly toward the last end, but they do remove some obstacles to it, quelling certain kinds of temptation. Finally, moral philosophy presents likenesses to things treated in moral theology, such as that of human friendship to charity.[59]

Practical Reason, the Natural Order, and Politics

A striking instance of Thomas's taking a metaphysical viewpoint on the moral order is the proem of his commentary on Aristotle's *Politics*. As usual, he starts with an Aristotelian dictum: "art imitates nature."[60] But then he goes on to account for it in a way that Aristotle never does: as a result of the human mind's relation to the divine mind. The human intellect's intelligible light, he says, derives from the divine intellect according to a likeness. Hence there is a proportional likeness between the works of the human mind, which are works of art, and those of God's mind, which are

---

55. *STh*, II–II, q. 64, a. 5, ad 3. Here too, Thomas's thought is reminiscent of Plato; see *Phaedo*, 61c–63c.

56. See *STh*, I–II, q. 63, a. 3; q. 65, a. 2; II–II, q. 23, a. 7; II–II, q. 47, a. 13.

57. *STh*, I–II, q. 91, a. 4, ad 1; q. 99, a. 2, ad 1 & 2; q. 100, a. 1, & a. 3, ad 1; q. 106, a. 1, ad 2; q. 108, a. 2, ad 1.

58. *STh*, I–II, q. 65, a. 3, ad 2. On Thomas's account of the passions, see the excellent study by Robert Miner, *Thomas Aquinas on the Passions*.

59. More generally on the integration of Thomas's philosophy into his understanding of charity, see Sherwin, *By Knowledge and by Love*.

60. See *Physics*, II.2, 194a21–22.

natural things. Thomas compares natural things to examples fashioned by a master artisan for his apprentices to imitate. The human intellect "must be informed by the inspection of things done naturally, so as to work similarly." In effect, Thomas is explaining why, as Chesterton said, the artist is more intelligible than other men. As we saw, natural things contain our intellect's proper object—their whatness or nature—and this is nothing other than a conception of divine art instilled in things.[61] And so the works of the supreme artist are to us the first and supremely intelligible things. The human artist is the one who succeeds in harnessing that primordial intelligibility.

Thomas's proem goes on to remind us that the human mind cannot make natural things. It only knows them. They are objects of speculative science. The things that it both knows and effects, things that are by art, are objects of sciences that are "practical or operative according to the imitation of nature." Further on, he distinguishes between reason operating in the mode of production (*factionis*—Aristotle's *poiēsis*), i.e., transitive action, which passes into exterior matter and is properly the business of mechanical art, and reason operating in the mode of conduct (*actionis*—Aristotle's *praxis*), i.e., immanent action, such as deliberating, choosing, and willing. Conduct is the sphere of the moral sciences, among which is political science.

Here too the imitation of nature is at work. This is rather remarkable, because the natural actions that we can inspect are those of physical nature, and these are productions, exercised by physical agencies upon exterior matter. Nevertheless, Thomas finds moral and political action imitating them.[62] Nature, he observes, proceeds from simple and imperfect things to composite and perfect things, and so does practical reason; and this holds not only of reason's disposal of the things that man uses, but also of its disposal of men themselves, who are ruled by reason. Reason orders men into communities, and of these, the most composite and perfect, and the end of the others, is civic community. He is explaining why, among the practical disciplines, politics is highest.

Implied here is a metaphysics of civic community, a conception of its mode of being, that merits consideration. A city is a composite whole

---

61. See above, 124.

62. Thomas also sees imitation of nature in the operation of reason itself, as falling under reason's own direction and pertaining to the art of logic; see *In Post. an.*, I, Proem., §5[5].

whose elements or simplest components are human persons. It is, as he said in the *Ethics* commentary, a multitude with a "unity of order." The ordering principle is reason. But even though human persons are the elements, the "matter" of this whole (the form being its order), we should not think of this as a case of reason working in the mode of action that passes into exterior matter, the mode of production. This whole exists, not through production, but through action remaining in the agent, conduct. This entails that the whole's own form remains in the agent. But here the form is an order, and the subject of an order is each of the things ordered.[63] Hence, each of the persons out of which this whole is formed is also an agent of it. Indeed, each is a voluntary agent, the sort that moral science considers. Evidently, then, there is no such thing as a person's being a citizen, or a multitude's being a city, involuntarily. A city's unity, and therefore its very being, reside chiefly in the citizens' souls, the dispositions of their wills.

This is not only to say that the city is an effect of their wills. It is also to say that their having the unity of a city is chiefly their very wanting to have it. The city is an effect of their wills, but not a product, in the strict sense. A product can go on existing after the action of producing it has ceased. If the city were a mere product of the citizens' wills, its continuance would not necessarily depend on their wills. It might even continue against their wills, by despotic force (whether wielded by one man or by several). But in that case they would be slaves, not citizens. They would be human tools, "things that man uses." And such a multitude would be, not a city, but the corruption of a city.[64] Civil unity is an order seated in the ongoing action of the citizens' wills. It is a kind of friendship.[65] A friendship is not a product, and neither is a true city.

On this point it is instructive to set the proem to the *Politics* commentary alongside the Introduction to Hobbes's *Leviathan*. Hobbes, too, starts from the idea that art imitates nature. But he does not distinguish between action and production—nor, for that matter, between complete activity and motion. These distinctions seem to have no place in his thought at all. He speaks wholly in terms of production and motion. And the likeness that he signals is not in the orders according to which nature and art operate, but in their products. His city is an "artificial man," with parts like human parts,

---

63. See *STh*, III, q. 75, a. 4, ad 1.

64. *In Polit.*, III, lect. 5, §390.

65. *In Eth.*, VIII, lect. 9–11.

and whose "soul" or giver of "life and motion" is the sovereign.[66] Further on, Hobbes says that a sovereign and a despot have the same rights, and that they differ only in how they are instituted.[67] Strikingly, but not too surprisingly, *Leviathan* contains no treatment of friendship at all. The very word scarcely appears. By contrast, about a fifth of Aristotle's *Ethics* is on friendship.

It would be hard to overstate the role that Thomas assigns, as a constitutive factor not just of politics but of the moral order generally, to the natural human need for friendship or to man's natural sociability. The dominant human goods are all "common" goods, apt to be shared by many, and on the whole they take priority over purely individual goods.[68] To a large extent, rendering judgment on the good or evil of human conduct is a matter of determining its relation to the true common goods to which the person is ordered.[69]

Metaphysical Resolution of Practical Principles and a Natural Law Leading to God

For Thomas, the expression *imitation of nature* does not always refer to the production of copies of natural products in different materials. As it applies to the moral field, it refers to principles of order that reason first discerns in the actions of physical nature and applies to voluntary actions. The reason why voluntary action can be ordered in ways similar to those of nature is evidently that its intrinsic condition, as he calls it, is at least analogous to that of natural action. This condition consists of the features common to all voluntary action, whether morally good or bad—that is, whether falling within or outside the order of reason. Thomas subjects the condition of voluntary action to a lengthy analysis.[70] Both there and elsewhere he draws numerous comparisons between voluntary and natural action.[71] For

---

66. Thomas Hobbes, *Leviathan*, Introduction, xviii.

67. Ibid., II.20, 139–44. The soul's having a kind of despotic rule over the body is actually an Aristotelian idea; see Aristotle, *Politics*, I.2, 1254b4–5.

68. See De Koninck, *De la primauté du bien commun*.

69. *STh*, I, q. 90, a. 2, ad 3; see Jensen, *Good and Evil Actions*.

70. *STh*, I–II, qq. 6–17. On the important distinction between interior and exterior acts of the will, see Kenny, *Aquinas on Mind*, 83–88. On Thomas on how voluntary actions are specified, see Pilsner, *The Specification of Human Actions in St. Thomas Aquinas*.

71. This is the general theme of my *Action and Conduct*.

instance, both voluntary and natural agents act for the sake of ends. This feature is common to them only by analogy, not univocally, because it belongs to them in unequal modes. Natural actions are naturally determined to their ends, whereas voluntary actions are ordered to their ends by the free determination of their own agents, typically through deliberation.[72]

Quite frequently, Thomas presents basic principles of order or rectitude in human conduct as applications to the voluntary domain of principles that also apply to natural things. Thus, in many places he determines rules for specific virtues, or against specific vices—habits of acting according or contrary to reason—by appeal to orders commonly observed in natural things.[73] Even the general principle that moral goodness consists in following reason, and moral badness, in deviating from it, is an application of the general principle that "for each thing whatsoever, that is good which suits it according to its form, and bad, that which is outside the order of its form"—man's form being reason.[74] In a famous passage, Thomas presents practical reason's first, "naturally apprehended" rules as functions of the objects of man's natural inclinations, many of which are common to man and non-rational things.[75] The most basic rule of all, "good is to be done and sought, and evil, avoided," is founded on the conception of the good, which is "what all desire"; and the word for "all," *omnia*, being neuter, means absolutely all beings.[76]

Another such principle is the love of God above all else. "Each and every thing, in its own mode, naturally loves God more than itself."[77] This is the primary instance of the still more general principle that insofar as a thing belongs to another according to what it naturally is, it naturally seeks the other's good more than its own. Non-rational things do so, and "the natural inclination in things without reason manifests the natural inclination in the will of intellectual nature."[78] Here, in fact, the topic is the love that angels have. But in the same text Thomas also points to an analogous

---

72. *STh*, I–II, q. 1, a. 2; q. 6, a. 2.

73. Examples: *STh*, II–II, q. 50, a. 4 (military prudence); q. 64, aa. 1 & 2 (killing); q. 65, a. 1 (mutilation); q. 104, a. l (obedience); q. 108, a. 2 (vindication); q. 130, a. 1 (presumption); q. 133, a. 1 (pusillanimity).

74. *STh*, I–II, q. 18, a. 5. See I–II, q. 21, a. 1; I–II, q. 94, a. 3; *In Eth.*, I, lect. 10.

75. *STh*, I–II, q. 94, a. 2.

76. Ibid.; see I, q. 5, a. 1.

77. *STh*, I, q. 60, a. 5.

78. Ibid.

principle at work in the political order, which he explains by the fact that reason imitates nature.

In these discussions, Thomas is not saying that we ought to act in this or that way because natural things do. To say this would be to posit, as the fundamental practical principle, that human actions ought to conform to the actions of nature. It would be as much as to say that such conformity is practical reason's own end. Thomas posits no such principle. Rather, he is analyzing practical reason's fundamental principles into more general truths, seeing them as applications of these truths. The general truths also apply to natural things. He is considering the practical order from a more universal, metaphysical perspective. The true measure to which human reason should conform is not physical nature itself, but the divine reason from which nature's order derives.[79]

Moreover, in presenting the fundamental practical principles as applications of more general principles, Thomas is not demonstrating them. He regards them as indemonstrable, *per se nota*—known in virtue of themselves.[80] This means that their truth is secured immediately by the understanding of their own terms. They are, so to speak, too true to be demonstrable. A demonstrable truth about a given matter is one whose truth is accounted for by means of a different truth about that same matter. For example, the moon's being eclipsed is accounted for by means of its being blocked from sunlight by the earth. But even an indemonstrable truth may be a particular application of a more general truth. The more general truth is not a different truth about the same matter; it is almost the same truth, only taken more abstractly, as bearing upon a more general matter. For example, a properly practical principle would be that the simpler communities to which people are apt to belong should be formed prior to the more complex ones. The more general principle would be that the simpler wholes to which a set of elements are apt to belong should be formed prior to the more complex ones. This principle applies to everything, including natural things.

Again, the idea is not that the reason why the principle is true and applies to human action is that it applies to natural things. Once we get the idea of starting from simple, imperfect things and proceeding to composite, perfect ones, we see at once that it makes sense, in any application. We

---

79. *STh*, II–II, q. 31, a. 3; q. 130, a. 1.

80. *STh*, I–II, q. 94, a. 2. For a thorough study of Thomas's notion of *per se notum*, see Tuninetti, 'Per se notum.'

do not have to go back and check to make sure that natural things work that way. On the other hand, even though Thomas is not demonstrating the practical principles, in resolving them into more general formulations he is indeed confirming them, exhibiting foundations upon which they rest. On the whole, more general considerations are better known to us, prior in our understanding to more particular ones. To say that truths are *per se nota* does not mean that there is no order among them or that grasping some of them does not suppose grasping others. None is demonstrated by means of others, but some may still be understood in light of others. Thus, in *Summa theologiae*, I–II, q. 94, a. 2, Thomas orders the first practical principles themselves, from the more general to the more particular. The one upon which all others are founded is that good is to be done and sought, and evil, avoided. This is the most general practical principle of all. In the other principles, it is applied to particular goods and evils. The other principles are not demonstrated by means of it, but grasping them supposes grasping it.

In the same article, Thomas also refers to the principle of non-contradiction, saying that upon it are founded all of our other truths whatsoever, whether speculative or practical. An example involving this principle may make the overall idea clearer. Take the proposition, "being a citizen is incompatible with not being a citizen." This is true, and there is no other truth about being a citizen on account of which it is true. It is an immediate truth about being a citizen, *per se nota*, indemonstrable. Nevertheless it is also an application of the utterly general truth that being such-and-such is incompatible with not being such-and-such. And we know the general truth better. We knew it long before we even had the concept of a citizen.

The reason why the more general principles are better known is the very fact that their terms are more general, more abstract, and hence simpler. Their formation in our minds is thus naturally prior to the formation of the more concrete or particular truths in which those terms are implied.[81] To be sure, Thomas thinks we are born not knowing anything. And in order to grasp even the simplest, most general principles, we have to experience singular instances from which their terms can be gathered.[82] But he is sure that practical principles are particular applications of general principles that we first gather, not from practical things that our own reason causes, but from things that we only observe—sensible, natural things. By pointing to the presence of the general principles in the commonly observed natural

81. See *STh*, I, q. 85, a. 3.
82. *STh*, I–II, q. 51, a. 1.

world, he shows that our access to them is itself quite natural. No special instruction is needed. In this way he shows that their applications to the practical domain are practical principles known "commonly to all."[83] Moral science can therefore take them for granted.

The general principles rest upon general terms, and there is order also among the terms. The very first term, as we considered in a previous chapter, is being. Truth is close on its heels. The good is a little farther behind, though not much. Between the notions of being and true, on the one hand, and good on the other, lies the notion of perfect; for the good is what all desire, and the desire that is common to all things is desire for their perfection. Perfection is "fullness of being." Of course the perfection of one kind of thing differs from that of another. What perfection is, for this or that thing, is a function of what the thing itself is, its nature or form. Think of the inner shape or boundary of a container; this sets the measure for what the container's being full amounts too. So in this way too, nature is a principle of practical thinking. It is a principle of the very notion of the good.

With regard to this, something should be said about the so-called is-ought fallacy that Hume is said to have exposed. Now, even if Hume did expose a genuine fallacy, the larger argument that he was engaged in is itself nothing short of sophistry. What he showed was that the notion of *according to nature* does not contain the notion of *good*. But what he actually needed was the sophistical inference from this, which he leaves tacit, that the notion of *good* does not contain the notion of *according to nature*. For it is really only this inference that provides grounds for his main thesis, which is that the notion of *good* has no rational or intelligible basis at all—that it is a mere function of sentiment or feeling.[84]

As for Thomas, he is certainly not guilty of the fallacy, because he does not present the notion of the good as implied by that of nature or even that of perfection, as though one could simply derive the good from these other

---

83. *STh*, I–II, q. 94, a. 2.

84. See Hume, *A Treatise of Human Nature*, Book III, Part I, Section i, esp. 469–70, and Section ii, 470–76. For Thomas, the appetite or desire to which the notion of the good most properly or adequately responds is the will, intellectual appetite. This differs from sense-appetite, which is the seat of the passions, inasmuch as its activity presupposes reason's grasp of the universal notion of the good and the application of this notion to the judgment of something. One implication of this is that when Thomas associates precepts of natural law with natural human inclinations, the inclinations that he has in mind must be inclinations of the will, and they must follow, not give rise to, the understanding of the goodness of their objects or the knowledge expressed in the precepts. I discuss this in "Natural Inclination and the Intelligibility of the Good in Thomistic Natural Law."

notions by some kind of conceptual analysis. It is the notion of the perfect that is included in the notion of the good, and the notion of nature that is included in both of those notions. The notion of the good adds something new to the notions of a being, the nature of a being, and the fullness of a being according to its nature. It adds the final causality, the aptitude for being desired and pursued. However, this novelty definitely has the status of an addition, a "natural growth" in the human intellect. The good is intelligible because nature and being, to which it points, are intelligible. And all of these notions are first grasped in natural things, objects of speculative understanding.[85]

The work of ordering principles, confirming the posterior ones on the basis of the prior ones, and tracing the very first ones and the concepts upon which these are based to their origins in our common experience, is a metaphysical task. Thomas's ultimate justification for considering speculative and practical things together in this way, as falling under a common order, is also eminently metaphysical: their both proceeding from the highest cause, divine wisdom. The actions of all things are naturally subject to the ordination of divine providence, which is called the eternal law, and they all somehow share in it. Thomas sees the first principles of practical reason as human nature's proper share in the eternal law. It results from the natural light of reason, which, as he said in the *Politics* commentary, derives from the divine light according to a likeness. It is as seen in this way, rational derivations from the eternal law, that the principles are properly called precepts of natural law.[86]

It is not that grasping the truth of these principles depends on having grasped their divine origin. In the case of those that do not refer to God, grasping them may not even suppose having yet considered Him. Nevertheless, the natural understanding of them does lead toward considering Him and tending to Him. How naturally it does so, even for our fallen nature, comes out in Thomas's account of what occurs when a child first reaches the "use of reason" and becomes morally responsible.[87] At that time, the child experiences a peremptory need to "deliberate about himself." This means that he understands himself to be something "for an end." That is

85. I argue for this point at some length in "Natural Law, the Understanding of Principles, and Universal Good."

86. *STh*, I–II, q. 91, a. 2. On reason's grasp of the precepts of natural law, see Jensen, *Knowing the Natural Law*. On natural law as a juridical principle, see Hittinger, "Thomas Aquinas on Natural Law and the Competence to Judge."

87. *STh*, I–II, q. 89, a. 6.

what deliberation investigates: things that are for an end.[88] He perceives that he exists for some purpose, and he wonders what it is and what it requires of him. Pursuing this question or not, however, is up to him. Having reached the use of reason, he now has some voluntary control over his own acts and even over his own thoughts. But if he does decide to seek the truth of the matter and "orders himself to his due end" as well as he can—according to his best lights—then he will, in effect, be "turning toward God." This is so true that, if he is unbaptized and was, until this moment, in the state of original sin, that will now be remitted through supernatural grace.[89]

This of course is Thomas the theologian speaking. He is by no means discounting sin's tendency to weaken the will's natural disposition to follow the truth. But he finds the natural light of reason still orienting us all in the right direction, Godward.

---

88. *STh*, I–II, q. 14, a. 2.

89. Needless to say, grace was also helping (not forcing) him to reach that decision; see *STh*, I-II, q. 109, a. 6.

Bibliography

Principal editions of Thomas Aquinas's works

Leonine

Sancti Thomae Aquinatis doctoris angelici Opera omnia iussu Leonis XIII. P. M. edita. Cura et studio fratrum praedicatorum. Rome/Paris: Leonine Commission, 1882–.

Still in progress, this is the most authoritative edition of Thomas's works, and it should be consulted whenever textual accuracy is crucial. About forty volumes have appeared to date. Volumes 2–15, which include four commentaries on physical works of Aristotle (2–3), the *Summa theologiae* (4–12), and the *Summa contra gentiles* (13–15), were produced without the full use of modern critical techniques. For the contents of the volumes, see the page devoted to the Leonine edition in the *Corpus Thomisticum* website (described below in the section on research tools).

Parma

Sancti Thomae Aquinatis Doctoris angelici ordinis praedicatorum Opera omnia ad fidem optimarum editionum accurate recognita. 25 vols. Parmae: typis Petri Fiaccadori, 1852–73. Reprint. New York: Musurgia, 1948–50.

Vivès

Doctoris angelici divi Thomae Aquinatis sacri Ordinis F.F. Praedicatorum Opera omnia. Studio ac labore Stanislai Eduardi Fretté et Pauli Maré Sacerdotum, Scholaeque thomisticae Alumnorum. 34 vols. Paris: apud Ludovicum Vivès, 1871–80.

Marietti

Handy editions of many of the major works were produced by the Marietti publishing house during the middle decades of the twentieth century. These are especially useful for the works that have not yet appeared in the Leonine edition. Some of the titles differ slightly (with little or no risk of confusion) from those given above, which follow the Leonine listing. For example:

S. Thomae Aquinatis. *In duodecim libros Metaphysicorum Aristotelis expositio.* Edited by M. R. Cathala and R. M. Spiazzi. 2nd ed. Turin/Rome: Marietti, 1971.

Sentences

Scriptum super Sententiis magistri Petri Lombardi. 4 vols. Edited by P. Mandonnet and M. F. Moos. Paris: P. Lethielleux, 1929–56. (This breaks off at Book IV, d. 22; for dd. 23–25, see the Parma edition, vol. 7/2, 872–1259.)

Other

There are other editions of many works; see Emery's catalogue in Torrell, *Initiation.* Two not included in the catalogue, being of only probable authenticity, are the following.

Thomas Aquinas. *Lectura romana in primum Sententiarum Petri Lombardi.* Edited by L. E. Boyle, O.P. and J. F. Boyle. Studies and Texts 152. Toronto: Pontifical Institute of Mediaeval Studies, 2006.

Thomas Aquinas. *Quaestio de immortalitate animae.* In Leonard A. Kennedy, "A New Disputed Question of St. Thomas Aquinas on the Immortality of the Soul." *Archives d'Histoire Doctrinale et Littéraire du Moyen Âge* 45 (1978) 205–23.

English translations

Bonin, Thérèse. "Thomas Aquinas in English. A Bibliography." No pages. Online: http://www.home.duq.edu/~bonin/thomasbibliography.html. This is a very well organized, complete, and up to date bibliography of Aquinas's works in English translation. Two other online resources of particular interest are the following:

Freddoso, Alfred J. "New English Translation of St. Thomas Aquinas's *Summa Theologiae* (*Summa Theologica*)." No pages. Online: http://www3.nd.edu/~afreddos/summa-translation/TOC.htm.

Kenny, Joseph, O.P. "St. Thomas Aquinas' Works in English." No pages. Online: http://www.dhspriory.org/thomas/.

Research tools

Alarcón, Enrique. *Corpus Thomisticum. Subsidia studii.* No pages. Online: http://www. corpusthomisticum.org/. This is an extremely useful website containing Thomas's writings, many of the doubtful or spurious works, an excellent search engine based on Roberto Busa's *Index Thomisticus,* a large and regularly updated bibliography, and other information.

Bourke, Vernon J., ed. *Thomistic Bibliography, 1920–1940.* Saint Louis: Saint Louis University, 1945.

Bulletin Thomiste. Soisy-sur-Seine: Le Saulchoir, 1924–65. (Continued by the *Rassegna di letteratura tomistica.*)

Ingardia, Richard, ed. *Thomas Aquinas: International Bibliography, 1977–1990.* Bowling Green, OH: Philosophy Documentation Center, 1993.

Kennedy, Leonard A., ed. *A Catalogue of Thomists, 1270–1900.* Notre Dame, IN: University of Notre Dame Press, 1987.

Mandonnet, Pierre, et al., eds. *Bibliographie thomiste.* Paris: Vrin, 1960.

Miethe, Terry L., and Vernon J. Bourke, eds. *Thomistic Bibliography, 1940–1978.* Westport, CT: Greenwood, 1980.

Rassegna di letteratura tomistica. Naples: Editrice domenicana italiana, 1966–93. (Continuation of the *Bulletin Thomiste.*)

Biographical sources

Calo, Petrus. *Vita S. Thomae Aquinatis.* In Calo, Petrus, et al. *Fontes vitae S. Thomae Aquinatis notis historicis et criticis illustrati.* Edited by D. M. Prümmer and M.-H. Laurent. Toulouse: Saint Maximin, 1911–37.

Chesterton, G. K. *Saint Thomas Aquinas: The Dumb Ox.* Garden City, NY: Image, 1964.

Foster, Kenelm, O.P., ed. *The Life of Saint Thomas Aquinas: Biographical Documents.* Translation and Introduction by Kenelm Foster, O.P. London: Longmans, 1959.

Guilelmus de Tocco. *Ystoria sancti Thome de Aquino.* Critical edition by C. le Brun-Gouanvic. Toronto: Pontifical Institute of Mediaeval Studies, 1996.

Torrell, Jean-Pierre, O.P. *Initiation à saint Thomas d'Aquin.* 3rd ed. Paris: Cerf, 2008.

Tugwell, Simon, O.P. "Thomas Aquinas: Introduction." In *Albert and Thomas: Selected Writings,* edited by S. Tugwell, 201–351. New York: Paulist, 1988.

Weisheipl, James A., O.P. *Thomas D'Aquino: His Life, Thought and Work.* Washington, DC: The Catholic University of America Press, 1983.

Introductions and overviews

Barron, Robert. *Thomas Aquinas. Spiritual Master.* New York: Crossroad, 2008.

Bird, Otto. "How to Read an Article of the *Summa.*" *The New Scholasticism* 27.2 (1953) 129–59.

Chenu, Marie-Dominique. *Toward Understanding St. Thomas.* Chicago: Regnery, 1964.

Copleston, Frederick C., S.J. *Aquinas.* London: Penguin, 1955.

Davies, Brian, O.P. *Thomas Aquinas's* Summa Theologiae: *A Guide and Commentary.* Oxford: Oxford University Press, 2014.

————. *The Thought of Thomas Aquinas*. Oxford: Clarendon, 1992.

Feser, Edward. *Aquinas. A Beginner's Guide*. Oxford: Oneworld, 2009.

Gardeil, Henri-Dominique. *Introduction to the Philosophy of St. Thomas Aquinas*. 4 vols. Herder, St. Louis 1956. Reprint of vols. 2–4. Eugene, OR: Wipf & Stock, 2009–12.

Geach, Peter. "Aquinas." In *Three Philosophers*, 65–125. Edited by G. E. M. Anscombe and P. T. Geach. Ithaca, NY: Cornell University Press, 1961.

Gilson, Étienne. *Thomism: The Philosophy of Thomas Aquinas*. Toronto: Pontifical Institute of Medieval Studies, 2002.

Maritain, Jacques. *St. Thomas Aquinas*. New York: Meridian, 1964.

Martin, Christopher. *The Philosophy of Thomas Aquinas: Introductory Readings*. London: Routledge Kegan & Paul, 1988.

McCabe, Herbert, O.P. *On Aquinas*. Edited and introduced by Brian Davies, O.P. London: Continuum, 2008.

McInerny, Ralph. *Aquinas*. Cambridge: Polity, 2004.

Pieper, Josef. *Guide to Thomas Aquinas*. New York: Pantheon, 1962.

Stump, Eleonore. *Aquinas*. London: Routledge, 2003.

Turner, Denys. *Thomas Aquinas: A Portrait*. New Haven: Yale University Press, 2014.

Vanni Rovighi, Sofia. *Introduzione a Tommaso d'Aquino*. 2nd ed. Rome: Laterza, 1981.

Other authors and works cited

Aertsen, Jan A. *Medieval Philosophy and the Transcendentals: The Case of Thomas Aquinas*. Leiden: Brill, 1996.

————. *Nature and Creature: Thomas Aquinas' Way of Thought*. Leiden: Brill, 1988.

Anscombe, G. E. M. "Analytical Philosophy and the Spirituality of Man." In *Human Life, Action and Ethics: Essays by G. E. M. Anscombe*, edited by M. Geach and L. Gormally, 3–16. Exeter, UK: Imprint Academic, 2005.

Ashworth, E. Jennifer. "Analogy and Equivocation in Thirteenth-Century Logic: Aquinas in Context." *Mediaeval Studies* 54 (1992) 94–135.

————. "Medieval Theories of Analogy." In *Stanford Encyclopedia of Philosophy*. No pages. Online: http://plato.stanford.edu/entries/analogy-medieval/.

Bergamino, Federica. "*Quaestio disputata de immortalitate animae*. Traduzione italiana e commento alla luce delle sue fonti e delle opere edite di Tommaso d'Aquino." *Acta Philosophica* 20.1 (2011) 73–120.

Berti, Enrico. *Studi Aristotelici. Nuova edizione riveduta e ampliata*. Brescia, Italy: Morcelliana, 2012.

Bowlin, John R. *Contingency and Fortune in Aquinas's Ethics*. Cambridge: Cambridge University Press, 1999.

Boyle, John. *Master Thomas Aquinas and the Fullness of Life*. South Bend, IN: St. Augustine's Press, 2014.

Bradley, Denis J. M. *Aquinas on the Twofold Human Good: Reason and Human Happiness in Aquinas's Moral Science*. Washington, DC: The Catholic University of America Press, 1997.

Brock, Stephen L. *Action and Conduct: Thomas Aquinas and the Theory of Action*. Edinburgh: T. & T. Clark, 1998.

————. "Causality and Necessity in Thomas Aquinas." *Quaestio* 2 (2002) 217–40.

——. "The Causality of the Unmoved Mover in Thomas Aquinas's Commentary on *Metaphysics* XII." *Nova et Vetera* (English) 10.3 (2012) 805–32.

——. "Harmonizing Plato and Aristotle on *Esse*: Thomas Aquinas and the *De hebdomadibus*." *Nova et Vetera* (English) 5.3 (2007) 465–94.

——. "How Many Acts of Being Can a Substance Have? An Aristotelian Approach to Aquinas's Real Distinction." *International Philosophical Quarterly* 54.3 (2014) 317–31.

——. "Intentional Being, Natural Being, and the First-Person Perspective in Thomas Aquinas." *The Thomist* 77.1 (2013) 103–33.

——. "Natural Inclination and the Intelligibility of the Good in Thomistic Natural Law." *Vera Lex* VI.1–2 (2005) 57–78. Reprinted in abridged form, in *The Natural Law Reader*, edited by J. A. Laing and R. Wilcox, 323–28. Oxford: Wiley Blackwell, 2014.

——. "Natural Law, the Understanding of Principles, and Universal Good." *Nova et Vetera* (English) 9.3 (2011) 671–706.

——. "On Whether Aquinas's *Ipsum Esse* is 'Platonism.'" *The Review of Metaphysics* 60.2 (2006) 269–303.

——. "The Physical Status of the Spiritual Soul in Thomas Aquinas." *Nova et Vetera* (English) 3.2 (2005) 305–32.

——. "Practical Truth and its First Principles in the Theory of Grisez, Boyle, and Finnis." *The National Catholic Bioethics Quarterly* 15.2 (2015) 303–29.

Brower, Jeffrey E. *Aquinas's Ontology of the Material World. Change, Hylomorphism, & Material Objects.* Oxford: Oxford University Press, 2014.

Chesterton, G. K. "An Apology for Buffoons." In *The Well and the Shallows*, 13–28. London: Sheed and Ward, 1935.

Cory, Therese Scarpelli. *Aquinas on Human Self-Knowledge.* New York: Cambridge University Press, 2014.

De Koninck, Charles. *De la primauté du bien commun contre les personnalistes.* Québec: Laval University Press, 1943.

Decosimo, David. *Ethics as a Work of Charity: Thomas Aquinas and Pagan Virtue.* Stanford: Stanford University Press, 2014.

Dewan, Lawrence, O.P. "The Distinctiveness of St. Thomas' 'Third Way.'" *Dialogue* 19 (1980) 201–18.

——. *Form and Being: Studies in Thomistic Metaphysics.* Washington, DC: The Catholic University of America Press, 2006.

——. "The Interpretation of St. Thomas's Third Way." In *Littera, sensus, sententia. Studi in onore del Prof. Clemente J. Vansteenkiste, O.P.*, edited by A. Lobato, 201–18. O.P. Milan: Massimo, 1991.

——. "St. Thomas and Creation: Does God Create 'Reality'?" *Science et Esprit* 51 (1999) 5–25.

——. "St. Thomas and the Divine Names." *Science et Esprit* 32.1 (1980) 19–33.

——. *St. Thomas and Form as Something Divine in Things.* The Aquinas Lecture 71. Milwaukee: Marquette University Press, 2007.

——. "St. Thomas, the Fourth Way, and Creation." *The Thomist* 59.3 (1995) 371–78.

——. *Wisdom, Law and Virtue: Essays in Thomistic Ethics.* New York: Fordham University Press, 2007.

Dodds, Michael J., O.P. *The Unchanging God of Love: A Study of the Teaching of St. Thomas Aquinas on Divine Immutability in View of Certain Contemporary Criticism of this Doctrine.* Fribourg: Éditions Universitaires de Fribourg, 1986.

Doolan, Gregory T. "Aquinas on the Demonstrability of Angels." In *A Companion to Angels in Medieval Philosophy*, edited by T. Hoffmann, 13–44. Leiden: Brill, 2012.

Eberl, Jason T. *Thomistic Principles and Bioethics*. London: Routledge, 2006.

Elders, Leo. *The Ethics of St. Thomas Aquinas*. Frankfurt am Main: Lang, 2005.

———. *The Metaphysics of Being of St. Thomas Aquinas in a Historical Perspective*. Leiden: Brill, 1993.

———. *The Philosophical Theology of St. Thomas Aquinas*. Leiden: Brill, 1990.

———. *The Philosophy of Nature of St. Thomas Aquinas*. Frankfurt am Main: Lang, 1997.

Feingold, Lawrence. *The Natural Desire to See God according to St. Thomas Aquinas and His Interpreters*. 2nd ed. Naples: Sapientia, 2010.

Finnis, John. *Aquinas: Moral, Political, and Legal Theory*. Oxford: Oxford University Press, 1998.

Flannery, Kevin, S.J. *Acts Amid Precepts: The Aristotelian Logical Structure of Thomas Aquinas's Moral Theory*. Washington, DC: The Catholic University of America Press, 2001.

Gallagher, David M. "Thomas Aquinas on Will as Rational Appetite." *Journal of the History of Philosophy* 29.4 (1991) 559–84.

Gendlin, Eugene T. *Line by Line Commentary on Aristotle's De Anima*. 2 vols. Spring Valley, NY: The Focusing Institute, 2012.

George, Marie I. "Mind Forming and *Manuductio* in Aquinas." *The Thomist* 57.2 (1993) 201–13.

Gilson, Étienne. *The Elements of Christian Philosophy*. New York: Doubleday, 1960.

———. "In Quest of Matter." In *Three Quests in Philosophy*, edited by A. Maurer and J. K. Farge, 75–130. Toronto: Pontifical Institute of Mediaeval Studies, 2008.

Goris, Harm J.M.J. *Free Creatures of an Eternal God. Thomas Aquinas on God's Infallible Foreknowledge and Irresistible Will*. Leuven: Peeters, 1996.

Grieco, John R. "An Analysis of St. Thomas Aquinas's 'Third Way.'" PhD diss., The Catholic University of America, 2006.

Haldane, John. *Mind, Metaphysics, and Value in the Thomistic and Analytical Traditions*. Notre Dame, IN: University of Notre Dame Press, 2002.

Henle, Robert J., S.J. *Saint Thomas and Platonism: A Study of the "Plato" and "Platonici" Texts in the Writings of Saint Thomas*. The Hague: Nijhoff, 1956.

Hittinger, Russell. "Thomas Aquinas on Natural Law and the Competence to Judge." In *St. Thomas Aquinas and the Natural Law Tradition: Contemporary Perspectives*, edited by J. Goyette and J. Latkovic, 261–84. Washington, DC: The Catholic University of America Press, 2004.

Hobbes, Thomas. *Leviathan: Or the Matter, Forme and Power of a Commonwealth, Ecclesiasticall and Civill*. Edited by A. R. Walter. Cambridge: Cambridge University Press, 1904.

Hochschild, Joshua P. *The Semantics of Analogy. Rereading Cajetan's De Nominum Analogia*. Notre Dame, IN: University of Notre Dame Press, 2010.

Hume, David. *A Treatise of Human Nature*. Edited by L. A. Selby-Bigge. Oxford: Oxford University Press, 1888.

Hütter, Reinhard. *Dust Bound for Heaven*. Grand Rapids: Eerdmans, 2012.

Jenkins, John. *Knowledge and Faith in Thomas Aquinas*. Cambridge: Cambridge University Press, 1997.

Jensen, Steven. *Good and Evil Actions: A Journey through Saint Thomas Aquinas*. Washington, DC: The Catholic University of America Press, 2010.

————. *Knowing the Natural Law: Precepts, Inclinations, and Deriving Oughts.* Washington, DC: The Catholic University of America Press, 2015.

————. *Living the Good Life: A Beginner's Thomistic Ethics.* Washington, DC: The Catholic University of America Press, 2013.

Kenny, Anthony. *Aquinas on Mind.* Topics in Medieval Philosophy. London: Routledge, 1993.

Klima, Gyula. "The Semantic Principles Underlying St. Thomas Aquinas's Metaphysics of Being." *Medieval Philosophy and Theology* 5.1 (1996) 87–141.

Kretzmann, Norman. *The Metaphysics of Theism: Aquinas's Natural Theology in* Summa contra gentiles I. Oxford: Clarendon, 1997.

————. *The Metaphysics of Creation: Aquinas's Natural Theology in* Summa contra gentiles II. Oxford: Clarendon, 1999.

Levering, Matthew. *Scripture and Metaphysics.* Malden, MA: Blackwell, 2004.

Lewis, C. S. *Studies in Words.* 2nd ed. Cambridge: Cambridge University Press, 1967.

Madden, James D. *Mind, Matter, and Nature: A Thomistic Proposal for the Philosophy of Mind.* Washington, DC: The Catholic University of America Press, 2013.

Marion, Jean-Luc. *God Without Being. Hors-Texte.* 2nd ed. Chicago: University of Chicago Press, 2012.

Maritain, Jacques. *De la philosophie chrétienne.* Paris: Desclée de Brouwer, 1933.

————. *Science et sagesse, suivi d'éclaircissements sur la philosophie morale.* Paris: Labergerie, 1935.

Martin, Christopher. *Thomas Aquinas: God and Explanations.* Edinburgh: Edinburgh University Press, 1997.

McInerny, Ralph. *Praeambula Fidei. Thomism and the God of the Philosophers.* Washington, DC: The Catholic University of America Press, 2006.

————, and John O'Callaghan. "Saint Thomas Aquinas." In *Stanford Encyclopedia of Philosophy.* No pages. Online: http://plato.stanford.edu/entries/aquinas/.

McLaughlin, Thomas. "Act, Potency, and Energy." *The Thomist* 75 (2011) 207–43.

Miner, Robert. *Thomas Aquinas on the Passions.* Cambridge: Cambridge University Press, 2009.

Murray, Paul, O.P. *Aquinas at Prayer: The Bible, Mysticism and Poetry.* London: Bloomsbury Academic, 2013.

O'Callaghan, John. *Thomist Realism and the Linguistic Turn: Toward a More Perfect Form of Existence.* Notre Dame, IN: University of Notre Dame Press, 2003.

Paterson, Craig, and Matthew S. Pugh, eds. *Analytical Thomism: Traditions in Dialogue.* Aldershot, UK: Ashgate, 2006.

Pegis, Anton. *St. Thomas and the Problem of the Soul in the Thirteenth Century.* Toronto: Pontifical Institute of Medieval Studies, 1934.

Pilsner, Joseph. *The Specification of Human Actions in St. Thomas Aquinas.* Oxford: Oxford University Press, 2006.

Porro, Pasquale. *Tommaso d'Aquino. Un profilo storico-filosofico.* Rome: Carocci, 2012.

Ramírez, Santiago. "De philosophia morali christiana." *Divus Thomas (Frib.)* 14 (1936) 87–122, 181–204.

————. "Sur l'organisation du savoir moral." *Bulletin Thomiste* 12 (avril–juin 1935) 423–32.

Schmidt, Robert W., S.J. *The Domain of Logic according to Saint Thomas Aquinas.* The Hague: Nijhoff, 1966.

Sherwin, Michael S., O.P. *By Knowledge and by Love: Charity and Knowledge in the Moral Theology of St. Thomas Aquinas.* Washington, DC: The Catholic University of America Press, 2005.

Sokolowski, Robert. "Soul and the Transcendence of the Human Person." In *Christian Faith and Human Understanding. Studies on the Eucharist, Trinity, and the Human Person*, 151–64. Washington, DC: The Catholic University of America Press, 2006.

Taylor, Richard C. "Aquinas, the *Plotiniana Arabica*, and the Metaphysics of Being and Actuality." *Journal of the History of Ideas* 59 (1998) 217–39.

te Velde, Rudi. *Aquinas on God: The "Divine Science" of the* Summa theologiae. Aldershot, UK: Ashgate, 2006.

———. "Metaphysics, Dialectics and the *Modus Logicus* according to Thomas Aquinas." *Recherches de Théologie ancienne et médiévale* 63 (1996) 15–35.

———. *Participation and Substantiality in Thomas Aquinas.* New York: Brill, 1995.

Torrell, Jean-Pierre, O.P. *Christ and Spirituality in St. Thomas Aquinas.* Translated by Bernhard Blankenhorn, O.P. Washington, DC: The Catholic University of America Press, 2011.

———. *Saint Thomas d'Aquin, maître spirituel.* Paris: Cerf, 1993.

Tuninetti, Luca F. "L'argomentazione dialettica e il compito del sapiente nella *Summa contra Gentiles*." In *Sapienza e libertà. Studi in onore del prof. Lluís Clavell*, edited by M. Pérez de Laborda, 435–45. Rome: ESC, 2012.

———. 'Per se notum'. *Die logische Beschaffenheit des Selbstverständlichen im Denken des Thomas von Aquin.* Leiden: Brill, 1996.

Turner, Denys. *Faith, Reason and the Existence of God.* Cambridge: Cambridge University Press, 2004.

Twetten, David B. "Aquinas's Aristotelian and Dionysian Definition Of 'God'." *The Thomist* 69.2 (2005) 203–50.

Vargas Della Casa, Rosa. "Thomas Aquinas on the Apprehension of Being: The Role of Judgement in Light of Thirteenth-Century Semantics." PhD diss., Marquette University, 2013. Dissertations (2009–). Paper 310. http://epublications.marquette.edu/dissertations_mu/310.

Villagrassa, Jesús. *Bibliografía sulla metafisica di Tommaso d'Aquino.* Rome: Ateneo Pontificio Regina Apostolorum, 2009.

Vogler, Candace. "Aristotle, Aquinas, Anscombe and the New Virtue Ethics." In *Aquinas and the* Nicomachean Ethics, edited by T. Hoffmann, J. Müller, and M. Perkams, 239–57. Cambridge: Cambridge University Press, 2013.

Wallace, William A., O.P. *The Elements of Philosophy: A Compendium for Philosophers and Theologians.* 1977. Reprint. Eugene, OR: Wipf & Stock, 2012.

———. *The Modeling of Nature.* Washington, DC: The Catholic University of America Press, 1996.

Weingartner, Paul. *God's Existence. Can it be Proven? A Logical Commentary on the Five Ways of Thomas Aquinas.* Heusenstamm: Ontos Verlag, 2010.

Weisheipl, James A., O.P. *Aristotelian Methodology: A Commentary on the* Posterior Analytics *of Aristotle.* Edited by J. R. Catan. River Forest, IL: Pontifical Institute of Philosophy, 1958. Online: http://pvspade.com/Logic/docs/Weisheipl.pdf.

———. *Nature and Gravitation.* River Forest, IL: Albertus Magnus Lyceum, 1955.

———. *Nature and Motion in the Middle Ages.* Studies in Philosophy and the History of Philosophy 11. Washington, DC: The Catholic University of America Press, 1985.

West, J. L. A. "The Functioning of Philosophy in Aquinas." *Journal of the History of Philosophy* 45.3 (2007) 383–94.

Wielockx, Robert. "Poetry and Theology in the *Adoro te deuote*: Thomas Aquinas on the Eucharist and Christ's Uniqueness." In *Christ among the Medieval Dominicans: Representations of Christ in the Texts and Images of the Order of Preachers*, edited by K. Emery and J. Wawrykow, 157–74. Notre Dame, IN: University of Notre Dame Press, 1998.

Wippel, John. *The Metaphysical Thought of Thomas Aquinas: From Finite Being to Uncreated Being*. Washington, DC: The Catholic University of America Press, 2000.

Name Index

Subject Index

abstraction, from matter, 78, 88
accidents
    as beings, 39–40, 42, 44, 99–100,
        105–6, 111
    predication and, 99–100
act
    and potency. See potency and act.
    being (esse) as, 104–6, 128–29
    form as, 35, 47–50, 62, 128–29
action
    first grasped in motion, 37–38
    immanent vs. transitive, 71, 147,
        155, 164–66
    natural and voluntary, 167–68
activity
    and being, 111–12
    motion as incomplete, 36
    perfect or complete, contrasted
        with motion, 70–71, 165
affirmation and denial. See judgment.
afterlife, 114–17
analogy, 84, 141–42
analytical philosophy, xvii, 101,
    146n3
angels, 37, 117–20, 167
    as ipsa forma subsistens, 126–27,
        136
appetite, 59, 61–62, 71–72, 170n84
    as a source of immanent action,
        71
    See also will.
artificial, vs. natural, 31–33

Arts masters (Paris), xvi–xvii, 10–11,
    16, 77
authority, of the auctores, 4–7
Averroists, 10–11, 77

beatitude. See bliss.
Beatitudes, 158
being (ens)
    as subject of metaphysics, 22–23,
        92–98, 103
    attributes of, 94–95, 97n63, 102–5
    does not always require matter,
        109
    first understood, by abstraction,
        95
    in unqualified sense, actual
        substance, 104–6
    taken as a whole, God's effect, 137
    See also being (esse).
being (esse)
    and ens, 92
    and essence, 127–29
    and form, 54, 109–10, 115,
        126–30
    and unity, 104
    as act, 104–6, 128–29
    as distinct from essence and form
        in creatures, 126–29
    as specifiable, 128–30
    concept of, 130–31, 137
    for living things, same as life, 55
    in general, a proportion, 131

CPSIA information can be obtained
at www.ICGtesting.com
Printed in the USA
LVHW091014240719
625155LV00001B/108/P